THE CAUSES OF THE CIVIL WAR

3rd revised edition

Edited By
KENNETH M. STAMPP

A TOUCHSTONE BOOK
Published by Simon & Schuster
New York   London   Toronto
Sydney   Tokyo   Singapore

TOUCHSTONE
Simon & Schuster Building
Rockefeller Center
1230 Avenue of the Americas
New York, New York 10020

Originally published by Prentice-Hall, Inc.
First Touchstone Edition 1986
TOUCHSTONE and colophon are registered trademarks
of Simon & Schuster Inc.

Designed by Deirdre C. Amthor

Manufactured in the United States of America

20 19 18 17 16 15 14 13 12 11

Library of Congress Cataloging in Publication Data

The Causes of the Civil War / edited by Kenneth M. Stampp.—3rd ed.
    p.   cm.
  "A Touchstone book."
  Includes bibliographical references.
    1. United States—History—Civil War, 1861–1865—Causes.
  2. United States—History—Civil War. 1861—1865—Sources.
  I. Stampp, Kenneth M. (Kenneth Milton)
  E458.C33   1991
  973.7'11—dc20   91-38819
                                                             CIP

ISBN: 0-671-75155-7

FOR AUDREY AND JIM

Contents

III *Economic Sectionalism* 85

Introduction

The steady stream of books, articles, movies, and television productions about the American Civil War is in part attributable to the fact that it, more than any other episode in our past, has all the poignant qualities of a tragic romance. It attracts both novelists and historians, the first because they find unlimited possibilities for plot situations and character analysis, the second because they understand the conflict's crucial significance to the whole of American history. And yet, in spite of all the attention given to the Civil War, historians seem to be nearly as far from agreement about its causes as were the partisans who tried to explain it more than a century ago.

Not even the facts of the sectional crisis—apart from their meaning and precise relevance to the war—can be summarized without risking some little controversy. But a factual summary is nonetheless worth trying as background for the documents brought together in this book. Here, in brief, is what had been developing prior to 1861:

As early as the summer of 1787, when the Constitutional Convention met in Philadelphia, delegates representing the commercial interests of the North clashed on a number of issues with delegates representing the planter interests of the South. On several occasions questions such as slavery, the slave trade, the counting of slaves in apportioning representation in the lower house of Congress, and the regulation of commerce were subjects of animated debate. An irritated South Carolinian once affirmed that the interests of North and South were "as different as the interests of Russia and Turkey." At the Virginia ratifying convention a delegate insisted that "so long as climate will have effect on man, so long will the different climates of the United States render us different." During the constitutional debates, however, sectional controversies were only minor irritants; few Americans then seemed to be much concerned about whether the Union could "endure permanently half slave and half free." In fact, several decades would pass before three Northern states—New York, Pennsylvania, and New Jersey—completed the emancipation of their own relatively small slave populations.

But eventually the conflict of sections reached such dimensions as to overshadow all else. During the 1790s Southern farmers and planters became Jeffersonian Republicans in order to fight Hamilton's policies, which they believed enriched only Northern merchants, manufacturers, bondholders, and speculators. Even then petitions from Northern antislavery societies provoked angry protests from Congressmen representing South Carolina and Georgia. At no time thereafter did the North lack a party, or at least an organized political faction, pledged to a legislative program that suited its economic needs—tariffs to protect manufacturers, navigation acts to encourage merchants and shipowners, subsidies to aid New England fishermen, and appropriations to finance internal improvements. Hardly a session of Congress passed without the slavery issue being raised in some form. Moreover, given the population trends—the rapid growth of the North in comparison with slow growth of the South—it seemed to be only a matter of time until Northerners would have complete control of the federal government.

Southerners, seeing their power declining, their interests in jeopardy, and their institutions under attack, soon began to behave in the manner of a "conscious minority." They were convinced that something had to be done to keep the two great sections in political balance. Perhaps a "strict" construction of the Constitution would limit the danger by keeping federal power at a minimum. Perhaps a vigorous defense of "state rights" against "federal encroachments," even to the extreme of nullification, would save the South. If nothing else worked, perhaps secession and the formation of two confederacies would be the final solution.

These sectional differences carried the country through a series of paroxysmal crises. Missouri's petition for admission as a slave state first made slavery expansion a major issue, as it continued to be for the next forty years. South Carolina's attempt to nullify the tariff of 1832 signified the persistence of economic antagonisms between North and South. During the 1830s, abolitionism, one of many movements of moral reform that swept the North, became a permanently significant political force. The moral indictment of slavery, the fear of slave rebellions, and the desire for internal unity drove Southern leaders to a defense of slavery as a "positive good" and to violent action against all critics. In effect, they created an "intellectual blockade," a hostility to nineteenth-century liberal thought that matched, said Northerners, the "unprogressive" nature of their agricultural economy.

To be sure, there were moderates in both sections who deplored "sectional agitation," who feared disunion and civil war, and who labored hard for compromise. With much difficulty they arranged sectional adjustments in 1820, in 1833, and again in 1850. But after each "settlement" a new crisis, more severe than the last, soon developed. The final crisis began in 1854, when, after a long and bitter debate, a Democratic Congress passed the Kansas-Nebraska Act, which opened to slavery territory in which it had been prohibited by the Missouri Compromise of 1820. Among the immediate consequences was the organization of the Republican party as a Northern sectional party committed to the exclusion of slavery, that "relic of barbarism," from all Western territories. A second consequence was a violent struggle between proslavery and antislavery partisans for control of Kansas Territory. The struggle culminated in the attempt of a proslavery constitutional convention to gain the admission of Kansas as a slave state in spite of the opposition of a large antislavery majority. Before the attempt was defeated in Congress, the Democratic party was temporarily destroyed as a national political organization, thus clearing the way in 1860 for the election of a Republican President, Abraham Lincoln. The secession of the states of the Deep South soon followed. This time the opponents of compromise controlled both sections, and in April 1861 war finally came.

One may ask, "What caused the Civil War?" in three different ways, all of them interdependent but each, nonetheless, a slightly different question: (1) What caused the North and South to engage in ceaseless controversy for more than a generation? (2) What caused the states of the Deep South to secede after Lincoln's election? (3) What caused the great majority of Northerners to prefer the use of force to the recognition of Southern independence? Most of the documents that I have selected attempt to answer only one of these questions rather than all three. I have organized the documents into seven broad categories of "causes," but, in addition to some inevitable overlap, the reader will detect many subtle shadings of interpretation within each category, as well as the sharper differences that often divide writers or speakers from the North and South.

American historians are sometimes criticized for not being sufficiently concerned about problems of methodology or sufficiently philosophical about the nature and meaning of history. Even though the results of their eclectic and empirical approach are often gratifying, some of this criticism is doubtless justified. They are particularly vulnerable for failing to think more about the problem of causation, and much of the literature about the Civil War illustrates this deficiency.

If the search for the causes of a great national crisis such as the Civil War is one of the most absorbing historical problems, it is also one of the most exasperating. The evidence on which the historian bases his interpretations does not come to him neatly evaluated and arranged so that he knows precisely when, where, and how to use it. Rather, the historian himself evaluates his evidence and unites historical occurrences in cause and effect relationships—the historian, for example, makes the link between the slavery controversy or economic sectionalism and the Civil War. Moreover, which of all the events prior to 1861 he decides are of prime causal significance results only in part from the evidence at his disposal; his decision also results from a variety of subjective factors. It results in part from what he knows, or thinks he knows, about individual and social psychology—about human behavior and human motivation. It results as well from what the life he has lived enables him to understand about the past, for his own life is the prism through which he views the past and develops his understanding of it. If there is truth to the proposition that knowing the past helps us to understand the present, I believe there is at least as much truth to the proposition that what we know of the present is crucial to our understanding of the past. What we have not ourselves experienced or observed we can at most only partially and imperfectly comprehend; and I suspect that there is much in history that is so remote from our own experiences or observations as to be largely beyond our understanding. But in spite of these formidable handicaps, historians sometimes speak of the causes—or even *the cause*—of the Civil War with more confidence and with a greater air of finality than would a scientist reporting the results of a controlled experiment in his laboratory.

In recent years some historians have attempted to solve the problems of historical causation with the analytical tools of modern social scientists. Professor Lee Benson, a leading exponent of the "scientific" study of history, insists that the failure of historians, after so much effort, to agree upon what caused the Civil War is not the result of insuperable problems but of the shortcomings of the "established historiographic system." If historians are to escape these "recurrent cycles of wheel-spinning revisionism," he argues, they must have a "good typology," a "good general analytic model," and "good general theories" applicable to internal wars. Though Benson may ultimately succeed, his efforts thus far have not carried us much closer to the definitive causal explanation that so many historians have sought. *

As one reflects upon the problem of causation one is driven to the conclusion that historians will never know, objectively and with mathematical precision, what caused the Civil War. Working with fragmentary evidence, possessing less than a perfect understanding of human behavior, viewing the past from the perspective of their

---

*Lee Benson, *Toward the Scientific Study of History* (Philadelphia: 1972), pp. 307–26.

own times, finding it impossible to isolate one historical event to test its significance apart from all others, historians must necessarily be somewhat tentative and conjectural in offering their interpretations.

It may then be asked whether there was any point to the enormous effort that has gone into the various attempts to find the causes of the Civil War. If after more than a century the debate is still inconclusive, would not the historian be wise to abandon his search for causes and confine himself to cataloguing facts and compiling statistics? Is it not all the more discouraging to find, as the documents in this book indicate, that historians often merely go back to interpretations advanced by partisans while the war was still in progress? I think not. Because the century of historical inquiry, if it leaves the causes of the Civil War still open to debate, has nevertheless been extremely illuminating. Uncertainty about the war's causes has driven historians back to the sources time and time again, with the result that we have gradually enlarged our knowledge and deepened our understanding of our greatest national crisis. Hence I find the prospect of a continuing debate, however much it may annoy those who find it disagreeable to live with uncertainties, the best promise that research and writing in this period of American history will continue to have vitality.

This selection of documents presents the views of those who lived through the sectional crisis as well as of postwar historians. The documents are usually arranged chronologically from contemporary opinion to the most recent historical interpretations. They constitute, of course, only a small sample—though, I trust, a representative one—of what has been said about the causes of the Civil War.

K.M.S.

I. The "Slave Power" and the "Black Republicans"

DURING THE YEARS of bitter sectional conflict that preceded the Civil War, Northern abolitionists, editors, and Republican politicians repeatedly charged that the South—in fact, the entire country—was ruled by a ruthless "Slave Power." This Slave Power, well organized and conspiratorial in its methods, consisted of the Southern slaveholding planters and political leaders who were determined to convert the whole United States into a nation of masters and slaves. Advancing from one conquest to another, they imperiled the rights and liberties of every freeman. They shaped national policy to serve only their own selfish ends. When, at last, the free states rebelled and elected Abraham Lincoln to the presidency, the Slave Power, unwilling to submit peacefully, attempted to destroy the Union and to establish a proslavery confederacy of its own. It was this, said contemporary Northern partisans, that caused the sectional crisis; and after the Civil War the first generation of Northern historians generally agreed with them.

Southern leaders interpreted the events that culminated in secession in quite another way. Far from the South being aggressive, they insisted that the aggression was all on the other side. It was Northern violation of Southern rights—the aggressions of "Black Republicans"—that endangered the Union. Or so thought contemporary Southerners, and some recent Southern historians as well.

1.   "THE GREAT SLAVE POWER CONSPIRACY"

Russel B. Nye, in his book Fettered Freedom (*East Lansing, Mich.: Michigan State University Press, 1949*), *presents one of the best historical analyses of the Northern concept of the Southern Slave Power. Extracts from pages 223–31 and 248–49 are reprinted with the permission of the publisher.*

. . . [It] was not until after 1845 that . . . [the abolitionists] discovered and developed an effective device to unite under one common heading all their arguments. Putting together all the evidence, the abolitionists came to the conclusion that there existed a secret agreement, a conspiracy among Southern slaveholders, to foist slavery upon the nation, destroy civil liberty, extend slavery into the territories (possibly to whites), reopen the slave trade, control the policies of the Federal government, and complete the formation of an aristocracy founded upon and fostered by a slave economy. . . .

The importance of the threat of this "Slave Power" in shaping Northern and Western thought on the slavery question during the decades 1840 to 1860 is not to be underestimated. Repeated accusations, revelations of "proofs" and "plots," and the seemingly convincing evidence of recent history, combined to give more than a veneer of truth to the abolitionist charge. The abolitionists, to perhaps a larger extent than many historians have believed, emerged in the popular mind as sole defenders of the democratic tradition against the machinations of this uncompromising, dangerous, secret cabal. . . .

The aggressive attitude of the Southern faction in Congress from the Texas dispute to the Dred Scott case increased rather than allayed suspicions, lending authenticity to the charges of "conspiracy." By 1858 a significantly large segment of the populace in the North and the West was of the opinion that unless the Slave Power was defeated by the abolition of slavery, the nation could no longer exist as a free republic. . . . As the fear of "black Republicanism" was used by the proslavery element in the South to unify opinion, so the threat of the Slave Power became an important factor in consolidating antislavery sentiment in the North, and in widening the sectional rift between North and South. . . .

What was the Slave Power, and from what conditions did it arise? One abolitionist called it "that control in and over the government of the United States which is exercised by a comparatively small number of persons, distinguished from the other twenty millions of free citizens, and bound together in a common interest, by being owners of slaves." Definitions agreed that it was fundamentally "an aristocracy constituted and organized on the basis of ownership of slaves." . . . This aristocracy was founded upon these principles: that slavery is not a moral wrong, that it is a right possessed by the slaveholder, that he holds the right of property in man, that slavery is legal, and that it is constitutional. Its power in the South rested upon such things as uneven representation in state legislatures, control of educational and opinion-forming media, and appeals to the economic interests of the non-slaveholder. . . .

After the Compromise of 1850, the Slave Power became a primary object of attack by the abolitionists, and the press and Congress were flooded with warnings of its increasing dominance in national affairs. John Rankin believed that "The Slave Power has already seized upon the General Government, and has overthrown the rights of the free States, and made the citizens slave citizens. . . . The struggle between the slave and the free institutions is for existence. They are antagonistic principles and cannot exist long together—one or the other must fall." In Congress the charge was frequently repeated, and abolitionist speakers and editors gave tongue throughout the land. *"The South is thoroughly in earnest,"* wrote William Goodell. "She is no land of *shams*. There is reality, terrible reality, there. The South has one object in view, and never loses sight of it for a single hour." . . .

The complete indictment against the Slave Power was impressive, and, so far as abolitionist logic was concerned, unanswerable. In the 'forties, Joshua Giddings listed ten proofs of its existence and its strength: the fugitive slave law of 1793; the Creek and Negro troubles in Florida in 1815; the Seminole War; the maintenance of slavery in the District of Columbia; the refusal to recognize Haiti;

the attempts to recapture fugitive slaves from Canada; the suppression of petitions in the House after 1836; the attacks on free speech and press, and the controversy over the mails; the extension of slavery into the Southwest; and the agitation for re-opening the slave trade. Seward, in 1855, added the Missouri Compromise, the annexation of Texas, the war with Mexico, the Kansas struggle, and the Compromise of 1850. The case of Dred Scott afforded another proof, and by 1858 a substantial number of Northerners were ready to agree with the non-abolitionist Cincinnati *Daily Commercial* that "There is such a thing as THE SLAVE POWER. It has marched over and annihilated the boundaries of the states. We are now one great homogeneous slaveholding community."

The aim of the Slave Power, maintained the abolitionists, was threefold: to re-open the slave trade; to extend the institution of slavery throughout the entire nation and beyond; and to remove from the free white man those constitutional and traditional guarantees of liberty which stood in the way of the exercise of control over the middle and lower classes by a privileged aristocracy of slave holder and capitalist. Successful realization of these aims, they warned, was not far in the future. . . .

The abolitionist contention that there existed a Slave Power conspiracy which threatened the existence of personal and civil liberty, and even of republican government itself, helped mold Northern opinion during the years of the slavery controversy. As the Southern charge that abolitionists were conspiring to foment revolt, miscegenation, and social disorder tended to unify certain classes of the South in support of slavery, so did the abolitionist accusation tend to enlist support of certain Northern classes for the antislavery movement. In some ways the "great Slave Power plot" overshadowed the importance in the public mind of "the abolitionist plot," by identifying the slaveholder with a greater conspiracy of infinitely more dangerous designs. Then, too, the abolitionist claim tended to discredit the proslavery argument, reading into it sinister implications; by carrying its logic to the ultimate and finding it apparently dangerous, the abolitionists robbed it of any possible appeal to Northern sympathizers. The "Slave Power Threat" helped to widen the schism between proslavery and antislavery men by making it more difficult than before to be neutral toward or tolerant of slavery or its extension. Neutrality or tolerance, in the abolitionist view, implied lack of interest in or positive hostility to the preservation of the liberal, democratic tradition.

The issue, as the abolitionists saw it, admitted of no compromise. Identifying their cause with the greater cause of freedom, and with the interests of large and relatively unorganized special groups such as laborers and immigrants, the abolitionists considered themselves to be, and convinced many others that they were, the sole remaining protectors of civil and political rights. The "Slave Power Threat" personified the proslavery argument, made it vivid and concrete, and dramatized the controversy into a contest between the forces of good and evil, of freedom and repression, of democracy and aristocracy. When war came, it was justified by the abolitionists and many others as the final phase of the contest, the final defense against the assaults of the Slave Power on traditional American liberties. The South waged war, it was said, ". . . not against Abolitionism or Republicanism, *per se,* but against free institutions and the democratic theory of government universally." Had it not been for the abolitionists, it was said, "We should have had a nation in which were only two classes, *masters and slaves.* The antislavery people contributed to enlighten the people in regard to the villainous purposes and character of slavery . . . , and educated and awakened the people to vigilance to preserve their own liberties."

Was there a Slave Power conspiracy, and were the abolitionists correct in ascribing to it the evil designs which formed so large and important a part of their propaganda? In the sense of the term as used by Wilson, Goodell, Bailey, Garrison, and others—a secret and highly organized group with conscious aims of imposing restrictions upon traditional liberties—the "Slave Power conspiracy" had no real existence. The South was never so completely unified as to reveal evidence of a definite conspiracy. There was Southern disagreement upon such vital issues as Texas annexation, the Mexican War, the Wilmot Proviso, the 1850 Compromise, and the Kansas question. Yet there evidently was agreement among certain Southern leaders that slavery was a good system, probably the best, and that it should be retained and possibly extended. Certainly the events of the period 1830 to 1860 showed that in preserving and extending it the South was willing to infringe upon basic civil and personal rights. The Calhoun-Fitzhugh school of thought, that slavery was "a positive good," was something more than a defense of slavery; it was a counterattack on free institutions. While the "conspiracy" of which the abolitionists warned was no doubt simply an alliance of common economic and political interests, its inherent threat seemed to the times more than idle. The alliance itself was motivated by and founded upon the cardinal principle of slavery—the master principle—and the abolitionists were perhaps not so far wrong in believing that its existence jeopardized the American tradition.

---

2.   "WHERE WILL IT END?"

Below are three contemporary Northern descriptions of the aggressive Southern Slave Power, the first from the Atlantic Monthly, I *(1857), pp. 22–46.*

. . . [That] the stronger half of the nation should suffer the weaker to rule over it in virtue of its weakness, that the richer region should submit to the political tyranny of its impoverished moiety because of that very poverty, is indeed a marvel and a mystery. That the intelligent, educated, and civilized portion of a race should consent to the sway of their ignorant, illiterate, and barbarian companions in the commonwealth, and this by reason of that uncouth barbarism, is an astonishment, and should be a hissing to all beholders everywhere. It would be so to ourselves, were we not so used to the fact, had it not so grown into our essence and ingrained itself with our nature as to seem a vital organism of our being. Of all the anomalies in morals and in politics which the history of civilized man affords, this is surely the most abnormal and the most unreasonable.

The entire history of the United States is but the record of the evidence of this fact. What event in our annals is there that Slavery has not set her brand upon it to mark it as her own? In the very moment of the nation's birth, like the evil fairy of the nursery tale, she was present to curse it with her fatal words. The spell then wound up has gone on increasing in power, until the scanty formulas which seemed in those days of infancy as if they would fade out of the parchment into which they had been foisted, and leave no trace that they ever were, have blotted out all beside, and statesmen and judges read nothing there but the awful and all-pervading name of Slavery. Once intrenched among the institutions of the country, this baleful power has advanced from one position to another, never losing ground, but establishing itself at each successive point more impregnably than before, until it has us at an advantage that encourages it to demand the surrender of our rights, our self-respect, and our honor. . . .

. . . The North, distracted by a thousand interests, has always been at the mercy of whatever barbarian chief in the capitol could throw his slave-whip into the trembling scale of party. The government having been always, since this century began, at least, the creature and the tool of the slaveholders, the whole patronage of the nation, and the treasury filled chiefly by Northern commerce, have been at their command to help manipulate and mold plastic Northern consciences into practicable shapes. . . .

The baleful influence . . . shed by Slavery on our national history and our public men has not yet spent its malignant forces. It has, indeed, reached a height which a few years ago it was thought the wildest fanaticism to predict; but its fatal power will not be stayed in the mid-sweep of its career. The Ordinance of 1787 torn to shreds and scattered to the winds,—the line drawn in 1820, which the slaveholders plighted their faith Slavery should never overstep, insolently as well as infamously obliterated,—Slavery presiding in the Cabinet, seated on the Supreme Bench, absolute in the halls of Congress,—no man can say what shape its next aggression may not take to itself. A direct attack on the freedom of the press and the liberty of speech at the North, where alone either exists, were no more incredible than the later insolences of its tyranny. The battle not yet over in Kansas, for the compulsory establishment of Slavery there by the interposition of the Federal arm, will be renewed in every Territory as it is ripening into a State. . . . Mighty events are at hand, even at the door; and the mission of them all will be to fix Slavery firmly and forever on the throne of this nation.

Is the success of this conspiracy to be final and eternal? Are the States which name themselves, in simplicity or irony, the Free States, to be always the satrapies of a central power like this? Are we forever to submit to be cheated out of our national rights by an oligarchy as despicable as it is detestable, because it clothes itself in the forms of democracy, and allows us the ceremonies of choice, the name of power, and the permission to register the edicts of the sovereign? We, who broke the sceptre of King George, and set our feet on the supremacy of the British Parliament, surrender ourselves, bound hand in foot in bonds of our own weaving, into the hands of the slaveholding Philistines! . . . Is our spirit effectually broken? is the brand of meanness and compromise burnt in uneffaceably upon our souls? and are we never to be roused, by any indignities, to fervent resentment and effectual resistance? The answer to these grave questions lies with ourselves alone. One hundred thousand, or three hundred thousand . . . [slaveholders], however crafty and unscrupulous, cannot forever keep under their rule more than twenty millions, as much their superiors in wealth and intelligence as in numbers, except by their own consent.

---

3.   THE FOLLY OF THE SOUTH

Speech of Representative John B. Alley of Massachusetts, January 26, 1861, in Congressional Globe, 36 Congress, 2 Session, I, p. 584.

Had the South used her power prudently and acted wisely, she would have controlled the destinies of this Government for generations yet to come. . . . But, flushed with victories so constant and thorough and maddened by every expression of opposition to their peculiar institution, they commenced a work of proscription and aggression upon the rights of the people of the North, which has finally forced them to rise in their might and drive them from power. They commenced their aggressions upon the North in some of the southern States by the enactment of unconstitutional laws, imprisoning colored seamen, and refusing to allow those laws to be tested before the proper tribunals. They trampled upon the sacred right of petition; they rifled and burnt our mails, if they suspected they contained anything in condemnation of slavery. They proscribed every northern man from office who would not smother and deny his honest convictions upon slavery, and barter his manhood for place. They annexed foreign territory avowedly to extend and strengthen their peculiar institution, and made war in defense and support of that policy. They refused admission into the Union of States with free constitutions, unless they could have, as an equivalent, new guarantees for slavery. They passed a fugitive slave bill, some of the provisions of which were so merciless, and unnecessary as they were inhuman, that they would have disgraced the worst despotism of Europe. They repealed that "Missouri compromise act," which they had themselves forced upon the North, against their wishes and their votes; and after having attained all their share of the benefit, they struck it down, against the indignant and almost unanimous protest of the whole North, for the purpose of forcing slavery upon an unwilling people. They undertook to prevent, by violent means, the settlement of Kansas by free-State men. They invaded that Territory, and plundered and murdered its citizens by armed force. . . . Not satisfied with all this, they tried to force upon them, against their consent, a constitution permitting and protecting slavery; and for "spurning the bribe," they have been kept out of the Union, and made to suffer all manner of indignities. Every new triumph of the South and every concession by the North has only whetted their appetite for still more, and encouraged them in making greater claims and more unreasonable demands, until to-day they are threatening the overthrow of the Government if we do not give them additional guarantees for protection to their slave property in territory which we do not now own.

---

4.   THE THIRTY YEARS' CONSPIRACY

Trenton Gazette (January 3, 1861).

The present attempt at a forcible dissolution of the Union, is the result of a conspiracy which has been brooded upon and actively conducted by ambitious men for nearly thirty years past—sometimes elated by prospects of success, sometimes chagrined by unexpected defeat, they have, since 1832, steadily pushed on their plot, recruited their forces, and at last, confident in their strength, they have openly announced their plans, and defied resistance to their execution. Their aim is to found a Southern Empire, which shall be composed of the Southern States, Mexico, Central America, and Cuba, of which the arch-conspirators are to be the rulers.

---

5.   THE RECORD OF THE SLAVE POWER

Henry Wilson of Massachusetts was one of the early Northern historians whose history of the sectional conflict contained a severe indictment of the Slave Power. Wilson, a "radical" Republican, was an active participant in the politics of that era, serving for many years as a United States senator and as vice-president in Grant's second administration until his death in 1875. Below are extracts from his massive History of the Rise and Fall of the Slave Power in America *(Boston: 1872–1877), I, pp. 1–2, 165–66, 567; II, pp. 174–75, 188, 406, 462–64, 534–35, 655–56, 666, 673–74, 703–704; III, pp. 1–2.*

• • •

God's Holy Word declares that man was doomed to eat his bread in the sweat of his face. History and tradition teach that the indolent, the crafty, and the strong, unmindful of human rights, have ever sought to evade this Divine decree by filching their bread from the constrained and unpaid toil of others. From inborn indolence, conjoined with avarice, pride, and lust of power, has sprung slavery in all its Protean forms. . . . Thus have grown and flourished caste and privilege, those deadly foes of the rights and well-being of mankind, which can exist only by despoiling the many for the benefit of the few.

American slavery reduced man, created in the Divine image, to property. . . . It made him a beast of burden in the field of toil, an outcast in social life, a cipher in the courts of law, and a pariah in the house of God. To claim himself, or to use himself for his own benefit or the benefit of wife or child, was deemed a crime. His master could dispose of his person at will, and of everything acquired by his enforced and unrequited toil.

This complete subversion of the natural rights of millions . . . constituted a system antagonistic to the doctrines of reason and the monitions of conscience, and developed and gratified the most intense spirit of personal pride, a love of class distinctions, and the lust of dominion. Hence arose a commanding power, ever sensitive, jealous, proscriptive, dominating, and aggressive, which was recognized and fitly characterized as the Slave Power.

This slavery and this Slave Power, in their economical, social, moral, ecclesiastical, and political relations to the people and to the government, demoralizing the one and distracting the councils of the other, made up the vital issues of that "irrepressible conflict" which finally culminated in a civil war. . . .

In the Missouri struggle freedom and slavery grappled for the mastery. Freedom lost, and slavery won. Freedom became timid, hesitating, yielding; slavery became bolder, more aggressive, and more dominating. Freedom retreated from one lost position to another; slavery advanced from conquest to conquest. Several years of unresisted despotism of the Slave Power followed this consummation of the Missouri compromise. The dark spirit of slavery swayed the policy of the republic. . . . Institutions of learning, benevolence, and religion, political organizations, and public men bent in unresisting submission before this all-conquering despotism, whose aggressive advances became more resistless, as its successive victories became more complete. But amid this general defection and complete surrender there were a few who kept the faith of the fathers, and firmly and bravely adhered to the doctrines of human rights. . . .

[Then] the startling issues growing out of the Texas plot, the increasing aggressions of the Slave Power, brought the various questions pertaining to slavery to the hearts and homes of hundreds of thousands who had heretofore given little heed to abolition movements. They broadened and deepened the public interest, so that the conflicts of opinion and the adoption of policies passed, in a large degree, from the arena and control of antislavery societies to the wider domain of general debate and political combinations. . . . And thus the subject which had been discussed only by the few became the theme of the many, and that which had been confined to scattered circles overspread the land. . . .

The years intervening between the opening of negotiations for the annexation of Texas in 1843 and the close of the Presidential election in 1852 have no parallel for the intensity, variety, and disastrous results of the slavery struggle. During those years the successful attempt was made to annex the foreign nation of Texas to the United States; the war with Mexico was fought; vast accessions of territory were secured, and the effort to devote them to freedom was made and failed; the Fugitive Slave Law was enacted and mercilessly executed; the misnamed compromise measures proposed by the slave-masters were adopted and accepted as a "finality" by the conventions of the great national parties; while the crowning act of those years of disaster and infamy was the indorsement by the people of this whole series of aggressions by the triumphant election of Franklin Pierce, whose whole public and partisan career had ever been fully and even ostentatiously committed to the purposes and plans of the Slave Power. . . .

These persistent efforts of the propagandists in behalf of slavery could not but fix attention upon it as the cause of all these constant and disturbing movements, while it challenged investigation anew into the merits of a system for which such efforts were made and such sacrifices called for. Especially did this result from the relinquishment by its defenders of the former arguments that slavery was an entailed evil, for which the present generations were not responsible,—a temporary evil, that carried within itself the seeds of its own destruction, and which must soon pass away in the presence and by the workings of free institutions. The new dogmas that slavery was a good, and not an evil; that it was not temporary, but to be permanent; that it was not sectional, but national; and that the Constitution carried it wherever it went, presented the whole subject in a new light. Many felt that it must be re-examined, and that the arguments and considerations that formerly reconciled could satisfy them no longer. . . .

Reflecting men . . . saw, as never before, that there must be some malignant and potent agency at work, that could accomplish such results and give such a character to the nation's history. They called it the Slave Power. . . . They saw that there existed a commanding power in the land, which made its influence everywhere felt, . . . and before which all other interests were compelled in greater or less degree to bend. It was as if *somewhere* some imperious autocrat or secret conclave held court or council, in which slavery's every interest, necessity, and demand were considered and cared for, and from which were issued its stern and inexorable decrees. . . .

The determined purpose of the Slave Power to make slavery the predominating national interest was never more clearly revealed than by the proposed repeal of the Missouri compromise. This was a deliberate and direct assault upon freedom. Many, indeed, under the pleas of fraternity and loyalty to the Union, palliated and apologized for this breach of faith; but the numbers were increasing every hour, as the struggle progressed, who could no longer be deceived by these hollow pretences. They could not close their eyes to the dangers of the country, and they were compelled to disavow what was so manifestly wrong, and to disconnect themselves from men and parties who were making so little concealment of their nefarious purposes and of their utter profligacy of principle. . . .

The Kansas-Nebraska Act was no mere abstraction. Though its most prominent and persistent advocates, in their noisy clamor and claim in its behalf, pleaded chiefly its vindication of the principle of local self-government, it soon became apparent that its ultimate purpose occupied a far higher place in their regard. Slavery, and not popular sovereignty, was the object aimed at. . . . Calculating that this action of Congress and the close contiguity of slaveholding Missouri, with such co-operation as the known sympathy of the other slaveholding States would afford, could easily throw into Kansas a sufficient population to give to slavery the necessary preponderance, the slave propagandists regarded their victory in the halls of legislation as tantamount to the final success of their deep-laid schemes. . . . When, therefore, Congress had been dragooned into the adoption of the Kansas-Nebraska Act, with its newly invented and much-vaunted doctrine of popular sovereignty, it was supposed . . . that it was only a question of time when Kansas should become a slave State. . . . But they miscalculated. They did not fully comprehend the forces which freedom had at command, nor the purposes of Providence concerning the nation. . . .

The purpose to make Kansas a free State and the systematized efforts to carry that purpose into effect mark an important era in the progress of the slavery struggle. It was a deliberate and successful stand made by the friends of freedom against the aggressions of the Slave Power. . . . But it was a purpose that foretokened a fearful contest, fierce encounters, and bloody strifes. . . .

When the prohibition of slavery embodied in the Missouri compromise was repealed, it was declared to be the intent to leave the people of Kansas and Nebraska "perfectly free to form and regulate their domestic institutions in their own way, subject only to the Constitution of the United States." But this was a pretext, a device, a trick. The slavemasters who believed that the Constitution carried slavery into the Territories used this artifice as a temporary expedient to secure the overthrow of the principle of its prohibition, and to open a vast Territory to its polluting touch. . . . The Dred Scott decision and the Lecompton constitution . . . revealed the real character of the "sovereignty" involved, or, rather, it made apparent the utter insincerity of all pretensions of regard for the popular will, and the shameless duplicity that characterized the course of those who conceived and engineered that astounding fraud. . . .

During the closing days of the rule of the Slave Power in America madness seemed to rule in the counsels of the Southern leaders. . . . As if assured that they had but to speak to be heeded, had but to command to be obeyed, they seemed to regard the results already achieved as but stepping-stones to a higher position and more complete control, the advances already made as only affording a new base of operations. . . . Not satisfied with past concessions, the obliteration of the landmarks of freedom and the refusal of all discrimination in behalf of human rights, they seemed resolved that slavery should become emphatically national, that no part of the Republic should be beyond the reach of its encroachments, . . . and that the flag of the Union should wave only over the land of the slave. . . .

The proscription, lawlessness, and barbarism of slavery were the necessary conditions of its existence. Its essential injustice and inevitable cruelties, its malign and controlling influences upon society and the state, its violence of word and conduct, its unfriendliness to freedom of thought and its repression of free speech . . . , its stern and bloody defiance of all who questioned its action or resisted its behests, were specially manifest during the closing years of its terrible reign. Statutes, however severe, and courts, however servile, were not enough. The mob was sovereign. Vigilance committees took the law into their own hands, prompting and executing the verdicts and decisions of self-constituted judges and self-selected juries. Merchants on lawful business, travellers for pleasure, teachers and day-laborers, all felt alike the proscriptive ban. A merciless vindictiveness prevailed, and held its stern and pitiless control over the whole South. The privileges and immunities of citizenship were worthless, and the law afforded no protection. Southern papers were filled with accounts of the atrocities perpetrated, and volumes alone could contain descriptions of all that transpired during this reign of terror. . . .

The Democratic national convention of 1860 was memorable . . . because it marked an epoch in the history of the Slave Power.

It was the culmination of the irrepressible conflict, the turning-point in the tide of oppression which had flooded the land for so many years, and which from that hour began to subside. . . . The Slave Power went into that convention master of the situation, with the prestige of almost uninterrupted victories on its banners, in possession of every department of the government . . . ; and yet it recklessly abandoned its vantage-ground, threw away the sceptre it had so long and so remorselessly wielded, and with suicidal hands began the work of its own destruction.

The . . . question that distracted and at length divided the convention, was that of nominating Mr. Douglas as the Democratic candidate in the pending canvass. His acknowledged ability, his prominence in the party, his leadership in the Kansas-Nebraska struggle, his long and loudly proclaimed Southern proclivities, all pointed to him as the Democratic standard-bearer in the coming strife. But with all his devotion to Southern interests, his record was not sufficiently clean to satisfy their exacting demands. He had faltered, and for once had failed to come up to their full measure of fealty upon the Lecompton issue; and it became an unpardonable sin, not to be forgotten or forgiven. Though consistency, the instinct of self-preservation and a wise regard for the preservation of his party's ascendency in the Northern States demanded this course, Mr. Douglas was made the victim of the most unrelenting opposition, and that from the very men for whom he had made the greatest sacrifices. . . . That they were unwisely violent, that their vaulting ambition o'erleaped itself, and that they themselves inflicted fatal wounds upon their own cause, which no opposition then organized could have done, are matters of general belief, if not of historic record. . . .

The canvass . . . closed on the 6th of November by the election of Abraham Lincoln. . . . The slave-masters . . . fully comprehended the real significance of the result. They saw how much freedom had gained and how much slavery had lost. For more than two generations they had dictated principles, shaped policies, made Presidents and cabinets, judges of the Supreme Court, Senators, and Representatives. Now, for the first time, they had been beaten, the charm of invincibility was broken, the prestige of success was gone. Their cherished policy of slavery-expansion had been arrested, and their new dogma of slavery-protection had been forever defeated. . . . And slavery in the States, hedged in, surrounded, and pressed upon by the growing numbers and increasing vigor of free institutions and by the combined forces of advancing civilization and the manifest providences of God, must inevitably be put in process of ultimate, though it might be gradual extinction.

. . . [Hence Southern leaders], appealing to local interests, pandering to prejudices, painting in glowing colors the advantages of separation, . . . pleading the State-rights theory that it was one of their reserved powers to withdraw at will from the Union, . . . did not find it difficult to persuade the class of large slaveholders to make the rash experiment, and enter upon the perilous venture of revolution. Small slaveholders, too, and non-slaveholders even, confused by the blinding counsels and dominating influence of leaders they had been accustomed to follow, could not withstand the current, and were rapidly drifting into rebellion.

———

6. SECESSION AND THE "SOUTHERN REVOLUTIONARY NATIONALIST PARTY"

Lee Benson, in his book Toward the Scientific Study of History *(Philadelphia: J. B. Lippincott Co., 1972), approaches the problem of Civil War causation with an analytical model of a political community "that includes two or more relatively sizeable territorial culture groups." Tension between such groups, he believes, has more than once led to secessionist movements, or "separatist revolutions." In trying to determine why such a revolution occurred in the United States in 1860–1861, the proper question to ask is not what caused the Civil War but who caused it. In answering the question Benson uses the term "Southern Revolutionary Nationalist Party" rather than the term "Slave Power." Though his analysis is a good deal more sophisticated than Henry Wilson's, he does nevertheless seem to suggest that Wilson was on the right track.*

It seems as certain as anything can be in human affairs that the gradual abolition of black slavery in the North after 1790 and its flourishing state of development in the South after 1815 (particularly after 1833) constituted a *necessary* condition for The War for Southern Independence. It was a *sufficient* condition, however, only to insure the existence of a small group of elite Southerners passionately determined to bring about secession from a political community whose Constitution or Administration *officially, publicly* forbade black slavery in some geographic areas. To forbid—*officially, publicly*—slavery in the North, and later in parts of the West, was to stigmatize it. Inevitably, some Southerners whose social roles derived from the existence of a social system based upon slavery perceived its stigmatization as intolerably threatening to their honor and self-esteem. To a greater or lesser degree, it was also perceived as threatening to the honor and self-esteem of *all white* Southerners. . . .

That some significant proportion of Southern elites should have come to view the stigmatization of slavery as literally intolerable becomes even more understandable if we make this assumption: Particularly in respect to members of the master class, antebellum Southern society tended to develop individuals with *authoritarian* personality traits more strongly than it did individuals with *reconciling* personality traits. That assumption seems reasonable, particularly when we consider the functional requirements of a society in which white master-black slave relationships were dominant. . . .

Over time, who were the secessionists, and what did they do to achieve their goal, and why did they succeed? A second set of conditions greatly increased the *probability*, both that a dedicated group of Southern secessionists would form, and that the movement they set in motion would succeed. Summarily described, that set of conditions can be identified as the Constitutional revolution of 1787–1788 and the radically defective political system it created.

Given the heterogeneous, decentralized, libertarian, and *relatively* prosperous nature of American society, it was radically defective even during the 1790s; as American society developed in the nineteenth century, it became increasingly defective.

. . . Given the nature of American society in the late eighteenth century and its reasonably predictable evolution in the nineteenth, the governmental system created by the new constitution was almost certain to, and did actually, produce: 1) an incredibly irresponsible party system; 2) an extraordinarily disastrous concentration of real and symbolic power in the Presidential *office*. . . . Both developments contributed greatly to the formation of Northern and Southern territorial culture groups. Both made it far more likely that some political actors would successfully try to exacerbate, rather than reduce, tensions between Southerners and Northerners.

Given the evolution of American society after 1790, among the more radical defects of the American political system, first place must go to the cluster of features that facilitated the highly disproportionate concentration of national political power in a heterogeneous *coalition* of Southern political elites. That concentration of power particularly contributed to the formation of a Southern secessionist group. Among other reasons, it did so because, as late as the early 1830s, Southern elites strongly tended to be ideologically defensive about their society. . . .

During the nullification crisis . . . a very small number of Southern political elites converted to Southern nationalism. . . . After the nullification crisis passed in 1832–1833, with the Old Southern Republican anticentralization position increasingly dominant on the national level, the Presidential succession crisis of 1833–1836 created the basis for a powerful *coalition* of Southern "*provincials*," (i.e., men who viewed the State as the primary political community or "country" and out-of-staters as "foreigners"), *sectionalists* and *nationalists*. (The three groups are analytically distinct, but in practice, as a theory of separatist revolutions would predict, the lines between them blurred and shifted. As almost invariably occurs during the early stages of a separatist revolution, individuals wavered and oscillated in their commitment to Southern

Nationalism. Separatists strongly tend to experience genuine "identity crises," a consideration that helps us to understand not only the oscillation of the Southern Nationalists but their passion.)

Obviously, I use the terms "revolutionary" and "party" in a very loose sense, but I think it instructive to say that, in 1835–1836, a tiny group of Southern nationalists formed the "Southern Revolutionary Nationalist Party" that ultimately brought about secession in 1860–1861. . . .

Determined to heighten Southern national consciousness, the Southern Nationalists joined other disaffected Southern political elites in fierce opposition to the election of a Northerner, Martin Van Buren, to the presidency. . . . In December 1835, during the course of the presidential conflict and tremendously aided by it, . . . James H. Hammond [of South Carolina] accidentally stumbled on the issue of trying to prevent Congress from receiving or routinely disposing of antislavery petitions. Accidentally discovered by Hammond . . . what came to be known as the "Gag Rule" issue was consciously used to heighten sectional antagonisms and Southern national consciousness. If a small group of Northern abolitionists had not existed, Southern nationalists, sectionalists and provincials would have had to create them—as, in fact, they did.

As long as abolitionists concentrated upon trying to arouse intensely racist Northerners to force Southerners to right the wrongs done to black slaves, they were doomed to remain a tiny sect, politically impotent, their lives literally endangered in the North. But the fight over the Gag Rule on petitions, deliberately initiated by a loose coalition of disaffected Southern elites as a tactical maneuver in the larger strategy of the presidential succession crisis, transformed the "antislavery crusade."

Nicely illustrating action-reaction propositions about how conflicts escalate until they culminate in large-scale violence, to the mutual benefit of Northern abolitionists and Southern secessionists, the antislavery crusade became, as some leading actors on both sides hoped and other contemporaries feared that it would, no longer an impotent struggle for the rights of black slaves, but a basic conflict over the rights, principles, honor and self-esteem of Northern and Southern *white citizens.*

That conflict manifested itself in a variety of forms from 1835 to 1861. Understandably enough, to justify breaking away from the political community for which their forefathers "fought and died," most secessionists probably convinced themselves, erroneously, that their society was in "mortal danger" from Northern aggressors. Moreover, apart from misperceptions of reality, for tactical reasons Southern secessionists, sectionalists and provincials demanded that extremely "bold action" be taken to meet the danger posed by Northern aggressors "on the threshold." In turn, either out of conviction or expediency, some Northerners took the position that, unless "the North" took extremely bold action, a real danger existed that slavery would not only expand in the West but would be reinstituted in the North.

Predictably, the conflict deliberately stimulated by Southern Nationalists after 1830, particularly after 1835, had irrational aspects, involved serious misperceptions of reality, and increasingly was conducted in frenetic and hyperemotional fashion. But it was not basically irrational or pathological. . . . It was deeply-rooted in the objective reality of men's need for self-esteem. It was the type of conflict likely to develop in bicultural or multicultural political communities. In one form or another, its counterpart can be found today in large numbers of nation-states.

Once aroused, conflicts over the self-esteem and honor of members of territorial culture groups take on a life of their own. . . . In accounting for the ultimate success of the Southern Nationalists, however, I think that the greatest weight must be given to the extraordinarily irresponsible, extraordinarily defective character of the American political system during the antebellum decades. . . . And as Calhoun brilliantly observed in his theoretical works written during the 1840s, the most radically defective part of that system was the exalted role given to the indivisible presidency in a society that contained territorial culture groups with a strong latent propensity to conflict. . . .

To restate . . . [my] hypothesis in summary form:

A small group of Southern Nationalists ultimately succeeded in bringing about secession. They succeeded largely because the American political system, particularly the Presidency, developed in a way favorable to their cause. Among other defects, its irresponsible character, its built-in propensity to stimulate sectional cleavages, its incitement to demagoguery, its powerful inducements to and rich rewards for individual and group opportunism and amorality, its antidemocratic exaltation of "strong Presidents," its glorification of the cult of "the virile personality," all strengthened the ability of Southern Nationalists (and sectionalists and provincials) to initiate and intensify political conflicts over the self-esteem and honor of members of the two main territorial cultural groups that distinctly evolved after 1790—a development in itself strongly stimulated by the defects of the American political system. No group worked more consciously and more effectively than the Southern Nationalists to speed up that process. Who caused the Civil War? Living in a bicultural society with a radically defective political system, the Southern Nationalists, much more than any other group, caused it to occur by working unyieldingly, intensively, rationally, effectively, to achieve what later came to be known as "The Lost Cause."

-----

7. A WARNING TO THE NORTH

Senator John C. Calhoun of South Carolina, the ablest champion of the South's slaveholders, firmly believed that the sectional crisis resulted not from Southern but from Northern aggressions. His last speech in the Senate, read on March 4, 1850, was a denunciation of the Compromise of 1850 and a warning to Northerners that their encroachments upon Southern rights were endangering the Union. The speech is printed in Richard K. Cralle (ed.), The Works of John C. Calhoun (New York: 1853–56), IV, pp. 542–73.

I have, Senators, believed from the first that the agitation of the subject of slavery would, if not prevented by some timely and effective measure, end in disunion. Entertaining this opinion, I have, on all proper occasions, endeavored to call the attention of both the two great parties which divide the country to adopt some measure to prevent so great a disaster, but without success. The agitation has been permitted to proceed, with almost no attempt to resist it, until it has reached a point when it can no longer be disguised or denied that the Union is in danger. You have thus had forced upon you the greatest and the gravest question that can ever come under your consideration—How can the Union be preserved?

To give a satisfactory answer to this mighty question, it is indispensable to have an accurate and thorough knowledge of the nature and the character of the cause by which the Union is endangered. . . . The first question then, . . . is—What is it that has endangered the Union?

To this question there can be but one answer,—that the immediate cause is the almost universal discontent which pervades all the States composing the Southern section of the Union. This widely-extended discontent is not of recent origin. It commenced with the agitation of the slavery question, and has been increasing ever since. The next question, going one step further back, is— What has caused this widely diffused and almost universal discontent? . . .

One of the causes is, undoubtedly, to be traced to the long-continued agitation of the slave question on the part of the North, and the many aggressions which they have made on the rights of the South during the time. . . .

There is another lying back of it—with which this is intimately connected—that may be regarded as the great and primary cause. This is to be found in the fact that the equilibrium between the two sections, in the Government as it stood when the constitution was ratified and the Government put in action, has been destroyed. At that time there was nearly a perfect equilibrium between the two, which afforded ample means of each to protect itself against the aggression of the other; but, as it now stands, one section has the exclusive power of controlling the Government, which leaves the other without any adequate means of protecting itself against its encroachment and oppression. . . .

As, then, the North has the absolute control over the Government, it is manifest, that on all questions between it and the South, where there is a diversity of interests, the interests of the latter will be sacrificed to the former, however oppressive the effects may be; as the South possesses no means by which it can resist, through the action of the Government. But if there was no question of vital importance to the South, in reference to which there was a diversity of views between the two sections, this state of things might be endured, without the hazard of destruction to the South. But such is not the fact. There is a question of vital importance to the Southern section, in reference to which the views and feelings of the two sections are as opposite and hostile as they can possibly be.

I refer to the relation between the two races in the Southern section, which constitutes a vital portion of her social organization. Every portion of the North entertains views and feelings more or less hostile to it. . . . On the contrary, the Southern section regards the relation as one which cannot be destroyed without subjecting the two races to the greatest calamity, and the section to poverty, desolation, and wretchedness; and accordingly they feel bound, by every consideration of interest and safety, to defend it.

This hostile feeling on the part of the North towards the social organization of the South long lay dormant, but it only required some cause to act on those who felt most intensely that they were responsible for its continuance, to call it into action. The increasing power of this Government, and of the control of the Northern section over all its departments, furnished the cause. It was this which made an impression on the minds of many, that there was little or no restraint to prevent the Government from doing whatever it might choose to do. This was sufficient of itself to put the most fanatical portion of the North in action, for the purpose of destroying the existing relation between the two races in the South.

The first organized movement towards it commenced in 1835. Then, for the first time, societies were organized, presses established, lecturers sent forth to excite the people of the North, and incendiary publications scattered over the whole South, through the mail. . . . At the meeting of Congress, petitions poured in from the North, calling upon Congress to abolish slavery in the District of Columbia, and to prohibit, what they called, the internal slave trade between the States—announcing at the same time, that their ultimate object was to abolish slavery, not only in the District, but in the States and throughout the Union. At this period, the number engaged in the agitation was small, and possessed little or no personal influence. . . .

What has since followed are but natural consequences. With the success of their first movement, this small fanatical party began to acquire strength. . . . With the increase of their influence, they extended the sphere of their action. In a short time after the commencement of their first movement, they had acquired sufficient influence to induce the legislatures of most of the Northern States to pass acts, which in effect abrogated the clause of the constitution that provides for the delivery up of fugitive slaves. Not long after, petitions followed to abolish slavery in forts, magazines, and dockyards, and all other places where Congress had exclusive power of legislation. This was followed by petitions and resolutions of legislatures of the Northern States, and popular meetings, to exclude the Southern States from all territories acquired, or to be acquired, and to prevent the admission of any State hereafter into the Union, which, by its constitution, does not prohibit slavery. And Congress is invoked to do all this, expressly with the view to the final abolition of slavery in the States. . . .

Such is a brief history of the agitation, as far as it has yet advanced. Now I ask, Senators, what is there to prevent its further progress, until it fulfills the ultimate end proposed, unless some decisive measure should be adopted to prevent it? . . . Instead of being weaker, all the elements in favor of agitation are stronger now than they were in 1835, when it first commenced, while all the elements of influence on the part of the South are weaker. . . . Is it, then, not certain, that if something is not done to arrest it, the South will be forced to choose between abolition and secession?

Having now, Senators, explained what it is that endangers the Union, and traced it to its cause, and explained its nature and character, the question again recurs— How can the Union be saved? To this I answer, there is but one way by which it can be—and that is—by adopting such measures as will satisfy the States belonging to the Southern section, that they can remain in the Union consistently with their honor and their safety. . . . Do *this*, and discontent will cease—harmony and kind feelings between the sections be restored—and every apprehension of danger to the Union removed. The question, then, is— How can this be done? . . . There is but one way . . . and that is, by a full and final settlement, on the principle of justice, of all the questions at issue between the two sections. The South asks for justice, simple justice, and less she ought not to take. She has no compromise to offer, but the constitution; and no concession or surrender to make. She has already surrendered so much that she has little left to surrender. Such a settlement would go to the root of the evil, and remove all cause of discontent, by satisfying the South, she could remain honorably and safely in the Union, and hereby restore the harmony and fraternal feelings between the sections, which existed anterior to the Missouri agitation. Nothing else can, with any certainty, finally and for ever settle the questions at issue, terminate agitation, and save the Union.

But can this be done? Yes, easily; not by the weaker party, for it can of itself do nothing—not even protect itself—but by the stronger. The North has only to will it to accomplish it—to do justice by conceding to the South an equal right in the acquired territory, and to do her duty by causing the stipulations relative to fugitive slaves to be faithfully fulfilled—to cease the agitation of the slave question, and to provide for the insertion of a provision in the constitution, by an amendment, which will restore to the South, in substance, the power she possessed of protecting herself, before the equilibrium between the sections was destroyed by the action of this Government. There will be no difficulty in devising such a provision—one that will protect the South, and which, at the same time, will improve and strengthen the Government, instead of impairing and weakening it.

But will the North agree to this? It is for her to answer the question. But, I will say, she cannot refuse, if she has half the love of the Union which she professes to have, or without justly exposing herself to the charge that her love of power and aggrandizement is far greater than her love of the Union. At all events, the responsibility of saving the Union rests on the North, and not on the South. The South cannot save it by any act of hers, and the

North may save it without any sacrifice whatever, unless to do justice, and to perform her duties under the constitution, should be regarded by her as a sacrifice.

It is time, Senators, that there should be an open and manly avowal on all sides, as to what is intended to be done. If the question is not now settled, it is uncertain whether it ever can hereafter be; and we, as the representatives of the States of this Union, . . . should come to a distinct understanding as to our respective views, in order to ascertain whether the great questions at issue can be settled or not. If you, who represent the stronger portion, cannot agree to settle them on the broad principle of justice and duty, say so; and let the States we both represent agree to separate and part in peace. If you are unwilling we should part in peace, tell us so, and we shall know what to do, when you reduce the question to submission or resistance. If you remain silent, you will compel us to infer by your acts what you intend. In that case, California will become the test question. If you admit her, under all the difficulties that oppose her admission, you compel us to infer that you intend to exclude us from the whole of the acquired territories, with the intention of destroying, irretrievably, the equilibrium between the two sections. We would be blind not to perceive in that case, that your real objects are power and aggrandizement, and infatuated not to act accordingly.

I have now, Senators, done my duty in expressing my opinions fully, freely, and candidly, on this solemn occasion. In doing so, I have been governed by the motives which have governed me in all the stages of the agitation of the slavery question since its commencement. I have exerted myself, during the whole period, to arrest it, with the intention of saving the Union, if it could be done; and if it could not, to save the section where it has pleased Providence to cast my lot, and which I sincerely believe has justice and the constitution on its side. Having faithfully done my duty to the best of my ability, both to the Union and my section, throughout this agitation, I shall have the consolation, let what will come, that I am free from all responsibility.

8.   THE RECORD OF THE BLACK REPUBLICANS

New Orleans Daily Crescent (November 18, 1860), quoted in
Dwight L. Dumond (ed.), Southern Editorials on Secession (New
York: 1931), pp. 235–38.

The history of the Abolition or Black Republican party of the North
is a history of repeated injuries and usurpations, all having in direct
object the establishment of absolute tyranny over the slaveholding
States. And all without the smallest warrant, excuse or justification.
We have appealed to their generosity, justice and patriotism, but all
without avail. From the beginning, we have only asked to be let
alone in the enjoyment of our plain, inalienable rights, as explicitly
guaranteed in our common organic law. We have never aggressed
upon the North, nor sought to aggress upon the North. Yet every
appeal and expostulation has only brought upon us renewed insults
and augmented injuries. They have robbed us of our property, they
have murdered our citizens while endeavoring to reclaim that
property by lawful means, they have set at naught the decrees of the
Supreme Court, they have invaded our States and killed our
citizens, they have declared their unalterable determination to
exclude us altogether from the Territories, they have nullified the
laws of Congress, and finally they have capped the mighty pyramid
of unfraternal enormities by electing Abraham Lincoln to the Chief
Magistracy, on a platform and by a system which indicates nothing
but the subjugation of the South and the complete ruin of her
social, political and industrial institutions.

All these statements are not only true, but absolutely indisput-
able. The facts are well known and patent. Under these circumstances, in view of the dark record of the past, the threatening
aspect of the present, and the very serious contingencies which the
future holds forth, we submit and appeal to a candid and honorable
world, whether the Southern people have not been astonishingly
patient under gross provocation—whether they have not exhibited
remarkable forbearance—whether they have not been long suffering, slow to anger and magnanimous, on numerous occasions where

indignation was natural, and severe measures of retaliation justifiable? There can be no doubt on this point. For the sake of peace, for the sake of harmony, the South has compromised until she can compromise no farther, without she is willing to compromise away character, political equality, social and individual interest, and every right and franchise which freemen hold dear.

---

9. THE INJURED SOUTH

After the Civil War, Jefferson Davis of Mississippi, former president of the Confederate States of America, wrote a history of the crisis entitled The Rise and Fall of the Confederate Government (*New York: 1881*). *In it he presented the South's case against the North and refuted the concept of a Slave Power conspiracy. The following passages are from Volume I, pages 77–85.*

The reader of many of the treatises . . . which have been put forth as historical, if dependent upon such alone for information, might naturally enough be led to the conclusion that the controversies which arose between the States, and the war in which they culminated, were caused by efforts on the one side to extend and perpetuate human slavery, and on the other to resist it and establish human liberty. The Southern States and Southern people have been sedulously represented as "propagandists" of slavery, and the Northern as the defenders and champions of universal freedom, and this view has been so arrogantly assumed, so dogmatically asserted, and so persistently reiterated,- that its authors have, in many cases, perhaps, succeeded in bringing themselves to believe it, as well as in impressing it widely upon the world. . . .

. . . [The] sectional hostility which exhibited itself in 1820, on the application of Missouri for admission into the Union, which again broke out on the proposition for the annexation of Texas in 1844, and which reappeared after the Mexican war, never again to be suppressed until its fell results had been fully accomplished, was not the consequence of any difference on the abstract question of slavery. It was the offspring of sectional rivalry and political ambition. It would have manifested itself just as certainly if slavery had existed in all the States, or if there had not been a negro in America. . . .

Of course, the diversity of institutions contributed, in some minor degree, to the conflict of interests. There is an action and reaction of cause and consequence, which limits and modifies any general statement of a political truth. I am stating general principles—not defining modifications and exceptions with the precision of a mathematical proposition or a bill in chancery. The truth remains intact and incontrovertible, that the existence of African servitude was in no wise the cause of the conflict, but only an incident. In the later controversies that arose, however, its effect in operating as a lever upon the passions, prejudices, or sympathies of mankind, was so potent that it has been spread, like a thick cloud, over the whole horizon of historic truth.

As for the institution of negro servitude, it was a matter entirely subject to the control of the States. No power was ever given to the General Government to interfere with it, but an obligation was imposed to protect it. Its existence and validity were distinctly recognized by the Constitution. . . .

The President and Vice-President of the United States, every Senator and Representative in Congress, the members of every State Legislature, and "all executive and judicial officers, both of the United States and of the several States," were required to take an oath (or affirmation) to support the Constitution. . . . It is . . . impossible to reconcile with the obligations of honor or honesty the conduct of those who, having taken such an oath, made use of the powers and opportunities of the offices held under its sanctions to nullify its obligations and neutralize its guarantees. The halls of Congress afforded the vantage-ground from which assaults were made upon these guarantees. The Legislatures of various Northern States enacted laws to hinder the execution of the provisions made for the rendition of fugitives from service; State officials lent their aid to the work of thwarting them; and city mobs assailed the officers engaged in the duty of enforcing them. . . .

The preamble to the Constitution declared the object of its founders to be, "to form a more perfect union, establish justice, insure domestic tranquillity, provide for the common defense, promote the general welfare, and secure the blessings of liberty to ourselves and our posterity." Now, however (in 1860), the people of a portion of the States had assumed an attitude of avowed hostility, not only to the provisions of the Constitution itself, but to the "domestic tranquillity" of the people of other States. Long before the formation of the Constitution, one of the charges preferred in the Declaration of Independence against the Government of Great Britain, as justifying the separation of the colonies from that country, was that of having "excited domestic insurrections among us." Now, the mails were burdened with incendiary publications, secret emissaries had been sent, and in one case an armed invasion of one of the States had taken place for the very purpose of exciting "domestic insurrection."

It was not the passage of the "personal liberty laws," it was not the circulation of incendiary documents, it was not the raid of John Brown, it was not the operation of unjust and unequal tariff laws, nor all combined, that constituted the intolerable grievance, but it was the systematic and persistent struggle to deprive the Southern States of equality in the Union—generally to discriminate in legislation against the interests of their people; culminating in their exclusion from the Territories, the common property of the States, as well as by the infraction of their compact to promote domestic tranquillity. . . .

What resource for justice—what assurance of tranquillity—what guarantee of safety—now remained for the South? Still forbearing, still hoping, still striving for peace and union, we waited until a section President, nominated by a sectional convention, elected by a sectional vote—and that the vote of a minority of the people— was about to be inducted into office, under the warning of his own distinct announcement that the Union could not permanently endure "half slave and half free"; meaning thereby that it could not continue to exist in the condition in which it was formed and its Constitution adopted. The leader of his party [William H. Seward], who was to be the chief of his Cabinet, was the man who had first proclaimed an "irrepressible conflict" between the North and the South, and who had declared that abolitionism, having triumphed in the Territories, would proceed to the invasion of the States. Even then the Southern people did not finally despair until the temper of the triumphant party had been tested in Congress and found adverse to any terms of reconciliation consistent with the honor and safety of all parties.

No alternative remained except to seek the security out of the Union which they had vainly tried to obtain within it. The hope of our people may be stated in a sentence. It was to escape from injury and strife in the Union, to find prosperity and peace out of it.

------

10.   THE DEFENSIVE SOUTH

Chauncey S. Boucher, "In Re That Aggressive Slavocracy," Mississippi Valley Historical Review, *VIII (1921), pp. 13–79, insists that there was no Slave Power conspiracy, because the South was never united behind a political program. Most of the time, according to Boucher, Southerners were on the defensive against the aggressive action of the abolitionists. The following extracts are reprinted with the permission of the* Mississippi Valley Historical Review.

From most of the historical works covering the ante-bellum period one gains the impression that the dominant factor, controlling the course of events, is found in a powerful, united, well-organized, aggressive slavocracy. . . . It is the purpose of this monograph to examine the picture in detail and see whether it is true to facts. Was the south united throughout the ante-bellum period in its position on big questions of policy and action? Was it normally aggressive, or was it on the defensive?

Those historians who see in the ante-bellum south only an aggressive slavocracy admit that a primary requisite for that section to have been on the aggressive would seem to have been unity of purpose and action. . . . One does not read very far in newspaper files or correspondence collections of the ante-bellum period in the south before one encounters frequent complaints and laments, registered in all seriousness, that such a situation—unity of purpose and action politically—did not exist. Party divisions were not mere surface affairs; party ties did not hang loosely, and party allegiance was not renounced lightly. Indeed, the true state of affairs seems to have been that party divisions cut deeply through the body politic; party ties were strong, and party allegiance was renounced only under most abnormal and forceful circumstances. Personal political feuds between individuals and groups were as bitter and persistent as in any other section of the union. . . . Even in congress the south did not present a united front which might have enabled it to make demands with assurance of having them met; however, there was a nearer approach to unity of purpose and action among southern men in congress than among their constituents at home, the section over. It was difficult enough to get the people of a single state to agree upon and take a definite stand, as is witnessed by the history of South Carolina from 1828 to 1861; and as for getting several states to agree even upon an interpretation of the situation at any given time, to say nothing of concerted action, it seemed to be utterly hopeless. . . .

The ante-bellum period was characterized, in South Carolina and in the south generally, by waves of excitement. An examination of any one of these will reveal the same general story: much talk about necessity of action—of united action; but it never materializes. Always there are bitter party feuds, distrust of leaders, complaints of lack of proper leadership, et cetera, *ad infinitum*.

The story of the whig party in the south is a forceful proof of the lack of unity. When the "peculiar institution" was assailed from the north, of course the state-rights whigs came to its defense. As it was early seen that the northern whigs tended to be more actively hostile to slavery than were the northern democrats, the southern whigs were reminded of the fact and taunted with being traitors to their own interest. Quite naturally, perhaps, then, as long as the alliance between the southern and the northern wings of the party was continued, the southern whigs were more moderate in their defense of slavery than were the southern democrats. Throughout the struggle in congress over the gag resolutions the compact front of the south was broken again and again quite perceptibly by whig votes. The same was true of the votes in the house on the election of a speaker and in the senate on the ratification of appointments made by the president, when objection was raised that the man under consideration was an antislavery man. Indeed, through the eighteen-forties many southern whigs denounced the democrats for eternally dragging forth the slavery question to cover up the real issue, whatever it might be, and to stir up agitation. When the national whig party became irreparably split over the slavery question, it did not mean that from that time on there was a united south with a single purpose and a single policy. Though southern whigs agreed to disagree with their northern party brethren they could not agree among themselves nor with the southern democrats on a position to be held against the common foe; and, though the national democratic party continued its existence down to 1860, there was marked disagreement in the southern ranks of that party as to policy. . . .

It was the irony of fate that the southern statesman who saw, perhaps more clearly than any other, the necessity of southern unity for defense through the maintenance of the "true Republican principles," and who strove earnestly to promote such unity of action in support of basic principles, was the very one who perhaps caused more division and bitterness of strife within the section than any other man. No man ever had followers more devoted and enemies more bitter among the "people at home" than John C. Calhoun.

Instead of a united, aggressive slavocracy, one finds evidence at almost every turn that the true picture is quite the reverse, and that keen students of public affairs realized full well that cross-purposes and disorganization prevailed. Again and again, throughout the period from 1835 to 1860, complaint was registered that, vainly putting its trust in national parties, without unanimity of opinion either as to the dangers that menaced or the remedies to be applied, with no distinct issue, no certain aim, no wise plan of statesmanship, no well-defined ideas of what it might have to fear, to hope, or to do, the south was dragged along, ingloriously enough, by the fatal delusions of national partyism, a source of profit to its southern betrayers and a spoil and a mockery to its northern enemies. Though the opinion was frequently offered that if united the south would be invincible, at least in the protection of its rights, it was almost as frequently admitted that it seemed impossible to get the section to unite even for self-defense, let alone for a positive or an aggressive program, within the union. Hence it was that toward the end of the period some sincere believers in the preservation of the "Constitutional Union" as the best policy for both sections began to hope for secession by a single state as the only development that could bring about southern unity; and many of these men admitted at the same that they feared that such unity would last but a short time beyond the formation of a southern confederacy, and that disorganization and disintegration would soon follow.

When the historian finds that some southerners boasted of how they might control the nation if they could but secure unity among southern statesmen and politicians, and that individuals or groups urged this item or that one for a southern program and boasted of the wonders it would work, is the historian to interpret them literally? In most of such instances were they not in the mood of a small boy going down a dark alley, whistling as loud as he can to keep up his courage? Just as the boy's whistling is so forced and strained that he hits many false notes, so the boasting of southerners gives one the impression that it was forced, unnatural, not sincere, and hence false notes were struck.

When the south struggled for power in national councils, was it for political strength to be used aggressively? Did the south have a positive program to be put through in its own interest to the exclusion of, or the positive injury of, the other sections? Did not the south want political strength mainly or simply to block and stop the aggressions of its opponents? Did it ask anything more than to be let alone and not to be made to bear the burden of legislation injurious to itself alone? . . .

. . . From [the time of the Mexican War] . . . until 1861 the charge of aggression was hurled with ever increasing vigor against the south by the abolitionists, and the writer believes that the persistence of the charge from the end of the war to the present in historical works is due to the fact that most of these works have been based on sources which, in the final analysis, are really of abolitionist origin. The writer believes that the south, instead of being the aggressor, was on the defensive throughout almost the entire ante-bellum period; and that so far from having the unity which was a primary necessity for an offensive campaign, the south could not often, nor for long, agree upon even a defensive program, down to the very eve of the civil war. Individuals at times took a stand which may perhaps best be termed "aggressively defensive." The well-known individualism of the southerner, however, militated against united action to the extent that there was no organized, unified aggression.

---

11.   "Egocentric Sectionalism"

Though blaming both sections to some extent, Frank L. Owsley, in an article entitled "The Fundamental Cause of the Civil War: Egocentric Sectionalism," in the Journal of Southern History, VII *(1941), pp. 3–18, clearly implies that the North was guilty of the more serious aggression. The extracts below are reprinted by permission of the* Journal of Southern History.

. . . Looking immediately behind . . . [the] attempt of the South to establish a separate government, and of the attempt of the North to prevent it, we discover a state of mind in both sections which explains their conduct. This state of mind may be summed up thus: by the spring of 1861 the Southern people felt it both abhorrent and dangerous to continue to live under the same government with the people of the North. So profound was this feeling among the bulk of the Southern population that they were prepared to fight a long and devastating war to accomplish a separation. On the other hand, the North was willing to fight a war to retain their reluctant fellow citizens under the same government with themselves.

The cause of that state of mind which we may well call war psychosis lay in the sectional character of the United States. In other words, the Civil War had one basic cause: sectionalism. . . . Our national state was built, not upon the foundations of a homogeneous land and people, but upon geographical sections inhabited severally by provincial, self-conscious, self-righteous, aggressive, and ambitious populations of varying origins and diverse social and economic systems; and the passage of time and the cumulative effect of history have accentuated these sectional patterns.

Before accepting the possibility of future wars and national disintegration as inevitable because of the irrepressible conflict between permanent sections, let me hasten to say that there are two types of sectionalism: there is that egocentric, destructive sectionalism where conflict is always irrepressible; and there is that constructive sectionalism where good will prevails—two types as opposite from one another as good is opposite from evil, as the benign is from the malignant. It was the egocentric, the destructive, the evil, the malignant type of sectionalism that destroyed the Union in 1861. . . .

There were three basic manifestations of that egocentric sectionalism which disrupted the Union in 1861. First, was the habit of the dominant section—that is, the section which had the larger share in the control of the Federal government—of considering itself the nation, its people the American people, its interests the national interests; in other words, the habit of considering itself the sole possessor of nationalism, when, indeed, it was thinking strictly in terms of one section; and conversely the habit of the dominant section of regarding the minority group as factional, its interests and institutions and way of life as un-American, unworthy of friendly consideration, and even the object of attack.

The second manifestation of this egocentric sectionalism that led to the Civil War was the perennial attempt of a section to gain or maintain its political ascendancy over the Federal government by destroying the sectional balance of power which, both New England and the South maintained, had been established by the three-fifths ratio clause in the Federal constitution.

The third and most dangerous phase of this sectionalism, perhaps the *sine qua non*, of the Civil War, was the failure to observe what in international law is termed the comity of nations, and what we may by analogy designate as the comity of sections. That is, the people in one section failed in their language and conduct to respect the dignity and self-respect of the people in the other section. These three manifestations of sectionalism were so closely related that at times they can be segregated only in theory and for the sake of logical discussion. Indeed, as I have suggested, all were manifestations of that egocentric sectionalism that caused a section to regard itself as the nation. . . .

The . . . [first two manifestations] of that sectionalism which led to the Civil War, while causing a slow accumulation of sectional grievances, were not marked during the thirty years prior to the Missouri debates by excessive ill will or serious disregard for the comity of sections. Indeed, up until the time of the Missouri debates, despite the rivalry of sections which almost disrupted the Union, there was maintained a certain urbanity and self-restraint on the part of the leaders of the rival sections; for as long as the founding fathers lived and exercised influence over public affairs, there seems to have been a common realization—indeed, a common recollection—that the nation had been founded upon the principle of mutual tolerance of sectional differences and mutual concessions; that the nation had been constructed upon the respect of each section for the institutions, opinions, and ways of life of the other sections. But the years laid the founding fathers low and their places were taken by a new and impatient generation who had no such understanding of the essence of national unity. The result was that urbanity, self-restraint, and courtesy—the ordinary amenities of civilized intercourse—were cast aside; and in their gracious place were substituted the crude, discourteous, and insulting language and conduct in intersectional relations now familiar in the relations between the totalitarian nations and the so-called democracies. It was the Missouri debates in which intersectional comity was first violated; and it was the political leaders of the East, particularly the New Englanders and those of New England origin, who did it when they denounced in unmeasured terms slavery, the slaveholder, and

Southern society in general. It is noteworthy that the Southern leaders, with the exception of one or two, including John Randolph, ignored this first violent, denunciatory, insulting language of the Northerners during and immediately after the Missouri controversy; ignored them at least in that no reply in kind was made with the possible exception of two or three, including John Randolph, who demanded that the South withdraw from the Union before it was too late. The private correspondence of the Southerners, however, reveals them as resentful and apprehensive of future bad relations with the North.

Ten years after the Missouri Compromise debates the moral and intellectual leaders of the North, and notably those of New England origin, took up the language of abuse and vilification which the political leaders of that section had first employed in the Missouri debates. Quickly the political leaders resumed the tone of the Missouri controversy: and thus was launched the so-called anti-slavery crusade, but what in fact was a crusade against the southern people. For over three decades this attack upon slavery and the entire structure of southern society down to the custom of eating corn bread and turnip greens grew in volume and in violence. . . . One has to seek in the unrestrained and furious invective of the present totalitarians to find a near parallel to the language that the abolitionists and their political fellow travelers used in denouncing the South and its way of life. Indeed, as far as I have been able to ascertain, neither Dr. Goebbels nor Virginio Gayda nor Stalin's propaganda agents have as yet been able to plumb the depths of vulgarity and obscenity reached and maintained by George Bourne, Stephen Foster, Wendell Phillips, Charles Sumner, and other abolitionists of note. . . . All crimes were laid at the door of these [Southern] people: they were kidnappers, manstealers, pimps, robbers, assassins, freebooters, much more "despicable than the common horse thief." Neither time nor good taste permits any real analysis of this torrent of coarse abuse; but let it be said again that nothing equal to it has been encountered in the language of insult used between nations today—even those at war with one another.

This crusade against the South has often been brushed aside as the work of a few unbalanced fanatics. Such is not the case at all.

The genuine abolitionists were few in number in the beginning; but just as radicalism today has touched so many of the intellectuals of the East, so did abolitionism touch the intellectuals of the East and of the North generally. So did it touch the moral and political leaders. The effects upon the minds of those millions who did not consider themselves abolitionists were profound. In time the average Northerner accepted in whole or in part the abolitionist picture of Southern people: they became monsters and their children were not children but young monsters. Such a state of mind is fertile soil for war. The effect upon the minds of the Southern people was far more profound, since they were recipients of this niagara of insults and threats. To them the Northern people were a combination of mad fanatics and cold-blooded political adventurers. As years passed slow and consuming fury took hold of the Southern people; and this fury was combined with a deadly fear which John Brown's raid confirmed: a fear that most of the Northern people not only hated the Southern people but would willingly see them exterminated. This fear was further confirmed when such a kindly philosopher as Ralph Waldo Emerson approved of the incendiary, John Brown, by likening him to Jesus.

The political, intellectual, and moral leaders of the South did not remain silent under the abuse of the crusaders and the fellow travelers and well-wishers, but replied in a manner that added fuel to the roaring flames which were fast consuming the last vestiges of national unity. The language of insult which the so-called fire-eaters employed, however, was not usually coarse or obscene in comparison with the abolitionists; it was urbane and restrained to a degree—but insulting. Thus in language of abuse and insult was jettisoned the comity of sections: And let me repeat that peace between sections as between nations is placed in jeopardy when one nation or one section fails to respect the self-respect of the people of another section or nation.

II. State Rights and Nationalism

WAS THE UNION OLDER than the states? Or was it the other way around? Did the framers of the Constitution create a perpetual Union, a truly national government with substantial powers? Or did they create a mere voluntary federation of sovereign states? These questions, for which there were impressive and plausible arguments on both sides, were almost continuously debated from the birth of the Republic to the end of the Civil War. As John Quincy Adams once observed, "It is the odious nature of the question that it can be settled only at the cannon's mouth."

Post–Civil War Southern historians, who rarely agreed that slavery was a fundamental cause of the Civil War, found the real cause in conflicting interpretations of the Constitution. As they saw it, the South seceded to prevent the subversion of the rights of the states, not to save slavery. In recent years, however, some historians have expressed doubts that men really went to war in 1861 because of differing opinions about the nature of the Union. "State rights" and "national supremacy," they believe, were merely convenient sectional slogans. And, more important, neither section consistently supported one side or the other of this long constitutional debate; rather, each shifted its position when it was convenient to do so.

Whether or not the South fought for state rights, there can be no doubt that the attempt to break up the Union aroused the nationalist sentiments of many Northerners. To them secession was not only treason—not only defiance of legitimate political authority—but a denial of our national destiny.

12.   South Carolina's "Declaration of the Causes of Secession"

After unanimously adopting an Ordinance of Secession on December 20, 1860, the South Carolina convention issued a "Declaration of the Causes of Secession." This document presents both the argument which "proved" the sovereignty of the states and evidence that the Northern states had violated the federal "compact," i.e., the Constitution. Frank Moore (ed.), The Rebellion Record (New York: 1861–68), I, pp. 3–4.

In the year 1765, that portion of the British Empire embracing Great Britain undertook to make laws for the Government of that portion composed of the thirteen American Colonies. A struggle for the right of self-government ensued, which resulted, on the 4th of July, 1776, in a Declaration, by the Colonies, "that they are, and of right ought to be, FREE AND INDEPENDENT STATES; . . ."

In pursuance of this Declaration of Independence, each of the thirteen States proceeded to exercise its separate sovereignty; adopted for itself a Constitution, and appointed officers for the administration of government in all its departments—Legislative, Executive and Judicial. For purposes of defence they united their arms and their counsels; and, in 1778, they entered into a League known as the Articles of Confederation, whereby they agreed to intrust the administration of their external relations to a common agent, known as the Congress of the United States, expressly declaring, in the first article, "that each State retains its sovereignty, freedom and independence, and every power, jurisdiction, and right which is not, by this Confederation, expressly delegated to the United States in Congress assembled." . . .

In 1787, Deputies were appointed by the States to revise the

Articles of Confederation; and on 17th September, 1787, these Deputies recommended, for the adoption of the States, the Articles of Union, known as the Constitution of the United States.

The parties to whom this Constitution was submitted were the several sovereign States; they were to agree or disagree, and when nine of them agreed, the compact was to take effect among those concurring; and the General Government, as the common agent, was then to be invested with their authority. . . .

By this Constitution, certain duties were imposed upon the several States, and the exercise of certain of their powers was restrained. . . . But . . . an amendment was added, which declared that the powers not delegated to the United States by the Constitution, nor prohibited by it to the States, are reserved to the States respectively, or to the people. On the 23d May, 1788, South Carolina, by the Convention of her people, passed an ordinance assenting to this Constitution, and afterwards altered her own Constitution to conform herself to the obligations she had under-taken.

Thus was established, by compact between the States, a Government with defined objects and powers, limited to the express words of the grant. This limitation left the whole remaining mass of power subject to the clause reserving it to the States or the people, and rendered unnecessary any specification of reserved rights. We hold that the Government thus established is subject to the two great principles asserted in the Declaration of Independence; and we hold further, that the mode of its formation subjects it to a third fundamental principle, namely, the law of compact. We maintain that in every compact between two or more parties, the obligation is mutual; that the failure of one of the contracting parties to perform a material part of the agreement, entirely releases the obligation of the other; and that, where no arbiter is provided, each party is remitted to his own judgment to determine the fact of failure, with all its consequences.

In the present case, that fact is established with certainty. We assert that fourteen of the States have deliberately refused for years past to fulfill their constitutional obligations. . . . Thus the constitutional compact has been deliberately broken and disregarded by the non-slaveholding States; and the consequence follows that South Carolina is released from her obligation. . . .

We affirm that . . . [the] ends for which this Government was instituted have been defeated, and the Government itself has been destructive of them by the action of the non-slaveholding States. Those States have assumed the right of deciding upon the propriety of our domestic institutions; and have denied the rights of property established in fifteen of the States and recognized by the Constitution; they have denounced as sinful the institution of Slavery; they have permitted the open establishment among them of societies, whose avowed object is to disturb the peace of and eloign the property of the citizens of other States. They have encouraged and assisted thousands of our slaves to leave their homes; and those who remain have been incited by emissaries, books, and pictures, to servile insurrection. . . .

On the 4th of March next . . . [a sectional] party will take possession of the Government. It has announced that the South shall be excluded from the common territory, that the Judicial tribunal shall be made sectional, and that a war must be waged against Slavery until it shall cease throughout the United States.

The guarantees of the Constitution will then no longer exist; the equal rights of the States will be lost. The Slaveholding States will no longer have the power of self-government, or self-protection, and the Federal Government will have become their enemy. . . .

We, therefore, the people of South Carolina, by our delegates in Convention assembled, appealing to the Supreme Judge of the world for the rectitude of our intentions, have solemnly declared that the Union heretofore existing between this State and other States of North America dissolved, and that the State of South Carolina has resumed her position among the nations of the world, as a separate and independent State, with full power to levy war, conclude peace, contract alliances, establish commerce, and to do all other acts and things which independent States may of right do.

13. "A CONSTITUTIONAL VIEW"

Alexander H. Stephens of Georgia, who had served as vice-president of the Confederacy, was one of the most ardent defenders of the "Lost Cause." He neatly summarizes the state-rights interpretation of the Civil War in the Introduction to his book A Constitutional View of the Late War between the States *(Philadelphia: 1868–70), I, pp. 9–12.*

It is a postulate, with many writers of this day, that the late War was the result of two opposing ideas, or principles, upon the subject of African Slavery. Between these, according to their theory, sprung the "irrepressible conflict," in principle, which ended in the terrible conflict of arms. Those who assume this postulate, and so theorize upon it, are but superficial observers.

That the War had its origin in *opposing principles*, which, in their action upon the *conduct of men*, produced the ultimate collision of arms, may be assumed as an unquestionable fact. But the opposing principles which produced these results in physical action were of a very different character from those assumed in the postulate. They lay in the organic Structure of the Government of the States. The conflict in principle arose from different and opposing ideas as to the nature of what is known as the General Government. The contest was between those who held it to be strictly Federal in its character, and those who maintained that it was thoroughly National. It was a strife between the principles of Federation, on the one side, and Centralism, or Consolidation, on the other.

Slavery, so called, was but *the question* on which these antagonistic principles, which had been in conflict, from the beginning, on diverse *other questions*, were finally brought into actual and active collision with each other on the field of battle.

Some of the strongest Anti-Slavery men who ever lived were on the side of those who opposed the Centralizing principles which led to the War. Mr. Jefferson was a striking illustration of this, and a prominent example of a large class of both sections of the country, who were, most unfortunately, brought into hostile array against each other. No more earnest or ardent devotee to the emancipation of the Black race, upon humane, rational and Constitutional principles, ever lived than he was. . . . And yet Mr. Jefferson . . . is well known to have been utterly opposed to the Centralizing principle, when *first* presented, on *this question,* in the attempt to impose conditions and restrictions on the State of Missouri, when she applied for admission into the Union, under the Constitution. He looked upon the movement as a political manœuvre to bring this delicate subject . . . into the Federal Councils, with a view, by its agitation in a forum where it did not properly belong, to strengthen the Centralists in their efforts to revive their doctrines, which had been so signally defeated on so many other questions. The first sound of their movements on this question fell upon his ear as a "fire bell at night." . . .

It is the fashion of many writers of the day to class all who opposed the Consolidationists in *this,* their *first* step, as well as all who opposed them in all their subsequent steps, on *this question,* with what they style the Pro-Slavery Party. No greater injustice could be done any public men, and no greater violence be done to the truth of History, than such a classification. Their opposition to that measure, or kindred subsequent ones, sprung from no attachment to Slavery; but . . . from their strong convictions that the Federal Government had no rightful or Constitutional control or jurisdiction over such questions; and that no such action, as that proposed upon them, could be taken by Congress without destroying the elementary and vital principles upon which the Government was founded.

By their acts, they did not identify themselves with the Pro-Slavery Party (for, in truth, no such Party had, at that time, or at any time in the History of the Country, any organized existence). They only identified themselves, or took position, with those who maintained the Federative character of the General Government.

In 1850, for instance, what greater injustice could be done any one, or what greater violence could be done the truth of History, than to charge Cass, Douglas, Clay, Webster and Fillmore, to say nothing of others, with being advocates of Slavery, or following in the lead of the Pro-Slavery Party, because of their support of what were called the adjustment measures of that year?

Or later still, out of the million and a half, and more, of the votes cast, in the Northern States, in 1860, against Mr. Lincoln, how many, could it, with truth, be said, were in favor of Slavery, or even that legal subordination of the Black race to the White, which existed in the Southern States?

Perhaps, not one in ten thousand! It was a subject, with which, they were thoroughly convinced, they had nothing to do, and could have nothing to do, under the terms of the Union, by which the States were Confederated, except to carry out, and faithfully perform, all the obligations of the Constitutional Compact, in regard to it.

They simply arrayed themselves against that Party which had virtually hoisted the banner of Consolidation. The contest, so commenced, which ended in the War, was, indeed, a contest between opposing principles; but not such as bore upon the policy or impolicy of African Subordination. They were principles deeply underlying all consideration of that sort. They involved the very nature and organic Structure of the Government itself. The conflict, on *this question* of Slavery, in the Federal Councils, from the beginning, was not a contest between the advocates or opponents of that peculiar Institution, but a contest, as stated before, between the supporters of a strictly Federative Government, on the one side, and a thoroughly National one, on the other.

14.   "THE STATE RIGHTS FETISH"

An essay by Arthur M. Schlesinger entitled "The State Rights Fetish," which appears in his book New Viewpoints in American History *(New York: 1922), pp. 220–43, throws cold water on the interpretation of the Civil War presented by Alexander H. Stephens. Copyright 1922 by the Macmillan Company. Extracts reprinted by permission of the publishers.*

The doctrine of state rights is one that is intimately associated with American history, especially with certain movements and controversies that fell in the period before the Civil War. Writers and teachers of American history are accustomed to use the phrase as if it furnished a fundamental explanation of the motivation of events. That this is far from true any detailed examination of American history should make apparent; and indeed the expression itself has borne different meanings at different epochs or as understood by different leaders in the same epoch. . . .

Readers of the older American histories are likely to get the impression that the state rights theory, like cotton and slavery, was a peculiar product of the South, and that in the political field it has dominated the beliefs and policies of the Democratic party. On the basis of these assumptions the history of the United States prior to the Civil War, and to some extent since, is pictured as a great struggle between two schools of governmental theory, the Democrats, and the South generally, being wedded by temperament and intellect to the one view, and the rival party supported by a majority of the northerners having a psychological affinity for the other. There is, of course, a measure of truth in all this; but the picture as a whole is in wrong perspective and blurs the essential facts.

It is the purpose of the present discussion to show, as Alexander Johnston has so well said, that "almost every state in the Union in turn declared its own 'sovereignty,' and denounced as almost treasonable similar declarations in other cases by other states," and, secondly, that political parties have been almost as variable in this respect as the states. Throughout the discussion it will appear that economic interest or some other local advantage has usually determined the attitude of states and parties toward questions of constitutional construction.

The first notable attempt by any state legislatures to formulate the state rights doctrine appeared in the well-known Virginia and Kentucky resolutions of 1798 and 1799. We know now that these resolutions had a political animus behind them. Drafted respectively by Madison and Jefferson, they were adopted by the legislatures of Virginia and Kentucky as a spectacular protest against the action of the Federalists in Congress in passing the Alien and Sedition Acts and other laws which seemed to contravene a plain reading of the Constitution. Far from being carefully reasoned documents, these resolutions resorted to extravagant language in much the same manner as modern political platforms and for exactly the same purpose: the arousing of popular indignation against the party in power. . . .

The second important development of the state rights doctrine grew out of very different circumstances. In December, 1807, the Republican party in Congress under the leadership of President Jefferson passed the embargo as an act of retaliation against British and French interferences with American trade during the Napoleonic wars. New England was the center of the shipbuilding industry and the chief carrier of world commerce at this time, and the people there bitterly resented a regulation which meant the total destruction of their source of wealth. They therefore embarked upon a career of obstruction and opposition to the federal government, that was to last far into the war that the United States waged with Great Britain from 1812 to 1815. . . .

The festering discontent reached its climax in the Hartford Convention of December, 1814, made up of official delegates from Massachusetts, Connecticut and Rhode Island, and of representatives from local conventions in New Hampshire and Vermont. . . . Resolutions were adopted repeating the gist of the Virginia resolutions of 1798 and demanding seven amendments to the federal Constitution which, if adopted, would remove all of the New

England grievances. "If the Union be destined to dissolution," the convention announced to the world, ". . . it should, if possible, be the work of peaceable times, and deliberate consent." . . .

It was the tariff question . . . that was soon to cause the planters of South Carolina the same bitterness of spirit that the merchants of New England had felt toward the embargo. A high tariff to foster manufacturing could be of no possible assistance to the South, and indeed damaged that section by greatly raising the prices of the manufactures they must buy. So by December, 1825, the South Carolina legislature made the expedient discovery that a protective tariff was "an unconstitutional exercise of power." In a like category, it placed federal aid to internal improvements, a measure which was chiefly beneficial to northern merchants seeking to broaden their domestic markets. In the next few years South Carolina was joined in her new convictions by the nearby states of Virginia, Georgia, Alabama and Mississippi.

But South Carolina soon began to press forward to positions and views in advance of those of her sister states of the South. Having arrived at the opinion in 1827 that the Constitution was a compact of the states "as separate, independent sovereignties," the South Carolina legislature in the next year . . . [published] the famous "Exposition," written by John C. Calhoun, which explicitly announced the right of a state to nullify federal laws that were regarded by the state as unconstitutional. A few years later, in November, 1832, South Carolina put her threat into execution through the passage of an "Ordinance of Nullification" by a state convention expressly assembled for that purpose. In her opposition to the protective tariff South Carolina had carried her state rights views to lengths that had never been more than hinted at by any of her predecessors. When Congress granted her a measure of relief through the passage of the compromise tariff of 1833, the South Carolina convention solemnly repealed the Ordinance of Nullification and adopted a new ordinance nullifying the so-called Force Bill of Congress. . . .

From the close of the nullification episode of 1832–1833 to the outbreak of the Civil War, the agitation of state rights was intimately connected with a new issue of growing importance, the slavery question, and the principal form assumed by the doctrine was that of the right of secession. The pro-slavery forces sought refuge in the state rights position as a shield against federal interference with pro-slavery projects. . . . As a natural consequence, anti-slavery legislatures in the North were led to lay great stress on the national character of the Union and the broad powers of the general government in dealing with slavery. Nevertheless, it is significant to note that when it served anti-slavery purposes better to lapse into state rights dialectic, northern legislatures did not hesitate to be inconsistent.

Thus the legislature of Massachusetts resolved in 1844 that "the project of the annexation of Texas," if carried through to success by the pro-slavery forces, "may tend to drive these states into a dissolution of the union"; and when, notwithstanding, annexation was accomplished in the following year, the legislature resolved that "Massachusetts hereby refuses to acknowledge the act . . . authorizing the admission of Texas, as a legal act, in any way binding her from using her utmost exertions in coöperation with other States, by every lawful and constitutional measure, to annul its conditions, and defeat its accomplishment," Vermont, Ohio and Connecticut likewise protested that the federal government had exceeded its constitutional powers in annexing Texas as a state. With the outbreak of the Mexican War, the Massachusetts legislature denounced it as a pro-slavery war of conquest, and in 1847 resolved that the struggle was "unjust and unconstitutional in its origin and character" and that all good citizens should unite to stop it.

The New Jersey legislature found occasion as late as 1852 to declare, in solemn resolutions, that the Constitution was "a compact between the several States" and that the general government had been granted by the sovereign states only limited powers. The passage of the Fugitive Slave Act of 1850 called forth fresh evidences of latent state rights feeling in the North. Many of the legislatures of that section passed so-called Personal Liberty Laws, designed to obstruct the recovery of fugitive slaves under the federal act. "They were dangerously near the nullification of a United States law," James Ford Rhodes tells us. In 1855 and 1856, resolutions were passed by the legislatures of Massachusetts and Ohio pronouncing the Fugitive Slave Act unwarranted by the Constitution. In Wisconsin the state Supreme Court held the law to be "unconstitutional and void"; and when the federal Supreme Court reversed the decision, the state legislature resolved in 1859, on the verge of the war to preserve the Union, that the several states which had formed the federal compact, being "sovereign and independent," had "the unquestionable right to judge of its infractions" and to resort to "positive defiance" of all unauthorized acts of the general government. . . .

The same pervasive influences which played upon states and geographical sections and helped to mold their constitutional views have affected the attitude of political parties on questions of constitutional interpretation. But, in addition, another element must be taken into account, arising from the psychology of politics: the party in power always feels that the Constitution, however broadly construed, is perfectly safe in its keeping, while the minority party is convinced that the welfare of the people demands that the majority should be restrained to a very narrow exercise of governmental authority. Hence the "Ins" have always tended to be strong nationalists, and the "Outs" strict constructionists and advocates of state rights. . . .

The facts that have been presented in the foregoing discussion speak for themselves. There can be no doubt that the state rights agitation has played a large part in American history; but it is equally clear that the controversy must always be studied in its relation to time and circumstances. The state rights doctrine has never had any real vitality independent of underlying conditions of vast social, economic, or political significance. The group advocating state rights at any period have sought its shelter in much the same spirit that a western pioneer seeks his storm-cellar when a tornado is raging. The doctrine has served as a species of protective coloration against the threatening onslaughts of a powerful foe. As a well-known American historian has tersely said, "Scratch a Wisconsin farmer and you find a Georgia planter!"

15. What Price Union?

Weighing the costs of the Civil War and considering the evils of rampant nationalism in the modern world, Richard H. Shryock questions the assumption that a permanent division of North and South would have been a great disaster. The following passages from his essay "The Nationalistic Tradition of the Civil War: A Southern Analysis," South Atlantic Quarterly, XXXII (1933), pp. 294–305, explain his point of view. They are reprinted by permission of the South Atlantic Quarterly *and Richard H. Shryock.*

We have become almost smug about this greatest of American tragedies. It was, to be sure, a war of death and destruction; but also, was it not, a war of victory—a time suffused with "the glory of the coming of the Lord"? Then, if ever, right triumphed over wrong, the Union was saved, the slaves were freed, and those who survived lived more or less happily ever after. This optimistic tradition, ever orthodox in the best of Northern circles, has long since invaded the South as well. . . . This "after all" philosophy, which reconciles respect for Confederate sires with a reviving nationalism, is becoming characteristic of the New South.

It is obvious that such a view serves those who wish, laudably enough, to complete the reconciliation of the sections, or those who desire to promote patriotism in general. But those who would wish to see this thing clearly, who believe that in the long run it is actually more patriotic to seek the truth than to indulge in propaganda, may well ponder the premises of the whole tradition. After all, *was* it so glorious a thing that the Union was saved by means of civil war? . . . How often has an unprejudiced effort been made to estimate the real value of union and freedom over against the price paid for these in the waste of war and its aftermath? Yet only when this has been attempted can anyone be in a position to decide whether the American people struck a fair bargain with fate or whether, perchance, they paid too much for victory. . . .

. . . The first point to be noted here is that we inevitably underestimate the costs of the Civil War—at least present generations do so. This is partly due to the natural tendency to forget suffering and other unpleasant things in general. What was gained is still apparent and is therefore appreciated; what was lost is gone and therefore more or less forgotten. . . .

There are other reasons for underestimating costs, besides the obvious tendency to forget. Current historiography probably has much to do with it. The political and military traditions, plus the apparent necessity for abstraction, rob historical writings of that realism which alone can convey a sense of the suffering involved in a great war. An historian's description of the battle of Gettysburg is likely to tell of what occurred to Lee's right wing, or to Longstreet's corps, but rarely of what happened to the bodies of plain John Jones and the thousands like him. . . . The historians might, however, picture reality and convey a sense of the costs involved if, in describing campaigns, they gave less space to tactics in the field and more to tactics in the camp and hospitals. There, after all, is where most of the men were lost.

It is also possible that the traditional treatment of the post-bellum South, in the general histories, is responsible for the distortion under discussion. The dramatic Reconstruction era has long received due attention, but not so the dreary, discouraging years which followed. An entire generation had to struggle on under conditions of poverty which inevitably involved cultural as well as economic decline. . . . Much of all this is to be checked off on the debit side of our national accounting. . . .

It is trite to observe that nothing is more sacred in a nationalistic age than the nation, hence the sanctity of any development which preserved the Union. All this, however, is largely a matter of metaphysics suffused with emotion—an idealistic entity known as the State must be preserved! Such abstractions must be ignored if one is to come down to earth and real human interests. The American nation is doubtless larger and more powerful today than it would have been if certain Northern Republicans (who had previously blocked all compromise) had not decided to hold the Union together by force. We have today, as a result of their policy, a bigger state, but how a better one?

Many will reply that no worthwhile Union of any sort could have survived, once a precedent of peaceful secession had been established. . . . Yet consider the facts. There is little evidence that more than seven states would have gone out in '61, had Lincoln maintained a policy of peace. . . . The loss of the Gulf tier of states would hardly have been an irreparable blow to the rest of the nation. Is it not questionable, moreover, to assume that other sections would soon have followed them out, merely because they were privileged to do so? The values of the economic and political bonds obtaining between New England and the Middle Atlantic or Middle Western states were too genuine and too obvious to have made this likely. The advent of industrialism in the seaboard South (already apparent in the fifties) would probably have cemented similar bonds between that region and the North. . . .

Suppose the worst, however; that several border states had later joined the Confederacy, that the Pacific seaboard had erected a separate republic, and that the Middle West had broken from the East. Difficulties there would have been, concerning runaway slaves, tariffs, or outlets to the sea; but few sovereign states are exempt from the like, and various means to their solution less tragic than war might well have been found. It is obvious that each of these suggested republics would have been smaller and less powerful than the present one, but it hardly follows that they would have been less prosperous or happy. . . . On the whole, recent years have certainly demonstrated that size and power are no protection, in themselves, against war, poverty, or the other major causes of human misery.

Several historical illustrations occur to one in this connection, which while they are not complete analogies are at least suggestive. There was once a sort of indirect union between certain Canadian and the other "continental" colonies. Try to tell Canadians from the older provinces that their future was ruined when, in 1783, this union with the colonies southward was severed! Or, again, try to tell the people of Norway and Sweden that all is lost with them because the former seceded from the latter some years ago, and Sweden had the rare good sense to let her go in peace! . . .

The purport of this whole matter is that a vast, a literally inestimable price was paid in war and reconstruction for values of a decidedly uncertain nature. War was the worst possible solution—if it can be called a solution at all—for the sectional issue. This is not sentimentality but a matter of cold calculation; it is those who thrill over Platonic abstractions like Union and Freedom who are the real sentimentalists. It is this tragic bad bargain with fate, this payment of so much for so little, that nationalism cherishes as our tradition of triumph!

One should not, in concluding this analysis of a tradition, entirely forget one other factor which has promoted it. Something has been said of the sentimentalism of nationalists; something should be said in like manner of the sentimentalism of optimists. The great majority of those who think at all naturally desire that their thought should lead to ultimately optimistic conclusions. Applied to history, this means that most people like to feel that things turn out for the best "in the long run." An optimistic philosophy of history is thus an essential part of most men's general outlook on life—whether they recognize it as such or not. It is small wonder, then, that when men look back on some tragedy like the Civil War, they strive to interpret it as a blessing in disguise, an ultimate triumph—even as they try to interpret all phases of the world's evil. Such interpretations inevitably sanction whatever outcomes actually occurred, and therefore lend popular support to the supposedly unpopular doctrine that whatever is (or has been) is right.

We may therefore thank our natural optimism, as well as our growing nationalism, for the tradition of the War Between the States. Would it not be more intelligent to face the possibility that at times all things work for the worst, even for them that love the Union?

----

16. THE CONSEQUENCES OF DISUNION

The following editorial from the Philadelphia Public Ledger
(*November 21, 1860*), *and other selections from the Northern
press, indicate that many believed that disunion would in fact have
disastrous consequences.*

The proud Republic, strong only in union, would dwindle into
insignificant States, more contemptible than those of Germany or of
Central America. . . . Like Mexico, we should either become a prize
for some military adventurer to grasp at, or keep up a petty show of
distinct sovereignties, continually warring against each other, or
adopting foolish and injurious restrictions to check each other's
progress. The proud title of "a citizen of the United States" could be
claimed no longer, and having no nationality commanding the
respect of the world, our persons and property would be secure in no
part of the globe. . . . Our property would be exposed to robbery upon
the sea, our flag to insult without redress, or rather we should say flags,
for every seaboard State would have some special device of the kind
like those now flaunting in the breeze at Charleston, instead of the
glorious stripes and stars, the emblem of union and power, of security
everywhere, and of freedom and prosperity at home.

---

17. WHY WE LOVE THE UNION

New York Courier and Enquirer (*December 1, 1860*).

We love the Union, because at home and abroad, collectively and
individually, it gives us character as a nation and as citizens of the
Great Republic; because it gives us *nationality* as a People, renders us
now the equal of the greatest European Power, and in another half
century, will make us the greatest, richest, and most powerful
people on the face of the earth. We love the Union, because already

in commerce, wealth and resources of every kind, we are the equal of the greatest; and because, while it secures us peace, happiness and prosperity at home, like the Roman of old we have only to exclaim "I am an American Citizen" to insure us respect and security abroad. And so loving this great and glorious Union, we are ready if need be, to shed our blood in its preservation, and in transmitting it in all its greatness, to our latest posterity.

---

18.   OUR MANIFEST DESTINY

Letter of Henry J. Raymond to William L. Yancey, in New York Times (December 13, 1860).

We should be surrendering to a foreign and hostile power more than half of the Atlantic seaboard,—the whole Gulf,—the mouth of the Mississippi, with its access to the open sea, and its drainage of the commerce of the mighty West,—all the feasible railroad routes to the Pacific,—all chance of further accessions from Mexico, Central America or the West India islands,—and all prospect of ever extending our growth and national development in the only direction in which such extension will ever be possible. We should be limiting ourselves to that narrow belt of the continent which would be bounded by the British Colonies on the north, the Slave Empire on the South, and the Rocky Mountains on the west. Have you seen any indications which encourage the hope of so magnificent a self-sacrifice on the part of our people? What is there in our past history to lead you to consider us thus reckless of national growth and national grandeur? . . . Nine-tenths of our people in the Northern and Northwestern States would wage a war longer than the War of Independence before they will assent to any such surrender of their aspirations and their hopes. There is no nation in the world so ambitious of growth and of power,—so thoroughly pervaded with the spirit of conquest,—so filled with dreams of enlarged dominions, as ours. In New England these impulses have lost something of their natural force under the influences of culture and the peaceful arts. But in the Centre and the West, this thirst for national power still rages unrestrained.

———————

19. THE POWER OF PATRIOTISM

New York Herald (*April 19, 1861*).

There exists no principle, so potent to unite the sympathies, and concentrate the energies, of a civilized people, as that of national unity. . . . Patriotism, reverence for the past, respect for established authority, and beneficient institutions, as well as the law of self-preservation, are all motives for maintaining it. To impair it, appears a sacrilege from which the sensitive mind shudders, and the odiousness of the word treason, attaches to those who would rend the parts of the homogeneous whole asunder. To it, exclusively, is to be attributed the spontaneous outburst of enthusiasm, . . . in favor of a vigorous and efficient policy, to re-establish the Union upon its pristine basis. . . . The authorities at Washington, have . . . found no difficulty in exciting the public mind to fever heat, and the programme it has inaugurated is approved, because it is founded upon that imperishable love of country, which will not permit the relinquishment of any of its parts, but prefers any sacrifice to its disintegration.

———————

20. SECESSION IS POLITICAL SUICIDE

Cincinnati Commercial (*May 6, 1861*).

A *surrender to Secession is the suicide of government.* There is no one capable of putting two ideas together, but must admit the truth of this proposition. If we succumb to secession now—if we suffer these insurgents and usurpers to dictate to us the terms of a national dismemberment, our national government is gone—hopelessly, irretrievably gone. We shall never more have peace or public order at home—we shall never more lift our head among the nations of the earth. The great battle which is now joined, is to prove whether a Republic, founded on the will of the people, is capable of exerting power enough to enforce its laws and maintain its existence, or whether it contains within itself the seeds of its own destruction.

---

21.   THE AGE OF NATIONALITIES

Boston Post (*May 16, 1861*).

The great American nation has, for near three quarters of a century, been recognized and honored in the family of States as a first class power. Its flag has carried our adventurous commerce to the four quarters of the globe: it has carried war and oppression to no nation or people in the circuit of the sun. Less romantic than the French, less belligerent than the English, it has floated from the brow of the Republic as the ensign of peace, heralding at once the asylum of the oppressed and the home of the free. The nationality it symbolizes is peculiar in its features and grand in its associations. It was founded on the successes of no military or civil hero: it was reared on the free will and unbought fealty of millions of people, renowned, above all others, for intelligence, thrift, and independence. It is a nationality of public sentiment, not less than of public government. "I am an American citizen" is the proud boast of every son of the soil. When that nationality was set up as a target by a rebel army, and shot into the dust, it was felt that the blow fell on the heart of the American people. A deep sentiment of nationality was fired, and it blazes with fervent heat, and will blaze until that flag is righted. . . .

If the Union could be severed tomorrow, the same influence which formed it would commend its instant renewal. Upon that

Union, which thus makes us one people, hangs our prosperity and our importance abroad; and, more than we are accustomed to think, the progress of the age. And not interest alone, but the eternal order of things would seem to bind us in Union. . . .

This is the age of nationalities. Fired by our example, the oppressed of the world would have aspired to the dignity of nationalities. . . . Shall the first to set the example, and the grandest in the procession of the nations, suffer its nationality to depart, at the bidding not of a foreign foe, but of rebel traitors of the soil? Rather let us dispute every inch of ground and every blade of grass.

―――――――

22. "A CRISIS IN LAW AND ORDER"

Phillip S. Paludan, in "The American Civil War Considered as a Crisis in Law and Order," American Historical Review, *LXXVII (1972), pp. 1013–34, argues that the crucial question is not why the South seceded but why the North resisted secession. The decision of Northerners to resist, Paludan believes, resulted from their close identification with the nation's democratic institutions and from a determination to preserve "law and order." The following extracts are reprinted with the permission of the author and of the* American Historical Review.

If we are to understand the reason that the North went to war for the Union we need to . . . direct our attention toward the local experience, toward the environments in which the majority of Northerners lived. To focus locally is to ask the question about why men fought for the Union in a different and I hope more useful and precise way. The question changes from the general "Why fight for the Union?" to "What was there in the daily experience of most Northerners that made them sensitive and responsive to those images the Union evoked?"

As the North reacted to the secession crisis one theme was

repeated constantly, and it suggests a crucial fact about Northern society. Again and again newspaper editors and political leaders discussed the degree to which secession was likely to produce disorder, anarchy, and general disrespect for democratic government. The future president Andrew Johnson pictured for his congressional colleagues "this Union divided into thirty-three petty governments . . . with quarreling and warring amongst the little petty powers which would result in anarchy." Congressman Zachariah Chandler announced that if secession were tolerated "I shall arrange for emigration to some country where they have a government. . . . I will never live under a government that has not the power to enforce its laws." The conservative Philadelphia *North American* called secession "Lawlessness on a Gigantic Scale" and remarked, "The world must regard with profound astonishment the spectacle of national lawlessness which the southern States of this Union now exhibit." . . .

Did secession in fact threaten the order of society in the North? Not this particular secession; a section different in so many ways from the North might justify its departure by pointing to the conflicts that its presence produced. Whatever the reality, however, the factor motivating the Northern response was what men then believed secession might mean and what they foresaw as its consequences. The idea of secession, applied generally, suggested that conflicts between parties should be settled not by harmonizing differences in the service of higher ends but by ignoring those ends in the service of the quarrel of the moment. What community was safe if such a pattern were established and endorsed? . . . The issue after Sumter was, can the country permit force to settle its disputes, cannons to resolve its differences? No people so dependent for success and stability on respecting and adhering to the processes of self-government, in the absence of any other compulsion, could afford to say yes. . . .

. . . [Throughout] the disunion crisis of 1860–61 men spoke not merely of a national economy or of the ties of sentiment that bound them to their birthplace but constantly and passionately of the destruction of self-government should secession succeed. They were thus seriously concerned with the preservation of the institutions of government that they were a part of, and they linked their experiences with that government to the survival of the Union. Local personal experience was somehow bound to the preservation of national institutions. How?

First of all, they knew that the Union was a federal union, that local government performed administrative functions that Washington could not, and should not, supply. Local government was an inextricable part of the nation's governing process. . . . [This] division of power and responsibility existed not for its own sake but because men believed that a national government could not function, nor could it remain the government of a free people, if it took to itself the governing of a vast continent. Men wanted to preserve local government so that the nation could function and continue to be free.

Second, and perhaps of greatest importance in establishing the connection between local self-government and the survival of the Union, was this fact: not only was local government an administrative necessity; it was the fundamental characteristic of this nation. The country had been founded with the ideal of self-rule in mind, had fought a revolution to secure it, and had created a constitution that respected it. Americans endorsed and validated this national ideal every time they established institutions of self-government.

Americans were not attached to a place; constant migration demonstrated that. They were not devoted to the land; the image of the land as real estate, the continuing land speculation attested to that. What made them Americans was that they ruled themselves wherever they went. The Scotsman Alexander McKay saw this with notable insight. What distinguished this people, he observed, was "the feeling which they cherished towards their institutions." . . . McKay admitted that in places like New England there was strong local feeling but what was "astonishing" was "how readily even there an American makes up his mind to try his fortunes elsewhere, particularly if he contemplates removal to another part of the Union, no matter how remote . . . providing the flag of his country waves over it, and republican institutions accompany him on his wanderings." Local institutions of democratic self-government were thus a nationalizing force, and devotion to them was the imperative bond of union.

Of course not every Northern soldier would go to war against the South with the words "law and order" on his lips. Many would enlist in the excitement of the moment. . . . A response of simple outrage at being attacked was natural enough and was probably wide-spread. . . . The vast majority accepted the assertion of Richard Henry Dana that the North should not "buy the right to carry on the government, by any concession to slavery." For these reasons and others men went to war.

Yet admitting these expressions of anti-Southern sentiment does not weaken the argument so far advanced for the importance of the idea of law and order in generating a willingness to fight. The source of much of this sentiment was a widespread fear that the institutions of self-government that maintained ordered liberty were threatened by slavery and the South. To describe the incidents of the 1850s that spawned or encouraged anti-Southern feelings is practically to catalog apparent threats by slavery on such Northern institutions. . . .

Examining the strengths of democracy on the eve of secession one perceptive author hit the mark: More than any other government, wrote Henry Flanders, democracy identified the citizen with his government and thus instilled a powerful patriotism. The citizen in such a state was "an indirect but influential agent in the adminis-tration of its affairs, watches with eager interest its course and when-ever difficulty or danger impends, with something more than a sense of duty or spirit of loyalty, acts boldly and greatly in its service." Such people were deeply devoted to the law, he continued, for "in doing homage to law, they do homage to themselves, the creators and preservers of law." Three years later, with the war raging, Andrew Preston Peabody was equally struck by the way in which self-government created patriotic citizens. Men who made the laws themselves felt personally responsible for them and their survival. Peabody's language was ornate, but the meaning for the war was precise: "He in whom resides an aliquot portion of the sovereignty," he wrote, "will bear his kingly estate in mind on the numerous occasions in daily life on which he might else forget even his manhood."

Urging the energetic prosecution of the war, James Russell Lowell had observed that "our Constitution claims our allegiance because it is law and order." Northerners did not forget their responsibility for that law and order. Foreign observers might have doubted that the nation with the least powerful national government in the world, a nation apparently so centrifugal, could and would find soldiers for a struggle to maintain unity, but those who knew the nation were not surprised. Exulting in the proof of strength that was indubitable by 1864 an obscure writer in the *Atlantic Monthly* remarked, "The bubble of Republicanism, which was to display such alacrity at bursting, is not the childish thing it was once deemed. . . . We have proved that we are a nation equal to the task of self-discipline and self-control." The daily experience of Americans with self-government, with fashioning and maintaining law and order, had done its work well.

———

III. Economic Sectionalism

THE CONSIDERABLE ATTENTION that individuals and societies give to material problems has caused many twentieth-century historians to place great emphasis upon economic forces in history. In seeking the causes of the Civil War, they argue, one must consider the basic differences between the economies of the two great sections, the numerous practical issues upon which sectional leaders were divided. It was opposition to the protective tariff that drove South Carolina to the edge of rebellion in 1832; it was the fact that Southerners repeatedly blocked the passage of internal-improvement (rivers and harbors) bills that caused many Northerners to denounce the Slave Power so violently; and it was the payment to various Northern interests of subsidies from the federal treasury that prompted many Southerners to "calculate the value of the Union." Slavery and slavery expansion were, after all, economic as well as moral problems, for slavery was a labor system and represented a large investment of Southern capital. According to those who advance an economic interpretation of the Civil War, sectional leaders, while expounding great moral and constitutional issues, were often simply disguising economic self-interest with a thin veneer of idealism.

23.   FEDERAL ECONOMIC POLICY

As Southern leaders saw it, the economic exploitation of the South was aided by the policies of the federal government. Sectional legislation, such as subsidies to shipowners and manufacturers, took money from the pockets of the planters and farmers and transferred it to the pockets of Northern capitalists. Senator Robert Toombs of Georgia, in a speech before the legislature of his state in November 1860, explained how this was accomplished. The Rebellion Record, Supplement, pp. 362–68.

The instant the Government was organized, at the very first Congress, the Northern States evinced a general desire and purpose to use it for their own benefit, and to pervert its powers for sectional advantage, and they have steadily pursued that policy to this day. They demanded a monopoly of the business of ship-building, and got a prohibition against the sale of foreign ships to citizens of the United States, which exists to this day.

They demanded a monopoly of the coasting trade, in order to get higher freights than they could get in open competition with the carriers of the world. Congress gave it to them, and they yet hold this monopoly. And now, to-day, if a foreign vessel in Savannah offer to take your rice, cotton, grain or lumber to New York, or any other American port, for nothing, your laws prohibit it, in order that Northern ship-owners may get enhanced prices for doing your carrying. This same shipping interest, with cormorant rapacity, have steadily burrowed their way through your legislative halls, until they have saddled the agricultural classes with a large portion of the legitimate expenses of their own business. We pay a million of dollars per annum for the lights which guide them into and out of your ports. We built and kept up, at the cost of at least another million a year, hospitals for their sick and disabled seamen, when they wear them out and cast them ashore. We pay half a million per annum to support and bring home those they cast away in foreign lands. They demand, and have received, millions of public money to increase the safety of harbors, and lessen the danger of navigating our rivers. All of which expenses legitimately fall upon their business, and should come out of their own pockets, instead of a common treasury.

Even the fishermen of Massachusetts and New-England demand and receive from the public treasury about half a million of dollars per annum as a pure bounty on their business of catching codfish. The North, at the very first Congress, demanded and received bounties under the name of protection, for every trade, craft, and calling which they pursue, and there is not an artisan in brass, or iron, or wood, or weaver, or spinner in wool or cotton, or a calico-maker, or iron-master, or a coal owner, in all the Northern or Middle States, who has not received what he calls the protection of his government on his industry to the extent of from fifteen to two hundred per cent from the year 1791 to this day. They will not strike a blow, or stretch a muscle, without bounties from the government. No wonder they cry aloud for the glorious Union. . . . By it they got their wealth; by it they levy tribute on honest labor. It is true . . . that the present tariff was sustained by an almost unanimous vote of the South; but it was a reduction—a reduction necessary from the plethora of the revenue; but the policy of the North soon made it inadequate to meet the public expenditure, by an enormous and profligate increase of the public expenditure; and at the last session of Congress they brought in and passed through the House the most atrocious tariff bill that ever was enacted, raising the present duties from twenty to two hundred and fifty per cent above the existing rates of duty. That bill now lies on the table of the Senate. It was a master stroke of abolition policy; it united cupidity to fanaticism, and thereby made a combination which has swept the country. There were thousands of protectionists in Pennsylvania, New-Jersey, New-York, and in New-England, who were not abolitionists. There were thousands of abolitionists who were free traders. The mongers brought them together upon a mutual surrender of their principles. The free-trade abolitionists became protectionists; the non-abolition protectionists became abolitionists. The result of this coalition was the infamous Morrill bill—the robber and the incendiary struck hands, and united in joint raid against the South.

Thus stands the account between the North and the South.

Under its ordinary and most favorable action, bounties and protection to every interest and every pursuit in the North, to the extent of at least fifty millions per annum, besides the expenditure of at least sixty millions out of every seventy of the public expenditure among them, thus making the treasury a perpetual fertilizing stream to them and their industry, and a suction-pump to drain away our substance and parch up our lands.

---

24.   THE IMPERIAL NORTH

Vicksburg Daily Whig (*January 18, 1860*), *quoted in Dumond* (*ed.*), Southern Editorials on Secession, pp. 13–14.

By mere supineness, the people of the South have permitted the Yankees to monopolize the carrying trade, with its immense profits. We have yielded to them the manufacturing business, in all its departments, without an effort, until recently, to become manufacturers ourselves. We have acquiesced in the claims of the North to do all the importing, and most of the exporting business, for the whole Union. Thus, the North has been aggrandised, in a most astonishing degree, at the expense of the South. It is no wonder that their villages have grown into magnificent cities. It is not strange that they have "merchant princes," dwelling in gorgeous palaces and reveling in luxuries transcending the luxurious appliances of the East! How could it be otherwise? New York city, like a mighty queen of commerce, sits proudly upon her island throne, sparkling in jewels and waving an undisputed commercial scepter over the South. By means of her railways and navigable streams, she sends out her *long arms* to the extreme South; and, with an avidity rarely equaled, grasps our gains and transfers them to herself—taxing us at every step—and depleting us as extensively as possible without actually destroying us.

---

25. ECONOMIC INDEPENDENCE THROUGH SECESSION

Speech of Representative John H. Reagan of Texas, January 15, 1861, Congressional Globe, 36 Congress, 2 Session, I, p. 391.

You are not content with the vast millions of tribute we pay you annually under the operation of our revenue law, our navigation laws, your fishing bounties, and by making your people our manufacturers, our merchants, our shippers. You are not satisfied with the vast tribute we pay you to build up your great cities, your railroads, your canals. You are not satisfied with the millions of tribute we have been paying you on account of the balance of exchange which you hold against us. You are not satisfied that we of the South are almost reduced to the condition of overseers for northern capitalists. You are not satisfied with all this; but you must wage a relentless crusade against our rights and institutions. . . .

We do not intend that you shall reduce us to such a condition. But I can tell you what your folly and injustice will compel us to do. It will compel us to be free from your domination, and more self-reliant than we have been. It will compel us to manufacture for ourselves, to build up our own commerce, our own great cities, our own railroads and canals; and to use the tribute money we now pay you for these things for the support of a government which will be friendly to all our interests, hostile to none of them.

---

26. NORTHERN GRIEVANCES

Northerners, however, insisted that every other economic group was sacrificed to the slaveholders of the South. A solid bloc of Southern votes defeated measure after measure introduced in Congress to advance the "free-labor" interests of the North. It was to increase this power of obstruction that Southerners sought to create additional slave states. Representative Joshua R. Giddings of

Ohio, in 1844, used this as an argument against the annexation of Texas. Two years later, after the Texas senators had helped to reduce the tariff, Giddings reminded his colleagues of his prediction. Joshua R. Giddings, Speeches in Congress (Boston: 1853), pp. 254–57.

It is now more than two years since I declared to this House and the country, that if Texas were admitted, "our tariff would be held at the will of Texan advocates of free trade." . . . The . . . bill to repeal the tariff of 1842 . . . was carried through the Senate by a majority of only one vote, while both Senators from Texas voted for it. Thus was my prediction most amply fulfilled. As I have already remarked, I then felt that the annexation of Texas was to determine the fate of northern industry. I regarded that as the time for the friends of free labor to rally in behalf of northern interests. But, Sir, opposition to that measure proved unavailing. The resolutions annexing Texas were passed. Her representatives took their seats on this floor; and the first important vote given by them was to strike down the most vital interests of Pennsylvania, of New Jersey, New York, and New England, as well as of the northwestern States; for I regarded the interest of those States as much involved as I do those of New England. I do not, in these remarks, charge southern men with inconsistency. I have no doubt that the cotton-growing interest, separately considered, may be benefited by free trade. It is opposed to all the other great interests of the country. In order to strike down the industry of the North, they must have the numerical force. To obtain this, they must extend the slave-holding territory. . . . Sir, their political power was extended, and we now see the consequences. The people of the free States will soon feel its weight, and will realize the loss they have sustained by their inactivity.

I would not impugn the motives or the judgment of northern whigs, who hold out to their constituents the hope that they may by their political efforts regain the ascendancy, and restore the lost rights of the free States. I may, however, be permitted to say, that when they shall have watched the operations of the slave power as long and as carefully as I have; when they shall have made themselves as familiar with its influences, its designs, and the agencies used to effect its ulterior objects, they will change their views. . . . I should fail to express the solemn convictions of my heart if I were not to say, in the most emphatic terms, that the rights and the interests of the free States have been sacrificed; and will not be regained until the North shall be awakened to its interests, its honor, and to its political duties. . . .

27. THE COMMERCIAL CONSEQUENCES OF SECESSION

When the Southern states began to secede after Lincoln's election, it soon became evident that the great majority of Northerners considered disunion intolerable. Among other reasons, they foresaw disastrous economic consequences; and this explains in part their demand that Lincoln "enforce the laws" in the South. The Boston Herald (November 12, 1860) predicted some of the evils that would result from disunion.

Should the South succeed in carrying out her designs, she will immediately form commercial alliances with European countries who will readily acquiesce in any arrangement which will help English manufacturing at the expense of New England. The first move the South would make would be to impose a heavy tax upon the manufactures of the North, and an export tax upon the cotton used by Northern manufacturers. In this way she would seek to cripple the North. The carrying trade, which is now done by American vessels, would be transferred to British ships, which would be a heavy blow aimed at our commerce. It will also seriously affect our shoe trade and the manufacture of ready-made clothing, while it would derange the monetary affairs of the country.

28.   TARIFF COMPLICATIONS

Philadelphia Press (*March 18, 1861*).

One of the most important benefits which the Federal Government has conferred upon the nation is unrestricted trade between many prosperous States with divers productions and industrial pursuits. But now, since the Montgomery Congress has passed a new tariff, and duties are exacted upon Northern goods sent to ports in the Cotton States, the traffic between the two sections will be materially decreased. . . . Another, and a more serious difficulty arises out of our foreign commerce, and the different rates of duty established by the two tariffs which will soon be in force. . . .

The General Government, . . . to prevent the serious diminution of its revenues, will be compelled to blockade the Southern ports . . . and prevent the importation of foreign goods into them, or to put another expensive guard upon the frontiers to prevent smuggling into the Union States. Even if the independence of the seceding Commonwealths should be recognized, and two distinct nations thus established, we should still experience all the vexations, and be subjected to all the expenses and annoyances which the people of Europe have long suffered, on account of their numerous Governments, and many inland lines of custom-houses. Thus, trade of all kinds, which has already been seriously crippled, would be permanently embarrassed. . . .

It is easy for men to deride and underestimate the value of the Union, but its destruction would speedily be followed by fearful proofs of its importance to the whole American people.

––––––––

29.   THE SOUTHERN BID FOR COMMERCIAL POWER

Boston Transcript (*March 18, 1861*).

It does not require extraordinary sagacity to perceive that trade is perhaps the controlling motive operating to prevent the return of the seceding States to the Union, which they have abandoned. Alleged grievances in regard to slavery were originally the causes for the separation of the cotton States; but the mask has been thrown off, and it is apparent that the people of the principal seceding States are now for commercial independence. They *dream* that the centres of traffic can be changed from Northern to Southern ports. The merchants of New Orleans, Charleston and Savannah are possessed with the idea that New York, Boston and Philadelphia may be shorn, in the future, of their mercantile greatness, by a revenue system verging upon free trade. If the Southern Confeder-ation is allowed to carry out a policy by which only a nominal duty is laid upon imports, no doubt the business of the chief Northern cities will be seriously injured thereby.

The difference is so great between the tariff of the Union and that of the Confederated States, that the entire Northwest must find it to their advantage to purchase their imported goods at New Orleans rather than at New York. In addition to this, the manufacturing interest of the country will suffer from the increased importations resulting from low duties. . . . The . . . [government] would be false to all its obligations, if this state of things were not provided against.

---

30.   THE CLASH OF RIVAL ECONOMIES

When Charles A. and Mary R. Beard examined the background of the Civil War, they came to the conclusion that there had existed an "irrepressible conflict" between the static, agrarian, staple-producing South and the expanding, commercialized, industrializing North. The ultimate triumph of industry over agriculture—of North over South—they described as a "Second American Revolution." Here, in brief, is the Beards' interpretation, from The Rise of American Civilization (*New York: 1927*), *II, pp. 3–10. Copyright 1933 by the Macmillan Company. Reprinted by permission of the publishers.*

Had the economic systems of the North and the South remained static or changed slowly without effecting immense dislocations in the social structure, the balance of power might have been maintained indefinitely by repeating the compensatory tactics of 1787, 1820, 1833, and 1850; keeping in this manner the inherent antagonisms within the bounds of diplomacy. But nothing was stable in the economy of the United States or in the moral sentiments associated with its diversities.

Within each section of the country, the necessities of the productive system were generating portentous results. The periphery of the industrial vortex of the Northeast was daily enlarging, agriculture in the Northwest was being steadily supplemented by manufacturing, and the area of virgin soil open to exploitation by planters was diminishing with rhythmic regularity—shifting with mechanical precision the weights which statesmen had to adjust in their efforts to maintain the equilibrium of peace. Within each of the three sections also occurred an increasing intensity of social concentration as railways, the telegraph, and the press made travel and communication cheap and almost instantaneous, facilitating the centripetal process that was drawing people of similar economic status and parallel opinions into cooperative activities. . . .

As the years passed, the planting leaders of Jefferson's agricultural party insisted with mounting fervor that the opposition, first of the Whigs and then of the Republicans, was at bottom an association of interests formed for the purpose of plundering productive management and labor on the land. And with steadfast insistence they declared that in the insatiable greed of their political foes lay the source of the dissensions which were tearing the country asunder.

"There is not a pursuit in which man is engaged (agriculture excepted)," exclaimed Reuben Davis of Mississippi in 1860, "which is not demanding legislative aid to enable it to enlarge its profits and all at the expense of the primary pursuit of man—agriculture. . . . Those interests having a common purpose of plunder, have united and combined to use the government as the instrument of their operation and have thus virtually converted it into a consolidated empire. Now this combined host of interests stands arrayed against the agricultural states; and this is the reason of the conflict which like an earthquake is shaking our political fabric to its foundation." . . .

With challenging directness, [Jefferson] Davis [of Mississippi] turned upon his opponents in the Senate and charged them with using slavery as a blind to delude the unwary: "What do you propose, gentlemen of the Free-Soil party? Do you propose to better the condition of the slave? Not at all. What then do you propose? You say you are opposed to the expansion of slavery. . . . Is the slave to be benefited by it? Not at all. It is not humanity that influences you in the position which you now occupy before the country. . . . It is that you may have an opportunity of cheating us that you want to limit slave territory within circumscribed bounds. It is that you may have a majority in the Congress of the United States and convert the Government into an engine of northern aggrandizement. It is that your section may grow in power and prosperity upon treasures unjustly taken from the South. . . . You desire to weaken the political power of the southern states; and why? Because you want, by an unjust system of legislation, to promote the industry of the New England states, at the expense of the people of the South and their industry."

Such in the mind of Jefferson Davis, fated to be president of the Confederacy, was the real purpose of the party which sought to prohibit slavery in the territories; that party did not declare slavery to be a moral disease calling for the severe remedy of the surgeon; it merely sought to keep bondage out of the new states as they came into the Union—with one fundamental aim in view, namely, to gain political ascendancy in the government of the United States and fasten upon the country an economic policy that meant the exploitation of the South for the benefit of northern capitalism.

But the planters were after all fighting against the census returns, as the phrase of the day ran current. The amazing growth of northern industries, the rapid extension of railways, the swift expansion of foreign trade to the ends of the earth, the attachment of the farming regions of the West to the centers of manufacture and finance through transportation and credit, the destruction of state consciousness by migration, the alien invasion, the erection of new commonwealths in the Valley of Democracy, the nationalistic drive of interstate commerce, the increase of population in the North, and the southward pressure of the capitalistic glacier all conspired to assure the ultimate triumph of what the orators were fond of calling "the free labor system." This was a dynamic thrust far too powerful for planters operating in a limited territory with incompetent labor on soil of diminishing fertility. Those who swept forward with it, exulting in the approaching triumph of machine industry, warned the planters of their ultimate subjection.

To statesmen of the invincible forces recorded in the census returns, the planting opposition was a huge, compact, and self-conscious economic association bent upon political objects—the possession of the government of the United States, the protection of its interests against adverse legislation, dominion over the territories, and enforcement of the national fugitive slave law throughout the length and breadth of the land. No phrase was more often on the lips of northern statesmen than "the slave power." The pages of the Congressional Globe bristled with references to "the slave system" and its influence over the government of the country. But it was left for William H. Seward of New York to describe it with a fullness of familiar knowledge that made his characterization a classic.

Seward knew from experience that a political party was no mere platonic society engaged in discussing abstractions. "A party," he said, "is in one sense a joint stock association, in which those who contribute most direct the action and management of the concern. The slaveholders contributing in an over-whelming proportion to the capital strength of the Democratic party, they necessarily dictate and prescribe its policy. . . . The slaveholding class has become the governing power in each of the slaveholding states, and it practically chooses thirty of the sixty-two members of the Senate, ninety of the two hundred and thirty-three members of the House of Representatives, and one hundred and five of the two hundred and ninety-five electors of the President and Vice-President of the United States."

Becoming still more concrete, Seward accused the President [James Buchanan] of being "a confessed apologist of the slave-property class." Examining the composition of the Senate, he found

the slave-owning group in possession of all the important committees. Peering into the House of Representatives he discovered no
impregnable bulwark of freedom there. Nor did respect for judicial
ermine compel him to spare the Supreme Court. . . .

Seward then analyzed the civil service of the national government
and could descry not a single person among the thousands employed
in the post office, the treasury, and other great departments who was
"false to the slaveholding interest." Under the spoils system, the
dominion of the slavocracy extended into all branches of the federal
administration. "The customs-houses and the public lands pour
forth two golden streams—one into the elections to procure votes
for the slave-holding class; and the other into the treasury to be
enjoyed by those whom it shall see fit to reward with places in the
public service." . . .

Having described the gigantic operating structure of the slavocracy, Seward drew with equal power a picture of the opposing
system founded on "free labor." He surveyed the course of economy
in the North—the growth of industry, the spread of railways, the
swelling tide of European immigration, and the westward roll of free
farmers—rounding out the country, knitting it together, bringing
"these antagonistic systems" continually into closer contact. Then
he uttered those fateful words which startled conservative citizens
from Maine to California—words of prophecy which proved to be
brutally true—"the irrepressible conflict."

This inexorable clash, he said, was not "accidental, unnecessary,
the work of interested or fanatical agitators and therefore ephemeral."
No. "It is an irrepressible conflict between opposing and enduring
forces." The hopes of those who sought peace by appealing to slave
owners to reform themselves were as chaff in a storm. "How long and
with what success have you waited already for that reformation? Did
any property class ever so reform itself? Did the patricians in old
Rome, the noblesse or clergy in France? The landholders in Ireland?
The landed aristocracy in England? Does the slaveholding class even
seek to beguile you with such a hope? Has it not become rapacious,
arrogant, defiant?" All attempts at compromise were "vain and
ephemeral." There was accordingly but one supreme task before the

people of the United States—the task of confounding and over-throwing "by one decisive blow the betrayers of the Constitution and freedom forever." . . .

Given an irrepressible conflict which could be symbolized in such unmistakable patterns by competent interpreters of opposing factions, a transfer of the issues from the forum to the field, from the conciliation of diplomacy to the decision of arms was bound to come. Each side obdurately bent upon its designs and convinced of its rectitude, by the fulfillment of its wishes precipitated events and effected distributions of power that culminated finally in the tragedy foretold by Seward.

---

31. THE CIVIL WAR AND THE CLASS STRUGGLE

Marxist historians have generally stressed an economic interpretation of the Civil War, but their analyses have been more schematic than that of the Beards. In this national crisis each class played its historic role; the inevitable result was the triumph of the capitalist class, aided by the workers, over the feudal planter class of the South. Algie M. Simons, in Class Struggles in America *(Chicago: 1906), pp. 32–36, provides an example of this point of view.*

By 1850 a class began to appear, national in scope, compact in organization, definite in its desires and destined soon to seize the reins of political power. This was the capitalist class; not to be sure the monopolized solidified plutocracy of today, but rather the little competitive bourgeoisie that already had overthrown the feudalism of Europe. This class had now reached into the Mississippi valley and turned the currents of trade so that the political and industrial affiliations of that locality began to be with New York and New England. This class found its political expression in the Republican party.

This party naturally arose in the upper Mississippi valley where the old political ties were weakest and the new industrial interests were keenest. The people of this locality felt no such close allegiance to the recently organized states in which they lived, as did the seaboard states. Whether employers, wage workers, or small farmers they all possessed the small capitalist mind, and all hoped, and with infinitely better reason than ever since, to become capitalists. They saw in the unsettled West the opportunity to carve out new cities, locate new industries, build yet longer lines of railroad—in short infinite opportunity to "rise"—the highest ideal of the bourgeois mind.

The Republican party exactly corresponded to these industrial interests. It exaggerated the importance of the national government, opposed further extension of slavery and supported all measures for more rapid settlement and exploitation of the West. . . . [In 1860] the Republican party placed in nomination the man, who, more than any other man, typified the best of the capitalist system,— Abraham Lincoln. The finest fruit of the Golden age of American capitalism, he stands as the embodiment of all that is good in that system. "Rising from the people" by virtue of a fierce "struggle for existence" under frontier conditions, where that struggle was freer and fairer than anywhere else in the entire history of capitalism, he incarnates the best of the best days of capitalism. As such he must stand as the greatest American until some higher social stage shall send forth its representative. . . .

Once that the capitalist class had wrested the national government from the chattel slave holders, there was nothing for them to do but to secede. The margin of profits in chattel slavery was already too narrow to permit its continuance in competition with wage slavery unless the chattel slave owners controlled the national government. The Civil war therefore was simply a contest to secure possession of the "big stick" of the national government. The northern capitalists wanted it to collect tariffs, build railroads, shoot down workers, protect trusts, and, in short, to further the interests of plutocracy. The southern chattel slave owner wanted it to secure free trade, to run down fugitive slaves, to conquer new territory for cotton fields, and to maintain the supremacy of King Cotton.

To say that the Republican party was organized, or the Civil war waged to abolish chattel slavery is but to repeat a tale invented almost a decade after the war was closed, as a means of glorifying the party of plutocracy and maintaining its supremacy. . . .

One direct cause of secession whose importance was carefully suppressed, but which undoubtedly played its part, although not a dominant one, is to be found in the debts owed by southern traders to the North. These debts amounted to something between two hundred and four hundred million dollars. One of the first acts of the seceding states was to promptly repudiate all these debts. This at once brought to the support of the southern confederacy a large number of the little traders who had no direct interest otherwise in the supremacy of the slave holding class. . . .

To the student of industrial history the outcome of the Civil war is plain from the beginning. In military conflict, wage slavery is incomparably superior to chattel slavery. The wage workers with modern machinery produce such enormous quantities of surplus value that the expenses of war are little more than a spur to industry. The development of the transportation system, and indeed the whole industrial and financial situation of the North was of a higher social type, more complex, more effective, in producing results of all kinds than that of the South. . . .

In very many senses the Civil war was the father of modern plutocracy. It was fought that the capitalist class might rule. Its progress laid the foundations and mightily extended the scope of the capitalist system.

---

32.   "Revolutionary America"

Louis M. Hacker, "Revolutionary America," Harper's Magazine (March, 1935), pp. 438–40, 441. Extracts reprinted by permission of Louis M. Hacker.

Before the Civil War, . . . the prevailing tone of American society was set by the lower middle classes and the small farmers: leveling doctrines . . . held sway in the States; the central government regarded with a benevolent eye these assaults on privilege and, where it could, aided them—as in the war on the Second Bank of the United States; and every effort was made to encourage westward expansion. Indeed it is important to note that the abolitionist movement arose and received its most devoted allegiance not in the New England urban areas . . . but among this small trader, manufacturer, and farmer class of the less densely settled regions of the North and Middle West. Closely linked with the evangelical churches, and drawing its strength from sections of the country shot through with egalitarian-ism, the anti-slavery crusade was a moral and humanitarian impulse that was regarded with hostility not only by the Southern slave lords of course, but by Northern commercial and industrial capitalists as well. It was not until the middle 1850's that the latter class seized upon the anti-slavery agitation as a standard about which to rally all the hosts against the planter aristocracy; and even here its vacillation was so marked that it refused to declare it was entering the Civil War to free the black man.

The role of the American worker during this period was less clearly indicated. Occasionally and only in large urban centers, he showed an appreciation of his inferior class position and expressed his hostility toward the rising industrial capitalists by the formation of short-lived workingmen's parties; but as a rule he accepted supinely the ministrations of employer welfare devices, and when he followed leaders he listened most attentively to those whose programs were philanthropic, libertarian, and utopian. . . .

In fact so out of tune was American labor with the harmony of the times that when the Civil War—the second great American revolution—threatened, it was incapable of appreciating the impor-tant historical role it was in its power to assume. Marx, viewing the impending conflict from the distance of London, could see that the American worker never would be free until slavery had been torn up root and branch; not so even such a courageous and understanding labor leader as William H. Sylvis who feared the outbreak of hostilities and was willing to accept an absurd compromise on slavery that was only an underwriting of the *status quo*. Unable to sense what similar left factions had known in the English, American, and French Revolutions: that the underprivileged groups could gain great class victories and perhaps even succeed in diverting the revolution into truly radical channels if they entered the conflict, theoretically speaking, as a body captained by their own leaders and under their own revolutionary banners, American labor was plainly bewildered, took no part in the preliminaries of the revolutionary crisis, and when the storm broke joined the armies of the North as individual soldiers. . . .

Such were the more obvious and superficial aspects of American life during the decades of the 1840's and 1850's; running underneath, however, were swift currents which were sweeping the country unerringly into another great revolutionary struggle. . . . [The] Civil War was nothing less than a conflict between two different systems of economic production; and with the victory at the Presidential polls in 1860 of the higher order, the young industrial capitalism of the North and Middle West, a counter-revolutionary movement was launched by the defenders of the lower order, the slave lords of the South.

The politics of compromise of the two decades preceding the opening of hostilities have completely obscured the economics and class bases of the maneuvers: that the slave masters, in the interest of the maintenance of their peculiar institution, were using every agency at their command—legislative, executive, and judicial—to prevent the growth to power and maturity of rising industrial capitalism. The contest was being waged on a number of fronts; the South, of course, was hostile to the extension of free farming into the territories because free farming could be more profitably operated, economically speaking, than slave—hence its bitter opposition to a homestead law; it sold its cotton in a world market and wanted to buy its necessaries cheap—hence its refusal to permit the inauguration of a protective tariff system; it was a debtor class and constantly in need of cheap money—hence its willingness to continue State banks having the right of note issue; . . . it was local and sectional in its interests—hence it could see no need for the underwriting of a great governmental program of support for internal improvements and railroad building, a program whose financial burden would have to be borne by the whole country and which would succeed only in binding West to North by firmer economic ties. With its control over the instrumentalities of government in the decades before the war the South was able to frustrate every hope of the industrial capitalists of the North and block up their every possible avenue of expansion.

The Republican platform of 1860 and the activities of the rump Civil War Congresses plainly reveal the true character of the cleavage between the sections that every passing year had only tended to widen. The Republican platform spoke in timid and faltering accents about slavery . . . but on economic questions its voice rang out loud and clear: it was for a protective tariff, a homestead act, a liberal immigration policy, government subsidies for internal improvements, and a transcontinental railway. And once installed in office, while it presumably was bending every effort to win the war, the victorious party did not permit itself to lose sight of its class program. In 1861 a protective tariff was enacted; in 1862 a homestead law was passed; in the same year, supported from federal loans and land grants, the first Pacific railway was chartered; in 1863 and 1864 a national banking code was written; and in 1864 the bars were let down to the entry of immigrant contract labor. . . .

The Civil War had freed capitalism from the political and economic restraints upon free economic activity that the slave power had imposed; within the next half century it developed mightily. *

---

* This essay should be compared with Professor Hacker's revised interpretation of the causes of the Civil War in his *Triumph of American Capitalism* (New York: 1940), and in his review essay in *Fortune* (July, 1947), pp. 6–8.

33.　Modernization and Sectionalism

By 1860, Northerners engaged in agriculture and industry had made substantial progress toward "modernization"—that is, they welcomed technological innovations that reduced labor costs and increased productivity, they readily abandoned traditional methods, and they viewed change rather than stability as the normal state of social and economic life. The economy of the antebellum South, on the other hand, remained more conservative and traditional. James M. McPherson, in Ordeal by Fire: The Civil War and Reconstruction *(New York: Alfred A. Knopf, 1982), finds an important source of sectional tension in these economic discrepancies. Extracts from pages 13, 23, 27–28, 30–31, 44, reprinted with permission of McGraw-Hill, Inc.*

The antebellum United States was undergoing a process that today's social scientists term "modernization": heavy investment in social overhead capital, which transforms a localized subsistence economy into a nationally integrated market economy; rapid increases in output per capita, resulting from technological innovation and the shift from labor-intensive toward capital-intensive production; the accelerated growth of the industrial sector compared with other sectors of the economy; rapid urbanization; . . . an expansion of education, literacy, and mass communications; a value system that emphasized change rather than tradition; [and] an evolution from the traditional, rural, village-oriented system of personal and kinship ties, in which status is "ascriptive" (inherited), toward a fluid, cosmopolitan, impersonal, and pluralistic society, in which status is achieved by merit. . . .

The South was the great exception to many of the foregoing generalizations about American modernization. The slave states remained overwhelmingly rural and agricultural. Their economy grew, but it did not develop a substantial commercial and industrial sector. Southern agriculture was as labor-intensive in 1860 as it had been in 1800. Upward social mobility was impossible for the half of the Southern labor force who lived in slavery. In contrast to the vigorous educational system and near-universal literacy of the North, the South's commitment to education was weak, and nearly half of its population was illiterate. The proliferation of voluntary associations, reform movements, and self-improvement societies that flourished in the free states largely bypassed the South. The slave states valued tradition and stability more than change and progress. . . .

A crucial aspect of the Southern economy helps to explain its failure to modernize: slaves were both capital and labor. On a typical plantation, the investment in slaves was greater than the investment in land and implements combined. Slave agriculture could not follow the path blazed by Northern agriculture and become more capital-intensive because, paradoxically, an increase of capital became an increase in labor. Instead of investing substantial sums in machinery, planters invested in more slaves. . . .

Antebellum Southern agriculture underwent little technological change after the invention of the cotton gin in 1793. . . . The per capita output of Southern agriculture did increase between 1800 and 1860 . . . but the cause was not primarily technological change. Rather, it was the improved organization of the plantation labor force and the westward movement of the plantation frontier to virgin soil. . . .

Thus the Southern economy *grew*, but it did not *develop*. . . . The South failed to develop a substantial urban middle class and skilled-labor population to generate a diversified economy producing a wide variety of goods and services. . . .

In the South the voices of those calling for industrial development were often drowned out by the voices of those who branded the entrepreneurial ethic a form of vulgar Yankee materialism. The South's ideal image of itself portrayed country gentlemen as practicing the arts of gracious living, hospitality, leisure, the ride and the hunt, chivalry toward women, honor toward equals, and kindness toward inferiors. The Yankees, on the other hand, appeared as a nation of shopkeepers—always chasing the almighty dollar, shrewd but without honor, hard-working but lacking the graces of a leisure class. . . . A South Carolina planter rejected the concept of progress as defined in Northern terms of commerce, industry, internal improvements, cities, and reform. The goals of these "noisy, brawling, roistering, *progressistas,*" he warned, could be achieved in the South "only by destruction of the planter class." . . .

In short, slavery and modernizing capitalism were irreconcilable. After a trip through Virginia in 1835, the future Whig and Republican leader William H. Seward wrote of "an exhausted soil, old and decaying towns, wretchedly-neglected roads . . . an absence of enterprise and improvement. . . . Such has been the effect of slavery." . . . Just as European capitalism had to liberate itself from the outworn restrictions of feudalism, so a dynamic American capitalism could no longer coexist with the outworn institution of slavery.

This view of Northern virtues and Southern vices was of course distorted. Nevertheless, as the conflict over the expansion of slavery into new territories heated up after 1845, an increasing number of Northerners adopted this viewpoint. Those in the antislavery camp regarded the conflict as no less than a contest over the future of America.

IV. Blundering Politicians and Irresponsible Agitators

PARTISAN PROPAGANDA is not noted for its accuracy, and the propaganda disseminated by sectional leaders before the Civil War was no exception. Northern abolitionists probably exaggerated the physical cruelties that Southern masters inflicted upon their slaves. Southern "fire-eaters" doubtless distorted the true character of Northern "Yankees." Politicians in both sections kept the country in constant turmoil and whipped up popular emotions for the selfish purpose of winning elections. Irresponsible agitators generated hatreds and passions that made the rational settlement of sectional differences almost impossible, and thus encouraged an appeal to arms. Some conservatives of the 1850s and 1860s and some present-day so-called "revisionist" historians lay most of the blame for the sectional crisis upon these politicians and agitators.

Moreover, though every generation of statesmen makes decisions that seem stupid and irrational—blundering—to later generations, "revisionist" historians apparently believe that pre–Civil War political leaders were unusually incompetent, that their acts and decisions were grotesque and abnormal. Their exaggeration of sectional differences, their invention of allegedly fictitious issues (such as slavery expansion), created a crisis that was highly artificial and eventually precipitated a "needless war."

34.   A STATESMAN OF COMPROMISE

Senator Stephen A. Douglas, Democrat of Illinois, was one of a group of moderate leaders who opposed the extremists, North and South. Though hated by Northern foes of the Slave Power and by Southern fire-eaters, "revisionist" historians have praised and defended him. In a speech, delivered at Bloomington, Illinois, July 16, 1858, during his campaign for re-election to the United States Senate, Douglas defended his doctrine of popular sovereignty and, in words like those of the "revisionists," attacked Republicans for stirring up sectional strife. Political Debates between Hon. Abraham Lincoln and Hon. Stephen A. Douglas in the Celebrated Campaign of 1858, in Illinois (*Columbus, Ohio: 1860*), *pp. 24–40.*

I hold it to be a fundamental principle in all free governments . . . that every people ought to have the right to form, adopt and ratify the Constitution under which they are to live. When I introduced the Nebraska bill in the Senate of the United States, in 1854, I incorporated in it the provision that it was the true intent and meaning of the bill, not to legislate slavery into any Territory or State, or to exclude it therefrom, but to leave the people thereof perfectly free to form and regulate their own domestic institutions in their own way, subject only to the Constitution of the United States. In that bill the pledge was distinctly made that the people of Kansas should be left not only free, but perfectly free to form and regulate their own domestic institutions to suit themselves. . . . If the people of Kansas want a slaveholding State, let them have it, and if they want a free State they have a right to it, and it is not for the people of Illinois, or Missouri, or New York, or Kentucky, to complain, whatever the decision of the people of Kansas may be upon that point. . . .

[Mr. Lincoln] tells you, in his speech made at Springfield, before the Convention which gave him his unanimous nomination, that:

"A house divided against itself cannot stand."

"I believe this Government cannot endure permanently, half slave and half free."

"I do not expect the Union to be dissolved—I don't expect the house to fall—but I do expect it will cease to be divided."

"It will become all one thing or all the other." . . .

Thus Mr. Lincoln invites, by his proposition, a war of sections, a war between Illinois and Kentucky, a war between the free States and the slave States, a war between the North and the South, for the purpose of either exterminating slavery in every Southern State, or planting it in every Northern State. . . . My friends, is it possible to preserve peace between the North and the South if such a doctrine shall prevail in either section of the Union? . . . I have said on a former occasion, and I here repeat, that it is neither desirable nor possible to establish uniformity in the local and domestic institutions of all the States of this Confederacy. . . .

The difference between Mr. Lincoln and myself upon this point is, that he goes for a combination of the Northern States, or the organization of a sectional political party in the free States to make war on the domestic institutions of the Southern States, and to prosecute that war until they shall all be subdued, and made to conform to such rules as the North shall dictate to them. . . . I am opposed to organizing a sectional party, which appeals to Northern pride, and Northern passion and prejudice, against Southern institutions, thus stirring up ill feeling and hot blood between brethren of the same Republic. I am opposed to that whole system of sectional agitation, which can produce nothing but strife, but discord, but hostility, and, finally, disunion. . . .

There is but one possible way in which slavery can be abolished, and that is by leaving a State, according to the principle of the Kansas-Nebraska bill, perfectly free to form and regulate its institutions in its own way. That was the principle upon which this Republic was founded, and it is under the operation of that principle that we have been able to preserve the Union thus far. Under its operations, slavery disappeared from New Hampshire, from Rhode Island, from Connecticut, from New York, from New Jersey, from Pennsylvania, from six of the twelve original slaveholding States; and this gradual system of emancipation went on quietly, peacefully and steadily, so long as we in the free States minded our own business, and left our neighbors alone. But the moment the Abolition Societies were organized throughout the North, preaching a violent crusade against slavery in the Southern States, this combination necessarily caused a counter-combination in the South, and a sectional line was drawn which was a barrier to any further emancipation. Bear in mind that emancipation has not taken place in any one State since the Freesoil party was organized as a political party in this country. . . . And yet Mr. Lincoln, in view of these historical facts, proposes to keep up this sectional agitation. . . . I submit to you, my fellow-citizens, whether such a line of policy is consistent with the peace and harmony of the country? Can the Union endure under such a system of policy? He has taken his position in favor of sectional agitation and sectional warfare. I have taken mine in favor of securing peace, harmony, and good-will among all the States, by permitting each to mind its own business, and discountenancing any attempt at interference on the part of one State with the domestic concerns of the others. . . .

Mr Lincoln is alarmed for fear that, under the Dred Scott decision, slavery will go into all the Territories of the United States. All I have to say is that, with or without that decision, slavery will go just where the people want it, and not one inch further. You have had experience upon that subject in the case of Kansas. . . . Why has not slavery obtained a foothold in Kansas? Simply because there was a majority of her people opposed to slavery, and every slaveholder knew that if he took his slaves there, the moment that majority got possession of the ballot-boxes, and a fair election was held, that moment slavery would be abolished and he would lose them. For that reason, such owners as took their slaves there brought them back to Missouri, fearing that if they remained they would be emancipated. Thus you see that under the principle of popular sovereignty, slavery has been kept out of Kansas, notwithstanding the fact that for the first three years they had a Legislature in that Territory favorable to it. I tell you, my friends, it is impossible under our institutions to force slavery on an unwilling people. . . .

Hence, if the people of a Territory want slavery, they will encourage it by passing affirmatory laws, and the necessary police regulations, patrol laws and slave code; if they do not want it they will withhold that legislation, and by withholding it, slavery is as dead as if it was prohibited by a constitutional prohibition, especially if, in addition, their legislation is unfriendly, as it would be if they were opposed to it. They could pass such local laws and police regulations as would drive slavery out in one day, or one hour, if they were opposed to it, and therefore, so far as the question of slavery in the Territories is concerned, so far as the principle of popular sovereignty is concerned, in its practical operation, it matter not how the Dred Scott case may be decided with reference to the Territories. . . . The question was an abstract question, inviting no practical results, and whether slavery shall exist or shall not exist in any State or Territory, will depend upon whether the people are for or against it, and whichever way they shall decide it in any Territory or in any State, will be entirely satisfactory to me. . . .

Why should this slavery agitation be kept up? Does it benefit the white man or the slave? Who does it benefit except the Republican politicians, who use it as their hobby to ride into office? Why, I repeat, should it be continued? Why cannot we be content to administer this Government as it was made—a confederacy of sovereign and independent States? Let us . . . refrain from interfering with the domestic institutions and regulations of other States, permit the Territories and new States to decide their institutions for themselves, as we did when we were in their condition; blot out these lines of North and South, and resort back to these lines of State boundaries which the Constitution has marked out, and engraved upon the face of the country; have no other dividing lines but these, and we will be one united, harmonious people, with fraternal feelings, and no discord or dissension.

These are my views and these are the principles to which I have devoted all my energies since 1850, when I acted side by side with the immortal Clay and the god-like Webster in that memorable struggle in which Whigs and Democrats united upon a common platform of patriotism and the Constitution, throwing aside partisan feelings in order to restore peace and harmony to a distracted country. . . . I call upon the people of Illinois, and the people of the whole Union, to bear testimony, that never since the sod has been laid upon the graves of these eminent statesmen have I failed, on any occasion, to vindicate the principle with which the last great, crowning acts of their lives were identified, or to vindicate their names whenever they have been assailed; and now my life and energy are devoted to this great work as the means of preserving this Union. This Union can only be preserved by maintaining the fraternal feeling between the North and the States, the East and the West. If that good feeling can be preserved, the Union will be as perpetual as the fame of its great founders. . . . Bear in mind the dividing line between State rights and Federal authority; let us maintain the great principles of popular sovereignty, of State rights, and of the Federal Union as the Constitution has made it, and this Republic will endure forever.

---

35.   THE TESTIMONY OF AN EARLY "REVISIONIST"

After retiring from the presidency, James Buchanan wrote a small volume defending his policies during the secession crisis. Below are passages from his book which sketch the background of the "needless war." Mr. Buchanan's Administration on the Eve of the Rebellion (*New York: 1866*), pp. 9–14, 64.

That the Constitution does not confer upon Congress power to interfere with slavery in the States has been admitted by all parties and confirmed by all judicial decisions ever since the origin of the Federal Government. This doctrine was emphatically recognized by the House of Representatives in the days of Washington, during the first session of the first Congress, and has never since been called in question. Hence, it became necessary for the abolitionists, in order to furnish a pretext for their assaults on Southern slavery, to appeal to a law higher than the Constitution.

   Slavery, according to them, was a grievous sin against God, and therefore no human Constitution could rightfully shield it from destruction. It was sinful to live in a political confederacy which tolerated slavery in any of the States composing it. . . . This doctrine of the higher law was preached from the pulpits and disseminated in numerous publications throughout New England. At the first, it was regarded with contempt as the work of misguided fanatics. Ere long, however, it enlisted numerous and enthusiastic partisans. These were animated with indomitable zeal in a cause they deemed so holy. They constituted the movement party, and went ahead; because, whether from timidity or secret sympathy, the conservative masses failed in the beginning to resist its progress in a native and determined spirit. . . .

The Constitution having granted to Congress no power over slavery in the States, the abolitionists were obliged to resort to indirect means outside of the Constitution to accomplish their object. The most powerful of these was anti-slavery agitation. . . . This agitation was conducted by numerous anti-slavery societies scattered over the North. . . . Never was an organization planned and conducted with greater skill and foresight for the eventual accomplishment of its object. . . .

. . . Every epithet was employed calculated to arouse the indignation of the Southern people. The time of Congress was wasted in violent debates on the subject of slavery. In these it would be difficult to determine which of the opposing parties was guilty of the greatest excess. Whilst the South threatened disunion unless the agitation should cease, the North treated such threats with derision and defiance. It became manifest to every reflecting man that two geographical parties, the one embracing the people north and the other those south of Mason and Dixon's line, were in rapid process of formation—an event so much dreaded by the Father of his Country.

It is easy to imagine the effect of this agitation upon the proud, sensitive, and excitable people of the South. One extreme naturally begets another. Among the latter there sprung up a party as fanatical in advocating slavery as were the abolitionists of the North in denouncing it. . . . If the fanatics of the North denounced slavery as evil and only evil, and that continually, the fanatics of the South upheld it as fraught with blessings to the slave as well as to his master. . . .

Fanaticism never stops to reason. Driven by honest impulse, it rushes on to its object without regard to interposing obstacles. Acting on the principle avowed in the Declaration of Independence, "that all men are created equal," and believing slavery to be sinful, it would not hesitate to pass from its own State into other States, and to emancipate their slaves by force of arms. . . . In the present state of civilization, we are free to admit that slavery is a great political and social evil. If left to the wise ordinances of a superintending Providence, which never acts rashly, it would have been gradually extinguished in our country, peacefully and without bloodshed, as has already been done throughout nearly the whole of Christendom. . . .

But even admitting slavery to be a sin, have the adherents of John Brown never reflected that the attempt by one people to pass beyond their own jurisdiction, and to extirpate by force of arms whatever they may deem sinful among other people, would involve the nations of the earth in perpetual hostilities? . . . Their sins are not our sins. We must intrust their punishment and reformation to their own authorities, and to the Supreme Governor of nations.

---

36.   THE FRUITS OF ABOLITIONIST PROPAGANDA

Like the "revisionists," the New York Herald (*November 13, 1860*) *assigned most of the responsibility for the sectional crisis to Northern agitators.*

When it is remembered how steadily the public mind in the North has been educated in the idea that "slavery is an evil and a crime"; how for many years this has been inculcated by the school books and the churches; how under its influence the religious sects of the country, once united in their sessions and synods, have been divided and led to look upon each other as wicked; how the missionary and tract societies have been split; how the religious book concerns have been sundered into Northern and Southern organizations; how every system of moral propagandism in the North has been to a greater or less degree turned to the same object, and that at last political parties have come to be ranged on sectional and geographical grounds, we shall find good reason why the South should be in earnest in its present alarm.

---

37. A NEEDLESS WAR

Believing that slavery was blocked from further expansion by geographical conditions, "revisionists" insist that the prewar agitators had raised and exploited a fictitious issue. Moreover, they maintain, by 1860 slavery had passed its peak and would soon have died of natural causes if the Civil War had not destroyed it by force. This point of view is developed in Charles W. Ramsdell, "The Natural Limits of Slavery Expansion," Mississippi Valley Historical Review, XVI (1929), pp. 151-71. The following extracts are reprinted with the permission of the Mississippi Valley Historical Review.

In the forefront of that group of issues which, for more than a decade before the secession of the cotton states, kept the northern and southern sections of the United States in irritating controversy and a growing sense of enmity, was the question whether the federal government should permit and protect the expansion of slavery into the western territories. . . . It was upon this particular issue that a new and powerful sectional party appeared in 1854, that the majority of the Secessionists of the cotton states predicated their action in 1860 and 1861, and it was upon this also that President-elect Lincoln forced the defeat of the compromise measures in the winter of 1860–61. It seems safe to say that had this question been eliminated or settled amicably, there would have been no secession and no Civil War. . . .

Disregarding the stock arguments—constitutional, economic, social, and what not—advanced by either group, let us examine afresh the real problem involved. Would slavery, if legally permitted to do so, have taken possession of the territories or of any considerable portion of them? . . .

The causes of the expansion of slavery westward from the South Atlantic Coast are now well understood. The industrial revolution and the opening of world markets had continually increased the consumption and demand for raw cotton, while the abundance of fertile and cheap cotton lands in the Gulf States had steadily lured cotton farmers and planters westward. Where large-scale production was possible, the enormous demand for a steady supply of labor had made the use of slaves inevitable, for a sufficient supply of free labor was unprocurable on the frontier. . . . The most powerful factor in the westward movement of slavery was cotton, for the land available for other staples—sugar, hemp, tobacco—was limited, while slave labor was not usually profitable in growing grain. This expansion of the institution was in response to economic stimuli; it had been inspired by no political program nor by any ulterior political purpose. . . . The movement would go on as far as suitable cotton lands were to be found or as long as there was a reasonable expectation of profit from slave labor, provided, of course, that no political barrier was encountered.

The astonishing rapidity of the advance of the southern frontier prior to 1840 had alarmed the opponents of slavery, who feared that the institution would extend indefinitely into the West. But by 1849–50, when the contest over the principle of the Wilmot Proviso was at its height, the western limits of the cotton growing region were already approximated; and by the time the new Republican party was formed to check the further expansion of slavery, the westward march of the cotton plantation was evidently slowing down. The northern frontier of cotton production west of the Mississippi had already been established at about the northern line of Arkansas. Only a negligible amount of the staple was being grown in Missouri. West of Arkansas a little cotton was cultivated by the slaveholding, civilized Indians; but until the Indian territory should be opened generally to white settlement—a development of which there was no immediate prospect—it could not become a slaveholding region of any importance. The only possibility of a further westward extension of the cotton belt was in Texas. In that state alone was the frontier line of cotton and slavery still advancing. . . .

By the provisions of the Compromise of 1850, New Mexico, Utah, and the other territories acquired from Mexico were legally open to slavery. In view of well-known facts, it may hardly seem worth while to discuss the question whether slavery would ever have taken possession of that vast region; but perhaps some of those facts should be set down. The real western frontier of the cotton belt is still in Texas; for though cotton is grown in small quantities in New Mexico, Arizona, and California, in none of these states is the entire yield equal to that of certain single counties in Texas. In none is negro labor used to any appreciable extent, if at all. In New Mexico and Arizona, Mexican labor is cheaper than negro labor, as has been the case ever since the acquisition of the region from Mexico. It was well understood by sensible men, North and South, in 1850 that soil, climate, and native labor would form a perpetual bar to slavery in the vast territory then called New Mexico. Possibly southern California could have sustained slavery, but California had already decided that question for itself, and there was no remote probability that the decision would ever be reversed. As to New Mexico, the census of 1860, ten years after the territory had been thrown open to slavery, showed not a single slave; and this was true also of Colorado and Nevada. Utah, alone of all these territories, was credited with any slaves at all. Surely these results for the ten years when, it is alleged, the slave power was doing its utmost to extend its system into the West, ought to have confuted those who had called down frenzied curses upon the head of Daniel Webster for his Seventh-of-March speech.

At the very time when slavery was reaching its natural and impassable frontiers in Texas, there arose the fateful excitement over the Kansas-Nebraska Bill, or rather over the clause which abrogated the Missouri Compromise and left the determination of the status of slavery in the two territories to their own settlers. . . . But, in all candor, . . . [can] anyone who examines the matter objectively today say that there was any probability that slavery as an institution would ever have taken possession of either Kansas or

Nebraska? Certainly cotton could not have been grown in either, for it was not grown in the adjacent part of Missouri. Hemp, and possibly tobacco, might have been grown in a limited portion of eastern Kansas along the Missouri and the lower Kansas rivers; and if no obstacle had been present, undoubtedly a few negroes would have been taken into eastern Kansas. But the infiltration of slaves would have been a slow process.

Apparently there was no expectation, even on the part of the pro-slavery men, that slavery would go into Nebraska. Only a small fraction of the territory was suited to any crops that could be grown with profit by slave labor, and by far the great portion of Kansas— even of the eastern half that was available for immediate settlement—would have been occupied in a short time, as it was in fact, by a predominantly non-slaveholding and free-soil population. To say that the individual slaveowner would disregard his own economic interest and carry valuable property where it would entail loss merely for the sake of a doubtful political advantage seems a palpable absurdity. . . . The census of 1860 showed two slaves in Kansas and fifteen in Nebraska. In short, there is good reason to believe that had Douglas' bill passed Congress without protest, and had it been sustained by the people of the free states, slavery could not have taken permanent root in Kansas if the decision were left to the people of the territory itself.

The fierce contest which accompanied and followed the passage of Douglas' Kansas-Nebraska Bill is one of the sad ironies of history. Northern and southern politicians and agitators, backed by excited constituents, threw fuel to the flames of sectional antagonism until the country blazed into a civil war that was the greatest tragedy of the nation. There is no need here to analyze the arguments, constitutional or otherwise, that were employed. Each party to the controversy seemed obsessed by the fear that its own preservation was at stake. The northern anti-slavery men held that a legal sanction of slavery in the territories would result in the extension of the institution and the domination of the free North by the slave power; prospective immigrants in particular feared that they would never be able to get homes in this new West. Their fears were groundless; but in their excited state of mind they could neither see the facts clearly nor consider them calmly. The slaveholding Southerners, along with other thousands of Southerners who never owned slaves, believed that a victory in Kansas for the anti-slavery forces would not only weaken southern defenses—for they well knew that the South was on the defensive—but would encourage further attacks until the economic life of the South and "white civilization" were destroyed. Though many of them doubted whether slavery would ever take permanent root in Kansas, they feared to yield a legal precedent which could later be used against them. And so they demanded a right which they could not actively use—the legal right to carry slaves where few would or could be taken. The one side fought rancorously for what it was bound to get without fighting; the other, with equal rancor, contended for what in the nature of things it could never use. . . .

If the conclusions that have been set forth are sound, by 1860 the institution of slavery had virtually reached its natural frontiers in the West. Beyond Texas and Missouri the way was closed. There was no reasonable ground for expectation that new lands could be acquired south of the United States into which slaves might be taken. There was, in brief, no further place for it to go. In the cold facts of the situation, there was no longer any basis for excited sectional controversy over slavery extension; but the public mind had so long been concerned with the debate that it could not see that the issue had ceased to have validity. In the existing state of the popular mind, therefore, there was still abundant opportunity for the politician to work to his own ends, to play upon prejudice and passion and fear. Blind leaders of the blind! Sowers of the wind, not seeing how near was the approaching harvest of the whirlwind!

Perhaps this paper should end at this point; but it may be useful to push the inquiry a little farther. If slavery could gain no more political territory, would it be able to hold what it had? Were there not clear indications that its area would soon begin to contract? Were there not even some evidences that a new set of conditions were arising within the South itself which would disintegrate the institution? Here, it must be confessed, one enters the field of speculation, which is always dangerous ground for the historian. But there were certain factors in the situation which can be clearly discerned, and it may serve some purpose to indicate them. . . .

As long as there was an abundance of cheap and fertile cotton lands, as there was in Texas, and the prices of cotton remained good, there would be a heavy demand for labor on the new plantations. As far as fresh lands were concerned, this condition would last for some time, for the supply of lands in Texas alone was enormous. But at the end of the decade, there were unmistakable signs that a sharp decline in cotton prices and planting profits was close at hand. The production of cotton had increased slowly, with some fluctuations, from 1848 to 1857, and the price varied from about ten cents to over thirteen cents a pound on the New York market. But a rapid increase in production began in 1858 and the price declined. The crop of 1860 was twice that of 1850. . . . There was every indication of increased production and lower price levels for the future, even if large allowance be made for poor-crop years. There was small chance of reducing the acreage, for the cotton planter could not easily change to another crop. Had not the war intervened, there is every reason to believe that there would have been a continuous overproduction and very low prices throughout the sixties and seventies.

What would have happened then when the new lands of the Southwest had come into full production and the price of cotton had sunk to the point at which it could not be grown with profit on the millions of acres of poorer soils in the older sections? The replenishment of the soil would not have solved the problem for it would only have resulted in the production of more cotton. Even on the better lands the margin of profit would have declined. Prices of slaves must have dropped then, even in the Southwest; importation from the border states would have fallen off; thousands of slaves would have become not only unprofitable but a heavy burden, the market for them gone. Those who are familiar with the history of cotton farming, cotton prices, and the depletion of the cotton lands since the Civil War will agree that this is no fanciful picture.

What would have been the effect of this upon the slaveowner's attitude toward emancipation? No preachments about the sacredness of the institution and of constitutional guarantees would have compensated him for the dwindling values of his lands and slaves and the increasing burden of his debts. . . . With prosperity gone and slaves an increasingly unprofitable burden, year after year, can there be any doubt that thousands of slaveowners would have sought for some means of relief? How they might have solved the problem of getting out from under the burden without entire loss of the capital invested in their working force, it is hard to say; but that they would have changed their attitude toward the institution seems inevitable. . . .

In summary and conclusion: it seems evident that slavery had about reached its zenith by 1860 and must shortly have begun to decline, for the economic forces which had carried it into the region west of the Mississippi had about reached their maximum effectiveness. It could not go forward in any direction and it was losing ground along its northern border. A cumbersome and expensive system, it could show profits only as long as it could find plenty of rich land to cultivate and the world would take the product of its crude labor at a good price. It had reached its limits in both profits and lands. The free farmers in the North who dreaded its further spread had nothing to fear. Even those who wished it destroyed had only to wait a little while—perhaps a generation, probably less. It was summarily destroyed at a frightful cost to the whole country and one third of the nation was impoverished for forty years. One is tempted at this point to reflections on what has long passed for statesmanship on both sides of that long dead issue. But I have not had the heart to indulge them.

———

38. "A Blundering Generation"

The "revisionist" interpretation is perhaps best illustrated in an essay by James G. Randall entitled "A Blundering Generation," in Lincoln the Liberal Statesman, *pp. 36–64. Copyright 1947 by Dodd, Mead & Company, Inc. First printed in the* Mississippi Valley Historical Review, *XXVII (1940), pp. 3–28. Extracts reprinted by permission of the* Mississippi Valley Historical Review *and Dodd, Mead & Company, Inc.*

In the present vogue of psychiatry, individual mental processes and behavior have been elaborately studied. Psychiatry for a nation, however, is still in embryo, though it is much the fashion to have discussions of mass behaviorism, public opinion, pressure groups, thought patterns, and propaganda. Writers in the field of history tend more and more to speak in terms of culture; this often is represented as a matter of cultural conflict, as of German against Slav, of Japanese against Chinese, and the like. Scholars are doing their age a disservice if these factors of culture are carried over, as they often are, whether by historians or others, into justifications or "explanations" of war. . . .

As for the Civil War the stretch and span of conscious economic motive was much smaller than the areas or classes of war involvement. Economic diversity offered as much motive for union, in order to have a well rounded nation, as for the kind of economic conflict suggested by secession. One fault of writers who associated war-making with economic advantage is false or defective economics; another is the historical fault. It is surprising how seldom the economic explanation of war has made its case historically—i.e., in terms of adequate historical evidence bearing upon those points and those minds where actually the plunge into war, or the drive toward war, occurred. . . .

War causation tends to be "explained" in terms of great forces. Something elemental is supposed to be at work, be it nationalism, race conflict, or quest for economic advantage. With these forces predicated, the move toward war is alleged to be understandable, to be "explained," and therefore to be in some sense reasonable. Thought runs in biological channels and nations are conceived as organisms. Such thought is not confined to philosophers; it is the commonest of mental patterns. A cartoonist habitually draws a nation as a person. In this manner of thinking Germany does so and so; John Bull takes this or that course, and so on. When thought takes so homely a form it is hardly called a philosophical concept; on the level of solemn learning the very same thing would appear under a Greek derivative or Freudian label. However labeled, it may be questioned whether the concept is any better than a poor figure of speech, a defective metaphor which is misleading because it has a degree of truth. . . .

War-making is too much dignified if it is told in terms of broad national urges, of great German motives, or of compelling Italian ambitions. When nations stumble into war, or when peoples rub their eyes and find they have been dragged into war, there is at some point a psychopathic case. Omit the element of abnormality, of bogus leadership, or inordinate ambition for conquest, and diagnosis fails. . . .

There is no intention here to draw a comparison of the American Civil War with recent wars. The point is that sweeping generalizations as to "war causation" are often faulty and distorted, and that when such distortion is assisted by taking the Civil War as an alleged example, a word by the historian is appropriate. . . . The "explaining" of war is one of the most tricky of subjects. If the explanation is made to rest on the cultural or economic basis, it is not unlikely that the American war in the eighteen-sixties will be offered as a supposedly convincing example. The writer, however, doubts seriously whether a consensus of scholars who have competently studied that war would accept either the cultural or the economic motive as the effective cause. . . .

Clear thinking would require a distinction between causing the war and getting into it. Discussion which overlooks this becomes foggy indeed. It was small minorities that caused the war; then the regions and sections were drawn in. No one seems to have thought of letting the minorities or the original trouble makers fight it out. Yet writers who descant upon the "causation" of the war write grandly of vast sections, as if the fact of a section being dragged into the slaughter was the same as the interests of that section being consciously operative in its causation. Here lies one of the chief fallacies of them all. . . .

In writing of human nature in politics Graham Wallas has shown the potent effect of irrational attitudes. He might have found many a Civil War example. Traditional "explanations" of the war fail to make sense when fully analyzed. The war has been "explained" by the choice of a Republican president, by grievances, by sectional economics, by the cultural wish for Southern independence, by slavery, or by events at Sumter. But these explanations crack when carefully examined. The election of Lincoln fell so far short of swinging Southern sentiment against the Union that secessionists were still unwilling to trust their case to an all-Southern convention or to coöperation among Southern states. . . . Alexander H. Stephens stated that secessionists did not desire redress of grievances and would obstruct such redress. Prophets of sectional economics left many a Southerner unconvinced. . . . The tariff was a potential future annoyance rather than an acute grievance in 1860. What existed then was largely a Southern tariff law. Practically all tariffs are one-sided. Sectional tariffs in other periods have existed without producing war. Such a thing as a Southern drive for independence on cultural lines is probably more of a modern thesis than a contemporary motive of sufficient force to have carried the South out of the Union on any broadly representative or all-Southern basis. . . .

It was hard for Southerners to accept the victory of a sectional party in 1860, but it was no part of the Republican program to smash slavery in the South, nor did the territorial aspect of slavery mean much politically beyond agitation. Southerners cared little about taking slaves into the territories; Republicans cared so little in the opposite sense that they avoided prohibiting slavery in territorial laws passed in February and March of 1861. . . .

Let one take all the factors traditionally presented—the Sumter maneuver, the election of Lincoln, abolitionism, slavery in Kansas, prewar objections to the Union, cultural and economic differences, etc.—and it will be seen that only by a kind of false display could any of these issues, or all of them together, be said to have caused the war if one omits the elements of emotional unreason and overbold leadership. If one word or phrase were selected to account for the war, that word would not be slavery, or economic grievance, or state rights, or diverse civilizations. It would have to be such a word as fanaticism (on both sides), misunderstanding, misrepresentation, or perhaps politics. . . .

As to wars, the ones that have not happened are perhaps best to study. Much could be said about such wars. There has been as much "cause" for wars that did not happen as for wars that did. Cultural and economic difficulties *in wars that have not occurred* are highly significant. The notion that you must have war when you have cultural variation, or economic competition, or sectional difference is an unhistorical misconception which it is stupid to promote. Yet some of the misinterpretations of the Civil War have tended to promote it.

This subject—war scares, or vociferous prowar drives which happily fizzled out—is a theme for a book in itself. There was the slogan "Fifty-four Forty or Fight" in 1844. If it meant anything, it meant that, in the international territorial difficulty as to the far Northwest, the United States should demand all the area in dispute with England, should refuse diplomatic adjustment, and should fight England if the full demand was not met. The United States did not get Fifty-four Forty—i.e., an enormous area of Canada—but it did not fight. The matter was easily adjusted by treaty in 1846. In retrospect, the settlement made the earlier slogan, and war drive, seem no better than sheer jingoism.

That was in the roaring forties. In the sixties the arguments with England, despite war cries, were adjusted by diplomacy; after the war they became the subject of successful arbitration. In the nineties the Venezuelan trouble with England caused a good deal of talk of coming war, while at the same time there was patriotic advocacy of peaceful adjustment. In the result, the Monroe Doctrine was peaceably vindicated. If that war over Venezuela had happened, one cannot doubt that writers would impressively have shown, by history, economics, etc., that it was "inevitable." Previous troubles with England would have been reviewed with exaggerated emphasis on a hostile background and with neglect of friendly factors. . . .

It would be instructive to examine such episodes and to show how easily the country accepted peaceful adjustment, or how life simply went on with continued peace; then, after the frenzy of war agitation had passed, reasonable men everywhere either forgot the agitation altogether or recognized how artificially and how mistakenly the "issues" had been misrepresented by those who gave out the impression of "inevitable" war. All the familiar arguments, replete with social and economic explanations, could be mustered up for "wars" that were avoided or prospectively imagined. The whole subject of war "causation" needs far more searching inquiry than it has received.

---

39. "AN EXCESS OF DEMOCRACY"

David Donald disagrees with the "revisionists" when they seem to imply that prewar politicians were incompetent or evil men. Rather, he suggests that they were the inevitable products of antebellum American society—an atomized society without re- straining institutions or traditions. But he disagrees with the "fundamentalists" who explain the crisis in terms of "grand elemen- tal forces," and he stresses "how little was actually at stake." Thus, in a more sophisticated way, he reaches conclusions that are in essential agreement with the "revisionists." Donald's thesis is developed in An Excess of Democracy: The American Civil War and the Social Process *(Oxford, England: 1960). Extracts are printed below with the permission of the publisher, the Clarendon Press.*

. . . The Civil War, I believe, can best be understood neither as the result of accident nor as the product of conflicting sectional interests, but as the outgrowth of social processes which affected the entire United States during the first half of the nineteenth century.

It is remarkable how few historians have attempted to deal with American society as a whole during this critical period. Accustomed to looking upon it as a pre-war era, we have stressed divisive elements and factors of sectional conflict. Contemporary European observers, on the whole, had a better perspective. Some of these foreign travellers looked upon the American experiment with loathing; others longed for its success; but nearly all stressed the basic unity of American culture, minimizing the 10 per cent of ideas and traits which were distinctive to the individual sections and stressing the 90 per cent of attitudes and institutions which all Americans shared.

It is time for us to emulate the best of these European observers and to draw a broad picture of the common American values in the early nineteenth century. Any such analysis would have to start with the newness of American life. Novelty was the keynote not merely for the recently settled regions of the West but for all of American society. Though states like Virginia and Massachusetts had two hundred years of history behind them, they, too, were affected by social changes so rapid as to require each generation to start anew. In the Northeast the rise of the city shockingly disrupted the normal course of societal evolution. . . . In the Old South the long-settled states of the Eastern coast were undergoing a parallel evolution, for the opening of rich alluvial lands along the Gulf Coast offered bonanzas as surely as did the gold mines of California. In the early nineteenth century all sections of the United States were being transformed with such rapidity that stability and security were everywhere vanishing values; nowhere could a father safely predict what kind of a world his son would grow up in.

Plenty was another characteristic of this new American society. . . . The lands begged to be developed. . . . Mineral wealth surpassed men's dreams. . . . Some Americans made their fortunes in manufacturing; others in cotton and rice plantations; still others in the mines and lands of the West. Not everybody got rich, of course, but everybody aspired to do so. Both the successful and those less fortunate were equally ruthless in exploiting the country's natural resources, whether of water power, of fertile fields, of mineral wealth, or simply of human labor.

Rapid social mobility was another dominant American trait. . . . Surely in no other Western society of the period could a self-taught merchant's apprentice have founded the manufacturing dynasty of the Massachusetts Lawrences; or a semi-literate ferry-boatman named Vanderbilt have gained control of New York City's transportation system; or the son of a London dried-fish shopkeeper named Benjamin have become Senator from Louisiana; or a self-taught prairie lawyer have been elected President of a nation. . . .

A new society of plenty, with abundant opportunities for self-advancement, was bound to leave its hallmark upon its citizens, whether they lived in North, South, or West. The connexion between character and culture is still an essentially unexplored one, but it is surely no accident that certain widely shared characteristics appeared among Americans in every rank of life. In such a society, richly endowed with every natural resource, protected against serious foreign wars, and structured so as to encourage men to rise, it was inevitable that a faith in progress should be generally shared. . . .

Confidence in the future encouraged Americans in their tendency to speculate. A man of even very modest means might anticipate making his fortune, not through exertions of his own but through the waves of prosperity which seemed constantly to float American values higher and higher. A small initial capital could make a man another John Jacob Astor. . . . It was no wonder that Americans rejected the safe investment, the "sure thing," to try a flier into the unknown. In some cases the American speculative mania was pathological. . . .

. . . In nineteenth-century America all the recognized values of orderly civilization were gradually being eroded. Social atomization affected every segment of American society. . . .

Even the most intimate domestic relations were drastically altered in nineteenth-century America. For centuries the Western tradition had been one in which females were subordinate to males, and in which the wife found her full being only in her husband. But in the pre–Civil War United States such a social order was no longer possible. In Massachusetts, for example, which in 1850 had 17,480 more females than males, many women could no longer look to their normal fulfilment in marriage and a family; if they were from the lower classes they must labour to support themselves, and if they were from the upper classes they must find satisfaction in charitable deeds and humanitarian enterprises. It is not altogether surprising that so many reform movements had their roots in New England. In the West, on the other hand, women were at a great premium; however old or ugly, they found themselves marriageable. . . . It was, consequently, extremely difficult to persuade these ladies that, after marriage, they had no legal existence except as chattels of their husbands. Not surprisingly, women's suffrage, as a practical movement, flourished in the West.

Children in such a society of abundance were an economic asset. . . . Partly because they were so valuable, children were well cared for and given great freedom. Virtually every European traveller in the nineteenth century remarked the uncurbed egotism of the American child. . . .

This child was father of the American man. It is no wonder that Tocqueville, attempting to characterize nineteenth-century American society, was obliged to invent a new word, "individualism." This is not to argue that there were in pre–Civil War America no men of orderly, prudent, and conservative habits; it is to suggest that rarely in human history has a people as a whole felt itself so completely unfettered by precedent. In a nation so new that, as President James K. Polk observed, its history was in the future, in a land of such abundance, men felt under no obligation to respect the lessons of the past. . . .

Every aspect of American life witnessed this desire to throw off precedent and to rebel from authority. Every institution which laid claim to prescriptive right was challenged and overthrown. The Church, that potent instrument of social cohesion in the colonial period, was first disestablished, and then strange new sects . . . appeared to fragment the Christian community. The squirearchy, once a powerful conservative influence in the Middle States and the South was undermined by the abolition of primogeniture and entails. . . . All centralized economic institutions came under attack. The Second Bank of the United States, which exercised a healthy restraint upon financial chaos, was destroyed during the Jackson period, and at the same time the Supreme Court moved to strike down vested monopoly rights.

Nowhere was the American rejection of authority more complete than in the political sphere. The decline in the powers of the federal government from the constructive centralism of George Washington's administration to the feeble vacillation of James Buchanan's is so familiar as to require no repetition here. With declining powers there went also declining respect. . . . The national government, moreover, was not being weakened in order to bolster the state governments, for they too were decreasing in power. . . . By the 1850's the authority of all government in America was at a low point; government to the American was, at most, merely an institution with a negative role, a guardian of fair play.

Declining power of government was paralleled by increased popular participation in it. The extension of the suffrage in America has rarely been the result of a concerted reform drive, such as culminated in England in 1832 and in 1867; rather it has been part of the gradual erosion of all authority, of the feeling that restraints and differentials are necessarily antidemocratic, and of the practical fact that such restrictions are difficult to enforce. By the mid-nineteenth century in most American states white manhood suffrage was virtually universal.

All too rarely have historians given sufficient attention to the consequences of the extension of the franchise in America, an extension which was only one aspect of the general democratic rejection of authority. Different appeals must necessarily be made to a broad electorate than to an *élite* group. Since the rival parties must both woo the mass of voters, both tended to play down issues and to stand on broad equivocal platforms which evaded all subjects of controversy. Candidates were selected not because of their demonstrated statesmanship but because of their high public visibility. . . . If it is a bit too harsh to say that extension of the suffrage inevitably produced leaders without policies and parties without principles, it can be safely maintained that universal democracy made it difficult to deal with issues requiring subtle understanding and delicate handling. . . .

. . . Simply because Americans by the middle of the nineteenth century suffered from an excess of liberty, they were increasingly unable to arrive at reasoned, independent judgments upon the problems which faced their society. The permanent revolution that was America had freed its citizens from the bonds of prescription and custom but had left them leaderless. Inevitably the reverse side of the coin of individualism is labelled conformity. Huddling together in their loneliness, they sought only to escape their freedom. Fads, fashions, and crazes swept the country. Religious revivalism reached a new peak in the 1850's. Hysterical fears and paranoid suspicions marked this shift of Americans to "other-directedness." Never was there a field so fertile before the propagandist, the agitator, the extremist.

These dangerously divisive tendencies in American society did not of course, go unnoticed. Tocqueville and other European observers were aware of the perils of social atomization and predicted that, under shock, the union might be divided. Nor were all Americans indifferent to the drift of events. Repeatedly in the Middle Period conservative statesmen tried to check the widespread social disorganization. . . .

Possibly in time this disorganized society might have evolved a genuinely conservative solution for its problems, but time ran against it. At a stage when the United States was least capable of enduring shock, the nation was obliged to undergo a series of crises, largely triggered by the physical expansion of the country. The annexation of Texas, the war with Mexico, and the settlement of California and Oregon posed inescapable problems of organizing and governing this new empire. Something had to be done, yet any action was bound to arouse local, sectional hostilities. Similarly in 1854 it was necessary to organize the Great Plains territory, but, as Stephen A. Douglas painfully learned, organizing it without slavery alienated the South, organizing it with slavery offended the North, and organizing it under popular sovereignty outraged both sections.

As if these existential necessities did not impose enough strains upon a disorganized society, well-intentioned individuals insisted upon adding others. The quite unnecessary shock administered by the Dred Scott decision in 1857 is a case in point; justices from the anti-slavery North and the pro-slavery South, determined to settle the slavery issue once and for all, produced opinions which in fact settled nothing but only led to further alienation and embitterment. Equally unnecessary, of course, was the far ruder shock which crazy John Brown and his little band administered two years later when they decided to solve the nation's problems by taking the law into their own hands at Harpers Ferry.

These crises which afflicted the United States in the 1850's were not in themselves calamitous experiences. Revisionist historians have correctly pointed out how little was actually at stake: Slavery did not go into New Mexico or Arizona; Kansas, after having been opened to the peculiar institution for six years, had only two Negro slaves; the Dred Scott decision declared an already repealed law unconstitutional; John Brown's raid had no significant support in the North and certainly roused no visible enthusiasm among Southern Negroes. When compared to crises which other nations have resolved without great discomfort, the true proportions of these exaggerated disturbances appear.

But American society in the 1850's was singularly ill equipped to meet any shocks, however weak. It was a society so new and so disorganized that its nerves were rawly exposed. It was, as Henry James noted, a land which had "No sovereign, no court, no personal loyalty, no aristocracy, no church, no clergy, no army, no diplomatic service, no country gentlemen, no palaces, no castles, nor manors, nor old country houses, nor parsonages, nor thatched cottages, nor ivied ruins; no cathedrals, nor abbeys, nor little Norman churches; no great universities nor public schools. . . ; no literature, no novels, no museums, no pictures, no political society"—in short, which had no resistance to strain. The very similarity of the social processes which affected all sections of the country—the expansion of the frontier, the rise of the city, the exploitation of great natural wealth—produced not cohesion but individualism. The structure of the American political system impeded the appearance of conservative statesmanship, and the rapidity of the crises in the 1850's prevented conservatism from crystallizing. The crises themselves were not world-shaking, nor did they inevitably produce war. They were, however, the chisel strokes which revealed the fundamental flaws in the block of marble, flaws which stemmed from an excess of democracy.

40.   THE POLITICIANS' WAR

Michael F. Holt, in The Political Crisis of the 1850s (*New York: John Wiley & Sons, 1978*), *rejects the interpretations of the "fundamentalists," who stressed slavery and cultural differences as Civil War causes. Rather, responsibility rested with the politicians, North and South, who politicized and exploited sectional differences and ultimately caused the collapse of the political process. Extracts from pages 184–85 reprinted with permission of Michael F. Holt.*

The sectionalization of American politics was emphatically not simply a reflection or product of basic popular disagreements over black slavery. Those had long existed without such a complete polarization developing. Even though a series of events beginning with the Kansas-Nebraska Act greatly increased sectional consciousness, it is a mistake to think of sectional antagonism as a spontaneous and self-perpetuating force that imposed itself on the political arena against the will of politicians and coerced parties to conform to the lines of sectional conflict. Popular grievances, no matter how intense, do not dictate party strategies. Political leaders do. Someone has to politicize events, to define their political relevance in terms of a choice between or among parties, before popular grievances can have political impact. It was not events alone that caused Northerners and Southerners to view each other as enemies of the basic rights they both cherished. Politicians who pursued very traditional partisan strategies were largely responsible for the ultimate breakdown of the political process. Much of the story of the coming of the Civil War is the story of the successful efforts of Democratic politicians in the South and Republican politicians in the North to keep the sectional conflict at the center of political debate and to defeat political rivals who hoped to exploit other issues to achieve election.

For at least thirty years political leaders had recognized that the way to build political parties, to create voter loyalty and mobilize support, and to win elections was to find issues or positions on issues that distinguished them from their opponents and that therefore could appeal to various groups who disliked their opponents by offering them an alternative for political action—in sociological terms, to make their party a vehicle for negative reference group behavior. Because of the American ethos, the most successful tactic had been to pose as a champion of republican values and to portray the opponent as anti-republican, as unlawful, tyrannical, or aristo-cratic. . . . Republican politicians quite consciously seized on the slavery and sectional issue in order to build a new party. Claiming to be the exclusive Northern Party that was necessary to halt slavery extension and defeat the Slave Power conspiracy was the way they chose to distinguish themselves from Democrats, whom they denounced as pro-Southern, and from the Know Nothings, who had chosen a different organizing principle—anti-Catholicism and nativism—to construct their new party.

To say that Republican politicians agitated and exploited sectional grievances in order to build a winning party is a simple description of fact. It is not meant to imply that winning was their only objective or to be a value judgment about the sincerity or insincerity of their personal hatred of black slavery. . . . The antislavery pedigree of Republican leaders, however, was in a sense irrelevant to the triumph of the Republican party. . . . Much more important was the campaign they ran to obtain power, their skill in politicizing the issues at hand in such a way as to convince Northern voters that control of the national government by an exclusive Northern party was necessary to resist Slave Power aggressions.

V. The Right and Wrong of Slavery

MODERATE STATESMEN, such as Douglas, had no strong feelings of moral indignation about the existence of black slavery in America. Douglas did not care whether it was "voted up or down." But many Americans, even some Southerners, of the pre–Civil War generation looked upon slavery as a national disgrace and a great moral evil. During the 1830s, some of them united in the American Antislavery Society to wage a moral crusade against the South's "peculiar institution." In 1861, countless Northerners accepted war as an effective means of removing the curse of slavery and of creating a better and purer nation. Given such high moral purposes, they concluded that the war, whose prime cause was slavery, was both inevitable and justifiable. Recently some historians have criticized the "revisionists" for failing to appreciate the moral urgency of the slavery issue and for treating antislavery leaders who did as mere troublemakers. They have given renewed emphasis to slavery as a cause of the Civil War.

Could anything be said in defense of human slavery? Many antebellum Southerners thought so. Planters and politicians, preachers and publicists, developed elaborate arguments to prove that slavery was a highly moral institution—a "positive good." In this manner Southerners convinced themselves that morality was on *their* side and that abolitionists were nothing but hypocrites. What is more, unlike some of their postwar descendants, they believed that slavery was a crucial element in the sectional crisis.

41.   THE DISRUPTING POWER OF SLAVERY

As Stephen A. Douglas was one of the first to formulate an interpretation of the sectional crisis similar to that of twentieth-century "revisionist" historians, Abraham Lincoln was one of its earliest critics. In his debate with Douglas at Alton, Illinois, on October 15, 1858, Lincoln denied that the crisis had been brought on by political agitators. Rather, he argued, it was slavery that troubled the country and threatened to destroy the Union. Extracts from Roy P. Basler (ed.), The Collected Works of Abraham Lincoln (Springfield, Ill.: 1953), III, pp. 310–11.

. . . You may say . . . that all this difficulty in regard to the institution of slavery is the mere agitation of office seekers and ambitious Northern politicians. . . . I agree that there are office seekers amongst us. . . .

But is it true that all the difficulty and agitation we have in regard to this institution of slavery springs from office seeking—from the mere ambition of politicians? Is that the truth? How many times have we had danger from this question? Go back to the day of the Missouri Compromise. Go back to the Nullification question, at the bottom of which lay this same slavery question. Go back to the time of the Annexation of Texas. Go back to the troubles that led to the Compromise of 1850. You will find that every time, with the single exception of the Nullification question, they sprung from an endeavor to spread this institution. There never was a party in the history of this country, and there probably never will be of sufficient strength to disturb the general peace of the country. Parties themselves may be divided and quarrel on minor questions, yet it extends not beyond the parties themselves. But does *not* this question make a disturbance outside of political circles? Does it not enter into the churches and rend them asunder? What divided the great Methodist Church into two parts, North and South? What has raised this constant disturbance in every Presbyterian General Assembly that meets? What disturbed the Unitarian Church in this very city two years ago? . . . Is it not this same mighty, deep seated power that somehow operates on the minds of men, exciting and stirring them up in every avenue of society—in politics, in religion, in literature, in morals, in all the manifold relations of life? Is this the work of politicians? Is that irresistible power which for fifty years has shaken the government and agitated the people to be stilled and subdued by pretending that it is an exceedingly simple thing, and we ought not to talk about it? . . . [Where] is the philosophy or statesmanship which assumes that you can quiet that disturbing element in our society which has disturbed us for more than half a century, which has been the only serious danger that has threatened our institutions—I say, where is the philosophy or the statesmanship based on the assumption that we are to quit talking about it, and that the public mind is all at once to cease being agitated by it? Yet this is the policy here in the North that Douglas is advocating—that we are to care nothing about it! I ask you if it is not a false philosophy? Is it not a false statesmanship that undertakes to build up a system of policy upon the basis of caring nothing about *the very thing that every body does care the most about?*—a thing which all experience has shown we care a very great deal about?

---

42. The "Higher Law"

William H. Seward's speech in the United States Senate, March 11, 1850, contained the first of three classic Northern statements of the slavery issue in the sectional conflict. Congressional Globe, 31 Congress, 2 Session, appendix, pp. 262–76.

There is another aspect of the principle of compromise, which deserves consideration. It assumes that slavery, if not the only institution in a slave State, is at least a ruling institution, and that this characteristic is recognized by the Constitution. But *slavery* is only *one* of many institutions there—freedom is equally an institution there. Slavery is only a temporary, accidental, partial, and incongruous one; freedom, on the contrary, is a perpetual, organic, universal one, in harmony with the Constitution of the United States. . . . But the principle of this compromise gives complete ascendency in the slave States, and in the Constitution of the United States, to the subordinate, accidental, and incongruous institution over its paramount antagonist. . . .

But there is yet another aspect in which this principle must be examined. It regards the [public] domain only as a possession, to be enjoyed, either in common or by partition, by the citizens of the old States. It is true, indeed, that the national domain is ours; it is true, it was acquired by the valor and with the wealth of the whole nation; but we hold, nevertheless, no arbitrary authority over it. We hold no arbitrary authority over anything, whether acquired lawfully, or seized by usurpation. The Constitution regulates our stewardship; the Constitution devotes the domain to union, to justice, to defence, to welfare, and to liberty.

But there is a higher law than the Constitution, which regulates our authority over the domain, and devotes it to the same noble purposes. The territory is a part—no inconsiderable part—of the common heritage of mankind, bestowed upon them by the Creator of the universe. We are his stewards, and must so discharge our trust as to secure in the highest attainable degree, their happiness. . . .

You say that you will not submit to the exclusion of slaves from the new territories. What will you gain by resistance? Liberty follows the sword, although her sway is one of peace and beneficence. Can you propagate slavery, then, by the sword?

You insist that you cannot submit to the freedom with which slavery is discussed in the free States. Will war—a war for slavery—arrest, or even moderate, that discussion? No, sir; that discussion will not cease; war would only inflame it to a greater height. It is a part of the eternal conflict between truth and error—between mind and physical force—the conflict of man against the obstacles which oppose his way to an ultimate and glorious destiny. It will go on until you shall terminate it in the only way in which any State or nation has ever terminated it—by yielding to it—yielding in your own time, and in your own manner, indeed, but nevertheless yielding to the progress of emancipation.

---

43. "A House Divided"

Speech of Abraham Lincoln at Springfield, Illinois, June 16, 1858, in Roy P. Basler (ed.), The Collected Works of Abraham Lincoln (Springfield, Ill.: 1953), II, pp. 461–62.

If we could first know *where* we are, and *whither* we are tending, we could then better judge *what* to do, and *how* to do it.

We are now far into the *fifth* year, since a policy was initiated, with the *avowed* object, and *confident* promise, of putting an end to slavery agitation.

Under the operation of that policy, that agitation has not only, not *ceased*, but has *constantly augmented*.

In *my* opinion, it *will* not cease, until a *crisis* shall have been reached, and passed.

"A house divided against itself cannot stand."

I believe this government cannot endure, permanently half *slave* and half *free*.

I do not expect the Union to be *dissolved*—I do not expect the house to *fall*—but I *do* expect it will cease to be divided.

It will become *all* one thing, or *all* the other.

Either the *opponents* of slavery, will arrest the further spread of it, and place it where the public mind shall rest in the belief that it is in course of ultimate extinction; or its *advocates* will push it forward, till it shall became alike lawful in *all* the states, *old* as well as *new*—*North* as well as *South*.

---

44.   "An Irrepressible Conflict"

Speech of William H. Seward at Rochester, New York, October 25,
1858. George E. Baker (ed.), The Works of William H. Seward
(*New York: 1853–84*), *IV, p. 292.*

Our country is a theater which exhibits in full operation two
radically different political systems: the one resting on the basis of
servile labor, the other on the basis of voluntary labor of free
men. . . . Hitherto the two systems have existed in different States,
but side by side within the American Union. This has happened
because the Union is a confederation of States. But in another
aspect the United States constitutes only one nation. Increase of
population, which is filling the States out of their very borders,
together with a new and extended network of railroads and other
avenues, and an internal commerce which daily becomes more
intimate, is rapidly bringing the States into a higher and more
perfect social unity or consolidation. Thus, these antagonistic
systems are continually coming into closer contact, and collision
results.

Shall I tell you what this collision means? They who think it is
accidental, unnecessary, the work of interested or fanatical
agitators, and therefore ephemeral, mistake the case altogether. It
is an irrepressible conflict between opposing and enduring forces,
and it means that the United States must and will sooner or later
become either entirely a slave-holding nation or entirely a
free-labor nation.

---

45. No Compromise with Slavery!

During the secession crisis of 1860–1861 many antislavery North-erners believed that the decisive struggle between slavery and freedom had finally come. They believed that compromise was futile and that war was inevitable. William H. Herndon, Lincoln's Illinois law partner, expressed this opinion in a letter to Charles Sumner, December 10, 1860. Sumner Papers, Widener Library, Harvard University.

Liberty and slavery—Civilization and barbarism are *absolute* antag-onisms. One or the other must perish on this Continent. . . . If we make a thousand Compromises this civilization, or that higher and grander one just springing up . . . will spring at the throat of its foe, and choke the life out of it, or die in the attempt. Compromise—Compromise! why I am sick at the very idea. Fools may compromise and reason that all *is* peace; but those who have read human history—those who know human nature, . . . know that Compro-mise aggravates *in the end* all our difficulties. The pathway of the sweep of man is paved with the fragments of blasted agreements, which were made to impede the progress of right, or to bolster up despotism; and will not men learn a lesson from all this? . . . There is no dodging the question. Let the *natural* struggle, heaven high and "hell" deep, go on. . . . I am thoroughly convinced that two such civilizations as the North and the South cannot co-exist on the same soil and be co-equal in the Federal brotherhood. To expect otherwise would be to expect the Absolute to sleep with and tolerate "hell."

. . . I helped to make the Republican party; and if it forsakes its distinctive ideas, I can help to tear it down, and help to erect a new party that shall never cower to any slave driver. Let this natural war—let this inevitable struggle proceed—go on, till slavery is *dead—dead—dead.*

46.   "THE QUESTION OF THE HOUR"

James Russell Lowell, "The Question of the Hour," Atlantic Monthly, *VII (1861), pp. 120–21.*

We do not underestimate the gravity of the present crisis, and we agree that nothing should be done to exasperate it; but if the people of the Free States have been taught anything by the repeated lessons of bitter experience, it has been that submission is not the seed of conciliation, but of contempt and encroachment. . . . It is quite time that it should be understood that freedom is also an institution deserving some attention in a Model Republic, that a decline in stocks is more tolerable and more transient than one in public spirit, and that material prosperity was never known to abide long in a country that had lost its political morality. The fault of the Free States in the eyes of the South is not one that can be atoned for by any yielding of special points here and there. Their offence is that they are free, and that their habits and prepossessions are those of Freedom. Their crime is the census of 1860. Their increase in numbers, wealth, and power is a standing aggression. It would not be enough to please the Southern States that we should stop asking them to abolish slavery,—what they demand of us is nothing less than that we should abolish the spirit of the age. Our very thoughts are a menace. It is not the North, but the South, that forever agitates the question of Slavery. The seeming prosperity of the cotton-growing States is based on a great mistake and a great wrong; and it is no wonder that they are irritable and scent accusation in the very air. It is the stars in their courses that fight against their system. . . .

It is time that the South should learn, if they do not begin to suspect it already, that the difficulty of the Slavery question is slavery itself,—nothing more, nothing less. It is time that the North should learn that it has nothing left to compromise but the rest of its self-respect. Nothing will satisfy the extremists at the South short of a reduction of the Free States to a mere police for the protection of an institution whose danger increases at an equal pace with its wealth.

---

47.   GOD'S PENALTY FOR SLAVERY

Evansville, Ind., Journal (*April 20, 1861*).

. . . [Perhaps] God has instituted the present troubles to rid the country of the predominance of slavery in its public affairs. The whole country, North as well as South, has been instrumental in the endeavor to spread it over the continent, and to force it on unwilling people. While the South has been actively propagating and perpetuating the institution, the North has winked at the wrongful business and encouraged it.—Therefore, in the coming troubles, the North must not expect to escape the penalty of her lack of principle. She must suffer, like the South.

It may even be possible that Providence designs by means of these troubles to put a summary end to slavery. The institution has gone on to spread until it interferes materially with the progress of the Nation. Our country can never reach its full stature and importance so long as this baleful influence extends over it. It is a paradoxical state of things to see a country, which boasts of its freedom, nursing and sustaining the most odious system of slavery known on earth. . . . There is truly an "irrepressible conflict" between free and slave labor, and eventually the country must be all slave or all free, or the two parts must separate; which, we shall soon know. . . .

The people of the North as a body have been willing to let slavery alone—to have nothing to do with it one way or the other. They have no other desire now. But if the war goes on . . . the contest sound[s] the death-knell of slavery. Thomas Jefferson said, that, in such a contest as the present, God has no attribute that could cause him to take sides with the slave-owners. . . . And, if the peculiar institution is doomed to come to an end by the acts of its friends, who will mourn its loss? It has kept the country in a ferment since its organization and hindered its progress and it would be truly a God's blessing to be rid of it. So every patriot feels in his heart of hearts.

---

48. "THE SLAVEHOLDERS' REBELLION"

During the Civil War, abolitionists and "Radical" Republicans insisted that slavery alone caused the conflict, and that to permit the conflict to end without removing its cause would be pure folly. Frederick Douglass, the famous black abolitionist, in a speech at Himrods Corners, Yates County, New York, July 4, 1862, presented a typical abolitionist's interpretation of the Civil War. Quoted in Philip S. Foner, The Life and Writings of Frederick Douglass *(New York: 1952), III, pp. 244–46.*

It is hardly necessary at this very late day of the war . . . to enter now upon any elaborate enquiry or explanation as to whence came this foul and guilty attempt to break up and destroy the national Government. All but the willfully blind or the malignantly traitorous, know and confess that this whole movement which now so largely distracts the country, and threatens ruin to the nation, has its root and its sap, its trunk and its branches, and the bloody fruit it bears only from the one source of all abounding abomination, and that is slavery. It has sprung out of a malign selfishness and a haughty and imperious pride which only the practice of the most hateful oppression and cruelty could generate and develop. No ordinary love of gain, no ordinary love of power, could have stirred up this terrible revolt. . . . The monster was brought to its birth by pride, lust and cruelty which could not brook the sober restraints of law, order and justice. . . .

There is . . . one false theory of the origin of the war to which a moment's reply may be properly given here. It is this. The abolitionists by their insane and unconstitutional attempt to abolish slavery have brought on the war. All that class of men who opposed what they were pleased to call coercion at the first, and a vigorous prosecution of the war at the present, charge the war directly to the abolitionists. In answer to this charge, I lay down this rule as a basis to which all candid men will assent. Whatever is said or done by any class of citizens, strictly in accordance with rights guaranteed by the Constitution, cannot be fairly charged as against the Union, or as inciting to a dissolution of the Union.

Now the slaveholders came into the Union with their eyes wide open, subject to a Constitution wherein the right to be abolitionists was sacredly guaranteed to all the people. They knew that slavery was to take its chance with all other evils against the power of free speech and national enlightenment. They came on board the national ship subject to these conditions, they signed the articles after having duly read them, and the fact that those rights, plainly written, have been exercised is no apology whatever for the slaveholders' mutiny and their attempt to lay piratical hands on the ship and its officers. When therefore I hear a man denouncing abolitionists on account of the war, I know that I am listening to a man who either does not know what he is talking about, or to one who is a traitor in disguise.

There is something quite distinct and quite individual in the nature and character of this rebellion. In its motives and objects it stands entirely alone, in the annals of great social disturbances. Rebellion is no new thing under the sun. The best governments in the world are liable to these terrible social disorders. All countries have experienced them. Generally however, rebellions are quite respectable in the eyes of the world, and very properly so. They naturally command the sympathy of mankind, for generally they are on the side of progress. They would overthrow and remove some old and festering abuse not to be otherwise disposed of, and introduce a higher civilization, and a larger measure of liberty among men. But this rebellion is in no wise analogous to such.—The pronounced and damning peculiarity of the present rebellion, is found in the fact, that it was conceived, undertaken, planned, and persevered in, for the guilty purpose of handing down to the latest generations the accursed system of human bondage. Its leaders have plainly told us by words as well as by deeds, that they are fighting for slavery. They have been stirred to this perfidious revolt, by a certain deep and deadly hate, which they warmly cherish toward every possible contradiction of slavery whether found in theory or in practice. For this cause they hate free society, free schools, free states, free speech, the freedom asserted in the Declaration of Independence, and guaranteed in the Constitution.—Herein is the whole secret of the rebellion.—The plan is and was to withdraw the slave system from the hated light of liberty, and from the natural operations of free principles. While the slaveholders could hold the reins of government they could and did pervert the free principles of the Constitution to slavery, and could afford to continue in the union, but when they saw that they could no longer control the Union as they had done for sixty years before, they appealed to the sword and struck for a government which should forever shut out all light from the southern conscience and all hope of Emancipation from the southern slave. This rebellion therefore, has no point of comparison with that which has brought liberty to America, or with those of Europe, which have been undertaken from time to time, to throw off the galling yoke of despotism. It stands alone in its infamy.

---

49. "THE ALMIGHTY HAS HIS OWN PURPOSES"

By the time of his second inaugural address, March 4, 1865, Lincoln had committed himself to abolition as a war aim and to the abolitionist interpretation of the war. But he stated it with humility and compassion. Richardson (ed.), Messages and Papers of the Presidents, *VI, pp. 276–77.*

One eighth of the whole population was colored slaves, not distributed generally over the Union, but localized in the southern part of it. These slaves constituted a peculiar and powerful interest. All knew that this interest was somehow the cause of the war. To strengthen, perpetuate, and extend this interest was the object for which the insurgents would rend the Union even by war, while the government claimed no right to do more than to restrict the territorial enlargement of it. Neither party expected for the war the magnitude or the duration which it has already attained. Neither anticipated that the *cause* of the conflict might cease with or even before the conflict itself should cease. Each looked for an easier triumph, and a result less fundamental and astounding. Both read the same Bible and pray to the same God, and each invokes His aid against the other. It may seem strange that any men should dare to ask a just God's assistance in wringing their bread from the sweat of other men's faces, but let us judge not, that we be not judged. The prayers of both could not be answered. That of neither has been answered fully. The Almighty has His own purposes. "Woe unto the world because of offenses; for it must needs be that offenses come, but woe to that man by whom the offense cometh." If we shall suppose that American slavery is one of those offenses which, in the providence of God, must needs come, but which, having continued through His appointed time, He now wills to remove, and that He gives to both North and South this terrible war as the woe due to those by whom the offense came, shall we discern therein any departure from those divine attributes which the believers in a living God always ascribe to Him? Fondly do we hope, fervently do we pray, that this mighty scourge of war may speedily pass away. Yet, if God wills that it continue until all the wealth piled up by the bondsman's two hundred and fifty years of unrequited toil shall be sunk, and until every drop of blood drawn with the lash shall be paid by another drawn with the sword, as was said three thousand years ago, so still it must be said, "The judgments of the Lord are true and righteous altogether."

50.   PROSPECTS OF SLAVERY EXPANSION

Before and during the Civil War many Southerners accepted the view that slavery was the most crucial issue in the sectional crisis. Northerners, they said, by attacking slavery were endangering the Union. Moreover, Southern expansionists denied that the right they claimed to carry slavery into the territories was a meaningless abstraction. The Charleston Mercury (February 28, 1860) insisted that it was neither geography nor climate but Northern political interference that prevented slavery from entering new territories.

The right to have [slave] property protected in the territory is not a mere abstraction without application or practical value. In the past there are instances where the people of the Southern States might have colonized and brought new slave States into the Union had the principle been recognized, and the Government, the trustee of the Southern States, exercised its appropriate powers to make good for the slaveholder the guarantees of the Constitution. . . . When the gold mines of California were discovered, slaveholders at the South saw that, with their command of labor, it would be easy at a moderate outlay to make fortunes digging gold. The inducements to go there were great, and there was no lack of inclination on their part. But, to make the emigration profitable, it was necessary that the [slave] property of Southern settlers should be safe, otherwise it was plainly a hazardous enterprise, neither wise nor feasible. Few were reckless enough to stake property, the accumulation of years, in a struggle with active prejudices amongst a mixed population, where for them the law was a dead letter through the hostile indifference of the General Government, whose duty it was, by the fundamental law of its existence, to afford adequate protection— executive, legislative and judicial—to the property of every man, of whatever sort, without discrimination. Had the people of the Southern States been satisfied they would have received fair play and equal protection at the hands of the Government, they would have gone to California with their slaves. . . . California would probably now have been a Slave State in the Union. . . .

What has been the policy pursued in Kansas? Has the territory had a fair chance of becoming a Slave State? Has the principle of equal protection to slave property been carried out by the Government there in any of its departments? On the contrary, has not every appliance been used to thwart the South and expel or prohibit her sons from colonizing there? . . . In our opinion, had the principle of equal protection to Southern men and Southern property been rigorously observed by the General Government, both California and Kansas would undoubtedly have come into the Union as Slave States. The South lost those States for the lack of proper assertion of this great principle. . . .

New Mexico, it is asserted, is too barren and arid for Southern occupation or settlement. . . . Now, New Mexico . . . teems with mineral resources. . . . There is no vocation in the world in which slavery can be more useful and profitable than in mining. . . . [Is] it wise, in our present condition of ignorance of the resources of New Mexico, to jump to the conclusion that the South can have no interest in its territories, and therefore shall waive or abandon her right of colonizing them? . . .

We frequently talk of the future glories of our republican destiny on the continent, and of the spread of our civilization and free institutions over Mexico and the Tropics. Already have we absorbed two of her States, Texas and California. Is it expected that our onward march is to stop here? Is it not more probable and more philosophic to suppose that, as in the past, so in the future, the Anglo-Saxon race will, in the course of years, occupy and absorb the whole of that splendid but ill-peopled country, and to remove by gradual process, before them, the worthless mongrel races that now inhabit and curse the land? And in the accomplishment of this destiny is there a Southern man so bold as to say, the people of the South with their slave property are to consent to total exclusion. . . ? Our people will never sit still and see themselves excluded from all expansion, to please the North.

51.   No Union with Abolitionists

New Orleans Bee (*December 14, 1860*), *quoted in Dumond,*
Southern Editorials on Secession, *p. 336.*

[The chief obstacle to reconciliation] is the absolute impossibility of
revolutionizing Northern opinion in relation to slavery. Without a
change of heart, radical and thorough, all guarantees which might
be offered are not worth the paper on which they would be
inscribed. As long as slavery is looked upon by the North with
abhorrence; as long as the South is regarded as a mere slave-
breeding and slave-driving community; as long as false and perni-
cious theories are cherished respecting the inherent equality and
rights of every human being, there can be no satisfactory political
union between the two sections. If one-half the people believe the
other half to be deeply dyed in iniquity; to be daily and hourly in the
perpetration of the most atrocious moral offense, and at the same
time knowing them to be their countrymen and fellow-citizens,
conceive themselves authorized and in some sort constrained to
lecture them, to abuse them, to employ all possible means to break
up their institutions, and to take from them what the Northern half
consider property unrighteously held, or no property at all, how can
two such antagonistic nationalities dwell together in fraternal
concord under the same government? . . . The feelings, customs,
mode of thought and education of the two sections, are discrepant
and often antagonistic. The North and South are heterogeneous
and are better apart.

---

52.   Lincoln's Election a Menace to Slavery

In advocating secession if Lincoln should be elected President, the
Charleston *Mercury (October 11, 1860) emphasized the need to*
protect slavery.

Immediate danger will be brought to slavery, in all the Frontier States. When a party is enthroned at Washington . . . whose creed is, to repeal the Fugitive Slave Laws, the *under*-ground railroad will become an *over*-ground railroad. The tenure of slave property will be felt to be weakened; and the slaves will be sent down to the Cotton States for sale, and the Frontier States *enter on the policy of making themselves Free States.*

With the control of the Government of the United States, and an organized and triumphant North to sustain them, the Abolitionists will renew their operations upon the South with increased courage. The thousands in every country, who look up to power, and make gain out of the future, will come out in support of the Abolition Government. . . . They will have an Abolition Party in the South, of Southern men. The contest for slavery will no longer be one between the North and the South. It will be in the South, between the people of the South.

If, in our present position of power and unitedness, we have the raid of John Brown . . . what will be the measures of insurrection and incendiarism, which must follow our notorious and abject prostration to Abolition rule at Washington, with all the patronage of the Federal Government, and a Union organization in the South to support it? . . .

Already there is uneasiness throughout the South, as to the stability of its institution of slavery. But with a submission to the rule of Abolitionists at Washington, thousands of slaveholders will despair of the institution. While the condition of things in the Frontier States will force their slaves on the markets of the Cotton States, the timid in the Cotton States, will also sell their slaves. The general distrust, must affect purchasers. The consequence must be, slave property must be greatly depreciated. . . .

The ruin of the South, by the emancipation of her slaves, is not like the ruin of any other people. It is not a mere loss of liberty, like the Italians under the Bourbons. It is not heavy taxation, which must still leave the means of living, or otherwise taxation defeats itself. But it is the loss of liberty, property, home, country—everything that makes life worth having. And this loss will probably take place under circumstances of suffering and horror, unsurpassed in the history of nations. We must preserve our liberties and institutions, under penalties greater than those which impend over any people in the world.

———————

53.   THE CONFEDERATE CORNERSTONE

In a speech at Savannah, March 21, 1861, Alexander H. Stephens clearly implied that slavery was the chief cause of the sectional crisis. This speech was in striking contrast to his postwar constitutional interpretation. Moore (ed.), The Rebellion Record, *I, pp. 44–49.*

[The Confederate] Constitution has put at rest forever all the agitating questions relating to our peculiar institution—African slavery as it exists among us—the proper status of the negro in our form of civilization. This was the immediate cause of the late rupture and present revolution. Jefferson, in his forecast, had anticipated this, as the "rock upon which the old Union would split." He was right. What was conjecture with him, is now a realized fact. But whether he fully comprehended the great truth upon which that rock stood and stands, may be doubted. The prevailing ideas entertained by him and most of the leading statesmen at the time of the formation of the old Constitution were, that the enslavement of the African was in violation of the laws of nature; that it was wrong in principle, socially, morally, and politically. It was an evil they knew not well how to deal with; but the general opinion of the men of that day was, that, somehow or other, in the order of Providence, the institution would be evanescent and pass away. . . . Those ideas, however, were fundamentally wrong. They rested upon the assumption of the equality of races. This was an error. It was a sandy foundation, and the idea of a Government built upon it—when the "storm came and the wind blew, it fell."

Our new Government is founded upon exactly the opposite ideas;

its foundations are laid, its cornerstone rests, upon the great truth that the negro is not equal to the white man; that slavery, subordination to the superior race, is his natural and moral condition. This, our new Government, is the first, in the history of the world, based upon this great physical, philosophical, and moral truth. . . .

. . . It is the first Government ever instituted upon principles in strict conformity to nature, and the ordination of Providence, in furnishing the materials of human society. Many Governments have been founded upon the principles of certain classes; but the classes thus enslaved, were of the same race, and in violation of the laws of nature. Our system commits no such violation of nature's laws. The negro by nature, or by the curse against Canaan, is fitted for that condition which he occupies in our system. The architect, in the construction of buildings, lays the foundation with the proper material—the granite—then comes the brick or the marble. The substratum of our society is made of the material fitted by nature for it, and by experience we know that it is the best, not only for the superior but for the inferior race, that it should be so. It is, indeed, in conformity with the Creator. It is not for us to inquire into the wisdom of His ordinances or to question them.

---

54.   THE INDISPENSABLE SLAVES

In his message to the Confederate Congress, April 29, 1861, Jefferson Davis also cited the Northern threat to slavery as the cause of Southern secession. As in the case of Stephens, this should be compared with his postwar interpretation. Moore (ed.), The Rebellion Record, I, pp. 166–75.

As soon . . . as the Northern States that prohibited African slavery within their limits had reached a number sufficient to give their representation a controlling voice in the Congress, a persistent and organized system of hostile measures against the rights of the owners of slaves in the Southern States was inaugurated and gradually extended. A continuous series of measures was devised and prosecuted for the purpose of rendering insecure the tenure of property in slaves. . . . Senators and Representatives were sent to the common councils of the nation, whose chief title to this distinction consisted in the display of a spirit of ultra-fanaticism, and whose business was . . . to awaken the bitterest hatred against the citizens of sister States, by violent denunciation of their institutions; the transaction of public affairs was impeded by repeated efforts to usurp powers not delegated by the Constitution, for the purpose of impairing the security of property in slaves, and reducing those States which held slaves to a condition of inferiority. Finally a great party was organized for the purpose of obtaining the administration of the Government, with the avowed object of using its power for the total exclusion of the slave States from all participation in the benefits of the public domain acquired by all the States in common, whether by conquest or purchase; of surrounding them entirely by States in which slavery should be prohibited; of thus rendering the property in slaves so insecure as to be comparatively worthless, and thereby annihilating in effect property worth thousands of millions of dollars. This party, thus organized, succeeded in the month of November last in the election of its candidate for the Presidency of the United States.

In the meantime, the African slaves had augmented in number from about 600,000, at the date of the adoption of the constitutional compact, to upward of 4,000,000. In moral and social condition they had been elevated from brutal savages into docile, intelligent, and civilized agricultural laborers, and supplied not only with bodily comforts but with careful religious instruction. Under the supervision of a superior race, their labor had been so directed as not only to allow a gradual and marked amelioration of their own condition, but to convert hundreds of thousands of square miles of the wilderness into cultivated lands covered with a prosperous people; towns and cities had sprung into existence, and had rapidly increased in wealth and population under the social system of the South; . . . and the productions in the South of cotton, rice, sugar, and tobacco, for the full development and continuance of which the labor of African slaves was and is indispensable, had swollen to an amount which formed nearly three-fourths of the exports of the whole United States and had become absolutely necessary to the wants of civilized man. With interests of such overwhelming magnitude imperiled, the people of the Southern States were driven by the conduct of the North to the adoption of some course of action to avert the danger with which they were openly menaced.

---

55. SLAVERY THE "SINGLE CAUSE"

James Ford Rhodes, like other Northern historians of the post–Civil War generation, believed that slavery was the fundamental cause of the Civil War. His interpretation is summarized in the following passages from Lectures on the American Civil War *(New York: 1913), pp. 2–16, 76–77. Copyright 1913 by the Macmillan Company. Reprinted by permission of the publishers.*

There is a risk in referring any historic event to a single cause. . . . [But] of the American Civil War it may safely be asserted that there was a single cause, slavery. In 1862 John Stuart Mill in *Fraser's Magazine,* and Professor Cairnes in a pamphlet on the Slave Power, presented this view to the English public with force, but it is always difficult to get to the bottom of a foreign dispute, and it is not surprising that many failed to comprehend the real nature of the conflict. When in July, 1862, William E. Forster said in the House of Commons that he believed it was generally acknowledged that slavery was the cause of the war, he was answered with cries, "No, no!" and "The tariff!" Because the South was for free trade and the North for a protective tariff, this was a natural retort, though proceeding from a misconception, as a reference to the most acute tariff crisis in our history will show.

In 1832, South Carolina, by act of her Convention legally called, declared that the tariff acts passed by Congress in 1828 and 1832 were "null, void, no law," and that no duties enjoined by those acts should be paid or permitted to be paid in the State of South Carolina. It is a significant fact that she failed to induce any of her sister Southern States to act with her. By the firmness of President Jackson and a conciliatory disposition on the part of the high tariff party the act of nullification was never put in force; but the whole course of the incident and the yielding of South Carolina demonstrated that the American Union could not be broken up by a tariff dispute. . . .

Some of our younger writers, impressed with the principle of nationality that prevailed in Europe during the last half of the nineteenth century, have read into our conflict European conditions and asserted that the South stood for disunion in her doctrine of States' rights and that the war came because the North took up the gage of battle to make of the United States a nation. I shall have occasion to show the potency of the Union sentiment as an aid to the destruction of slavery, but when events are reduced to their last elements, it plainly appears that the doctrine of States' rights and secession was invoked by the South to save slavery, and by a natural antagonism, the North upheld the Union because the fight for its preservation was the first step toward the abolition of negro servitude. The question may be isolated by the incontrovertible statement that if the negro had never been brought to America, our Civil War could not have occurred. . . .

As slavery was out of tune with the nineteenth century, the States that held fast to it played a losing game. This was evident from the greater increase of population at the North. . . . The South repelled immigrants for the reason that freemen would not work with slaves. In the House of Representatives, chosen on the basis of numerical population, the North at each decennial census and appointment, gained largely on the South, whose stronghold was the Senate. Each State, irrespective of population, had two senators, and since the formation of the Constitution, States had been admitted in pairs by a tacit agreement, each free State being counterbalanced by a slave State. The admission of California [as a free State] which would disturb this equilibrium was resisted by the South with a spirit of determination made bitter by disappointment over California's spontaneous act. The Mexican War had been for the most part a Southern war; the South, as Lowell made Hosea Biglow say, was "after bigger pens to cram with slaves," and now she saw the magnificent domain of California escaping her clutches. She had other grievances which, from the point of view of a man of 1850 reverencing the letter of the Constitution, were undoubtedly well founded, but the whole dispute really hinged on the belief of the South that slavery was right and the belief of the majority of Northerners that it was wrong.

At the time of the formation of the Constitution the two sections were not greatly at variance. A large number of Southern men, among them their ablest and best leaders, thought slavery was a moral and political evil to be got rid of gradually. In due time, the foreign slave trade was prohibited, but the Yankee invention of the cotton-gin made slavery apparently profitable in the culture of cotton on the virgin soil of the new States in the South; and Southern opinion changed. From being regarded as an evil, slavery began to be looked upon as the only possible condition of the existence of the two races side by side and by 1850 the feeling had grown to be that slavery was "no evil, no scourge, but a great religious, social and moral blessing." As modern society required hewers of woods and drawers of water, the slave system of the South, so the argument ran, was superior to the industrial system of England, France and the North.

In 1831, William Lloyd Garrison began his crusade against slavery. In a weekly journal, the *Liberator*, published in Boston, he preached with fearless emphasis that slavery was wrong and, though his immediate followers were never many, he set people to thinking about the question, so that six years later Daniel Webster . . . said, the subject of slavery "has not only attracted attention as a question of politics, but it has struck a far deeper-toned chord. It has arrested the religious feeling of the country; it has taken strong hold on the consciences of men." . . . [The] opinion constantly gained ground at the North that slavery was an evil and that its existence was a blot on the national honor.

In 1850, there were at the South 347,000 slaveholders out of a white population of six millions, but the head and center of the oligarchy was to be found amongst the large planters, possessors of fifty or more slaves, whose elegance, luxury and hospitality are recited in tales of travellers, over whose estates and lives the light of romance and poetry has been profusely shed; of these, there were less than eight thousand. . . . The men composing this oligarchy were high-spirited gentlemen, with a keen sense of honor showing itself in hatred of political corruption, resentment of personal attack by speech or by pen, to the length of the fatal duel. . . . It is obvious that men of this stamp could not be otherwise than irritated when Northern speeches, books, and newspapers were full of the charge that they were living in the daily practice of evil, that negro chattel slavery was cruel, unjust and barbaric. This irritation expressed itself in recrimination and insolent demands at the same time that it helped to bring them to the belief that property in negroes was as right and sacred as the ownership of horses and mules. . . .

The Civil War in England, wrote Gardiner, "was rendered inevitable" because "a reconciliation between opposing moral and social forces" could not be effected. Here is an exact statement of our own case in 1861. The Civil War might have been averted had the North yielded to the South and in the words of Lincoln ceased references to "slavery as in any way wrong" and regarded it "as one of the common matters of property" speaking "of negroes as we do of our horses and cattle." In other words, the North must repress its own enlightened sentiment regarding slavery. . . . Or, on the other hand, the war might have been prevented had the Southerners had a change of heart, reverted to the sentiment of the founders of the republic that slavery was an evil and agreed to limit its extension. The logical result would have been gradual abolition and the North stood ready to bear her share in compensating the owners of slaves. But anybody who should have promulgated such a doctrine in the South in 1861 would have been laughed at, hooted and mobbed.

56. THE ESSENCE OF OUR TRAGEDY

*In 1946, Bernard DeVoto wrote a detailed criticism of the "revi-
sionists" for their alleged failure to understand the moral issue
underlying the Civil War. "The Easy Chair," Harper's Magazine
(February, 1946), pp. 123–26. Extracts reprinted by permission of
Mrs. Bernard DeVoto.*

Historians are mortal men. . . . The intellectual climate of their
time affects them. Fashions in thesis and dogma sift under their
study doors. Historians who are now mature, the generation to
which Mr. [James G.] Randall belongs, happened to be young and
impressionable at a time when an intellectual fashion was developing the (erroneous) thesis that the United States could and should
have stayed out of the First World War and the (false) theorem that
we were betrayed into it by propaganda. . . .

This generation of historians has built up a body of judgment
about the Civil War. Some of it is certainly sound, some certainly
unsound. . . . Let me call the body of judgment about the Civil
War as a whole "revisionism." Well, revisionism, this historical
generation's conclusions about the Civil War, contains much solid
truth but it also contains some grave fallacies, some of which suggest
an apt and accurate designation out of history, "doughface." My
point is that, as a result of those fallacies, general ideas about the
Civil War are less trustworthy today than they were a generation
ago. There has been a regression in history.

I can state here only a few theorems from this body of judgment.
The basic one holds that the Civil War was avoidable: that the
moral, economic, social, political, and constitutional crisis could
have been resolved short of war and within the framework of our
institutions. Corollaries follow: that it should have been resolved
and that therefore someone was to blame for the failure to resolve
it. Who were the villains? A fundamental thesis of revisionism is
that they were extremists, radicals, hotheads, agitators, manufacturers of inflammatory propaganda. It turns out that the decisive
ones . . . were Northerners: abolitionists, freesoilers, the Republi-

can Party, more radical reformers, in short, everyone who thought that the slavery issue was in some degree a moral issue. . . . An accessory theorem makes Stephen A. Douglas the tragic hero of the revisionists. His ideas ought to have prevailed: that they did not, which is the heart of our national tragedy, was due to the Republican or abolitionist agitation, which led the American people down a fatal path in pursuit of an unreal, a falsely represented, issue. . . .

. . . Now the Civil War is the crux of our history. . . . A few of the innumerable matters it involved were these: the successful functioning of constitutional government, the basic paradox and conflict in our social system, the basic conflict in our economy, the basic conflict and evasion in our political system. Whether or not the war was inevitable, the crisis was: these conflicts and paradoxes created problems which had to be solved. That they were not solved short of war is our greatest national tragedy. Our failure to solve them short of war is our greatest failure. The inescapable duty of historians is to explain that failure. But revisionist dogmas are carrying them farther from an explanation year by year.

Already those dogmas have made all but impossible the necessary first step, an accurate definition of the crisis. Take one which Mr. Randall accepts. The political conflict between the slave states and the free states entered a critical phase as soon as the invasion of Mexico made it clear that the United States was going to acquire an enormous new area by conquest. . . . The prospect . . . posed the question whether slavery should be legalized in it. . . . From that point on our central political, social, economic, and constitutional conflicts, all of which pivoted on slavery, were fought out on the question so posed, the status of slavery in the territories. So far as slavery was a cause of the Civil War or an issue of the conflict that ended in the war, it was nationally faced during the fifteen years before the war not primarily as slavery but as the question of slavery in the territories.

And that is a tragic fact. For it is clear to us today . . . that the economy of slavery could not possibly be adapted to or survive in the lands conquered from Mexico. And it is almost certain that slavery could not have been maintained in the territory of Nebraska and only a little less than certain that it could not have been maintained in the territory of Kansas, and these territories came to be the very vortex of strife. Therefore, according to revisionist dogma, the question of the legality of slavery in the territories was tangential, unreal, abstract, hypothetical, and almost immaterial. The pivotal strife in the fifteen tragic years that led to war resulted from the forcing of an unreal issue. . . .

But this is to miss the very essence of the national tragedy, and when history leads us off on this tangent it monstrously fails to explain our past. It is true that the question of slavery in the territories was a peripheral issue. But for historians and for those of us who try to learn from them *that is the point which must be explained.* It cannot be impatiently shrugged away or dismissed with a denunciation of some agitators whose blindness or wilfulness or bigotry is supposed to have dropped it in the path of men of good will and so switched them into the maelstrom. . . .

To pass this off as an irresponsible mischief of politicians on the make is to go so far astray that history is forced entirely out of orientation and nothing less than a new beginning is required. What was there in the nature of the American people, in their institutions, in their development and way of life, or in the sum of all these and more, that prevented them from facing their inescapable problem squarely, in the nakedest light, with the soberest realism? What was there in the sum of American life that forbade us to go to fundamentals and forced us to escape through subterfuges into war? That is the question which historians must answer. . . . But, because of the evolution of historical ideas which I have called revisionism, historians are farther from answering that question than their predecessors were a generation ago. . . .

. . . [The] process of revisionism has developed a habit of understating certain things and passing quickly over others. . . . Thus the inquiring mind notes the agility with which revisionism dodges the question of minority dictation. A generation ago history clearly recognized that first the maintenance and then the loss of control of the national government by the slaveholding states, a minority, were important in the oncoming of the war. These facts have now been retired to the shadowy fringe. But there is a more central slurring-over which repeats the tragic evasion itself. In its concern to show that the Civil War was a product of hotheads, radical agitators, and their propaganda, an almost incidental result which could have been avoided if some extremists could have been induced to hold their tongues, history is in imminent danger of forgetting that slavery had anything whatever to do with the war. The revisionist gospel finds little time, and seems to have little inclination, to discuss whether in trying to understand the war we should take account of slavery as a social anachronism in the nineteenth century and as an obsolescent or even obsolete economy. . . . As for considering even theoretically that the problem of slavery may have involved moral questions, God forbid. . . .

We have lately seen some younger historians whose specialty is the American Revolution come back forthrightly to the little red schoolhouse with a finding that, after all, the Revolution did have something to do with representative government, taxation without representation, and some of the things which the Declaration of Independence calls abuses of power. It is time to take a singularly radical, or reactionary, step and find some relation between slavery and secession on the one hand and the Civil War on the other.

---

57.   THE INEVITABILITY OF VIOLENCE

In another critique of the "revisionists," Arthur Schlesinger, Jr., suggests that they are being sentimental and unrealistic to think that a moral issue as complex as slavery could be solved by any means other than force. "The Causes of the Civil War: A Note on Historical Sentimentalism," Partisan Review, XVI (1949), pp. 969–81. Extracts reprinted by permission of the Partisan Review.

The Civil War was our great national trauma. A savage fraternal conflict, it released deep sentiments of guilt and remorse—sentiments which have reverberated through our history and our literature ever since. Literature in the end came to terms with these sentiments by yielding to the South in fantasy the victory it had been denied in fact; . . . But history, a less malleable medium, was constricted by the intractable fact that war had taken place, and by the related assumption that it was, in William H. Seward's phrase, an "irrepressible conflict," and hence a justified one.

As short a time ago as 1937, for example, even Professor James G. Randall could describe himself as "unprepared to go to the point of denying that the great American tragedy could have been avoided." Yet in a few years . . . Professor Randall would emerge as the leader of a triumphant new school of self-styled "revisionists." [The writings of this school] . . . brought about a profound reversal of the professional historian's attitude toward the Civil War. Scholars now denied the traditional assumption of the inevitability of the war and boldly advanced the thesis that a "blundering generation" had transformed a "repressible conflict" into a "needless war." . . .

The revisionist case . . . has three main premises. First:

1) that the Civil War was caused by the irresponsible emotionalization of politics far out of proportion to the real problems involved. . . .

If uncontrolled emotionalism and fanaticism caused the war, how did they get out of hand? Who whipped up the "whipped up crisis"? Thus the second revisionist thesis:

2) that sectional friction was permitted to develop into needless war by the inexcusable failure of political leadership in the fifties. . . .

It is hard to tell which was under attack here—the performance of a particular generation or democratic politics in general. But, if the indictment "blundering generation" meant no more than a general complaint that democratic politics placed a premium on emotionalism, then the Civil War would have been no more nor less "needless" than any event in our blundering history. The phrase "blundering generation" must consequently imply that the generation in power in the fifties was *below* the human or historical or democratic average in its blundering. Hence the third revisionist thesis:

3) that the slavery problem could have been solved without war. For, even if slavery were as unimportant as the revisionists have

insisted, they would presumably admit that it constituted the real sticking-point in the relations between the sections. They must show therefore that there were policies with which a non-blundering generation could have resolved the slavery crisis and averted war; and that these policies were so obvious that the failure to adopt them indicated blundering and stupidity of a peculiarly irresponsible nature. If no such policies could be produced even by hindsight, then it would seem excessive to condemn the politicians of the fifties for failing to discover them at the time. . . .

. . . The problem [of slavery] in America was peculiarly recalcitrant. The schemes for gradual emancipation got nowhere. Neither internal reform nor economic exhaustion contained much promise for a peaceful solution. The hard fact, indeed, is that the revisionists have not tried seriously to describe the policies by which the slavery problem could have been peacefully resolved. They have resorted instead to broad affirmations of faith: if only the conflict could have been staved off long enough, then somehow, somewhere, we could have worked something out. It is legitimate, I think, to ask how? where? what?—at least, if these affirmations of faith are to be used as the premise for castigating the unhappy men who had the practical responsibility for finding solutions and failed.

Where have the revisionists gone astray? . . . I cannot escape the feeling that the vogue of revisionism is connected with the modern tendency to seek in optimistic sentimentalism an escape from the severe demands of moral decision; that it is the offspring of our modern sentimentality which at once evades the essential moral problems in the name of a superficial objectivity and asserts their unimportance in the name of an invincible progress.

The revisionists first glided over the implications of the fact that the slavery system was producing a closed society in the South. Yet that society increasingly had justified itself by a political and philosophical repudiation of free society; southern thinkers swiftly developed the anti-libertarian potentialities in a social system whose cornerstone, in Alexander H. Stephens' proud phrase, was human bondage. In theory and in practice, the South organized itself with mounting rigor against ideas of human dignity and freedom, because such ideas inevitably threatened the basis of their own system. . . .

A society closed in the defense of evil institutions thus creates moral differences far too profound to be solved by compromise. Such a society forces upon every one, both those living at the time and those writing about it later, the necessity for a moral judgment; and the moral judgment in such cases becomes an indispensable factor in the historical understanding.

The revisionists were commendably anxious to avoid the vulgar errors of the post–Civil War historians who pronounced smug individual judgments on the persons involuntarily involved in the tragedy of the slave system. Consequently they tried hard to pronounce no moral judgment at all on slavery. . . .

Because the revisionists felt no moral urgency themselves, they deplored as fanatics those who did feel it, or brushed aside their feelings as the artificial product of emotion and propaganda. The revisionist hero was Stephen A. Douglas, who always thought that the great moral problems could be solved by sleight-of-hand. . . .

By denying themselves insight into the moral dimension of the slavery crisis, in other words, the revisionists denied themselves a historical understanding of the intensities that caused the crisis. It was the moral issue of slavery, for example, that gave the struggles over slavery in the territories or over the enforcement of the fugitive slave laws their significance. These issues, as the revisionists have shown with cogency, were not in themselves basic. But they were the available issues; they were almost the only points within the existing constitutional framework where the moral conflict could be faced; as a consequence, they became charged with the moral and political dynamism of the central issue. . . .

Let us be clear what the relationship of moral judgment to history is. Every historian . . . imports his own set of moral judgments into the writing of history by the very process of interpretation; and the phrase "every historian" includes the category "revisionist." . . . The whole revisionist attitude toward abolitionists and radicals, repeatedly characterized by Randall as "unctious" and "intolerant," overflows with the moral feeling which is so virtuously excluded from discussions of slavery. . . .

. . . Professor Randall [was guilty of] . . . uncritical optimism . . . when he remarked, "To suppose that the Union could not have been continued or slavery outmoded without the war and without the corrupt concomitants of war is hardly an enlightened assumption." We have here a touching afterglow of the admirable nineteenth-century faith in the full rationality and perfectibility of man; the faith that the errors of the world would all in time be "outmoded" . . . by progress. Yet the experience of the twentieth century has made it clear that we gravely overrated man's capacity to solve the problems of existence within the terms of history.

This conclusion about man may disturb our complacencies about human nature. Yet it is certainly more in accord with history than Professor Randall's "enlightened" assumption that man can solve peaceably all the problems which overwhelm him. The unhappy fact is that man occasionally works himself into a log-jam; and that the log-jam must be burst by violence. We know that well enough from the experience of the last decade. . . .

We delude ourselves when we think that history teaches us that evil will be "outmoded" by progress and that politics consequently does not impose on us the necessity for decision and for struggle. If historians are to understand the fullness of the social dilemma they seek to reconstruct, they must understand that sometimes there is no escape from the implacabilities of moral decision. When social conflicts embody great moral issues, these conflicts cannot be assigned for solution to the invincible march of progress; nor can they be bypassed with "objective" neutrality. Not many problems perhaps force this decision upon the historian. But, if any problem does in our history, it is the Civil War.

To reject the moral actuality of the Civil War is to foreclose the possibility of an adequate account of its causes. More than that, it is to misconceive and grotesquely to sentimentalize the nature of history. For history is not a redeemer, promising to solve all human problems in time; nor is man capable of transcending the limitations of his being. Man generally is entangled in insoluble problems; history is consequently a tragedy in which we are all involved, whose key-note is anxiety and frustration, not progress and fulfillment. Nothing exists in history to assure us that the great moral dilemmas can be resolved without pain; we cannot therefore be relieved from the duty of moral judgment on issues so appalling and inescapable as those involved in human slavery; nor can we be consoled by sentimental theories about the needlessness of the Civil War into regarding our own struggles against evil as equally needless.

One must emphasize, however, that this duty of judgment applies to issues. Because we are all implicated in the same tragedy, we must judge the men of the past with the same forbearance and charity which we hope the future will apply toward us.

----

58. THE PROBLEM OF INEVITABILITY

Pieter Geyl, a third critic of the "revisionists," subjects to analysis their contention that the Civil War was a "needless war." "The American Civil War and the Problem of Inevitability," New England Quarterly, XXIV (1951), pp. 147–68. Extracts reprinted by permission of the New England Quarterly.

. . . The American people had suddenly found themselves in the Civil War and the majority in none of the sections had deliberately willed it. But what does this prove? Does it prove that the war might therefore have been avoided? Is it not rather one more proof of the general truth that the course of history is not governed by the conscious will of the majority? . . .

And is not this indeed what we can read on every page of the book of history? . . . The large majority wanted peace. "The shipowner thought of his ships, the writer of his books, the manufacturer of his machines." Here, there and everywhere peace was what men wanted, "and the war came." The instinctive aversion of the mass of people is no evidence that it might have been avoided. It is possible to believe—note that I am not saying, one can prove—that there were forces at work, stronger than individual desires or fears, or than their sum as resulting from the ballot box, which made it inevitable. How striking in this connection is the example of recent American history. I need hardly recall the way in which the United States entered both the First and Second World Wars. This is a controversial subject, but to me it seems that in the light of his own country's experiences, Randall's postulate of a strict majority democracy as a fixed standard of historical judgment comes to wear a somewhat ghostly look of unreality.

"Forces? indeed!" Randall will say: "Name calling, shibboleths, epithets, tirades." An appeal, not to reason or to true interest, but to the emotions. And who will deny that sentiment, passion, extra-rational conviction, supply a fertile soil to the monster growths of misunderstanding and exaggeration, misrepresentation, hatred and recklessness! The question remains whether one is justified in labelling these extra-rational factors with contemptuous terms and deny to them, as Randall does, a rightful rôle in the drama of history, relegating them without further ado to the category of "artificial agitation," which can on no condition be reckoned among "fundamental causes."

Two histories might be written—so says the Count de la Gorce in his striking little book on Louis XVIII—about the Restoration. One would be the sober and serious history of the good services rendered by that régime to France from day to day and in an unsensational manner. The other one is the history of violent incidents . . . which, pictured in colorful prints, struck the popular imagination. And it is this second history which culminates in the revolution of 1830. You will notice here, in the writing of the French royalist, the same idea . . . that the historian's rational criticism, working after the events, can detach from the total of what happened the emotions which brought about the catastrophe and that in the other sequence he will retain the real, the proper history. The suggestion is at least that this ought to have been the real history.

Now this idea is the basic idea of Randall's work. He constantly comes back to it. The Americans of the fifties both surprise and irritate him. An essay in which he recapitulates his grievances against them bears the title A Blundering Generation. How was it possible for these people to work up such excitement over trifles! All problems are distorted by them. Look how they made mountains out of mole hills and exaggerated matters which seen in their true size would never have stood in the way of a peaceful settlement.

Take the Kansas-Nebraska Bill, with which Douglas in 1854 set going so fateful a controversy. Randall is much concerned to exculpate Douglas. Douglas is a man after his heart: a practical man, a man who wanted to do business, and with Northerners and Southerners alike. Can one wonder if Douglas was astonished at the hubbub? Was it such a crime that by his principle of popular sovereignty he created the possibility of slavery in those territories situated so far North? The very fact of the situation of Kansas and Nebraska made it most improbable that slavery would ever take root there. The raving in the North about a mere theoretical possibility was therefore, according to Randall, lacking in all sense of reality; it was an example of the hollowness of all that vehement quarreling.

But now let us try to picture to ourselves the state of affairs. Shortly before, in 1850, the new Compromise had been reached, intended to put an end to the dangerous tension that had been growing up over the disposal of the newly acquired Western lands. The Compromise was worthless if it did not confine the extension of slavery within limits accepted by both sides. But here in effect the demarcation line of 1820, which had been looked upon as fixed, was wiped out, among loud cheers from the South. Moreover, what dominated the situation was Southern fears of the rapid increase in power of the North, and Northern suspicions that the South, to ward off that danger, was trying by all means to fasten its grip on the Federal Government. Must one not wilfully blindfold one's historical imagination in order to avoid seeing that the excitement was natural? . . .

Even the Fugitive Slave Law [of 1850] is, according to Randall, all things considered, but a small matter. And, indeed, one can say: were a few hundred fugitive slaves worth the risk of getting enmeshed in a destructive civil war? Answer: neither for the slaveholders, nor for the Northerners, who had to look on, on very rare occasions and in very few localities, when one was seized and forcibly carried back. Lincoln himself said that we must not act upon all our moral or theoretical preferences. "Ungodly," he exclaimed sadly, when once he came into contact with a case; "but it is the law of the land!" One can accept a personality in which were united deep moral feeling with caution, a sense of responsibility, and a capacity for weighing for and against in the scales of reason. But is it not just as understandable that a crowd assembled when a captured fugitive in Boston is taken to the harbor and that a battalion of soldiers and a war vessel had to be commandeered to see that the law was executed? The Southerners clung to the law because they desired to have from the North an acknowledgment of their right rather than because of the material advantage. A moral revulsion in the North soon made the execution impracticable, and this in its turn created bad blood in the South. Seen in this way—and it seems a truer way than the merely statistical one—, this was a considerable matter. It carried grist to the mill of the Abolitionists. . . .

In his Second Inaugural . . . Lincoln, a month before he was assassinated, announced his intentions with respect to the vanquished: "With malice toward none, with charity for all"—this is still the best-remembered part. But the leading idea, expressed in religious terms, is that events had taken their course independently of human control. To me this humility in the face of the mighty happenings seems to be a truer proof of wisdom than Randall's rationalism. The conception in which it is founded may have its tragic implications; it has not, to anyone who accepts life in its entirety, anything depressing. What seems depressing is rather that attempt to show, over and over again, that those people could have been spared all their misfortunes, if they had only been sensible. For do we not know at long last that man is not a sensible being? Moreover, the wisdom which Randall preaches to his fellow countrymen of three generations ago does not strike me as very convincing. Compromise; and when the seemingly final concessions have been made, for heaven's sake make short work of the remaining scruples. The denial of contrasts which do not appear to have to do with the interest of the majority. The ignoring of moral facts. And, in short, crying peace where there is no peace. Could the conflict have been—I do not say postponed, but—solved in this way? One can easily imagine that out of a new Compromise, fabricated in 1861, after those of 1820 and 1850, . . . a new crisis would soon have sprung, and, who knows, an even worse war. . . .

. . . [The] vision of "a blundering generation" does not do justice to the past. That vision belittles what had real greatness; it ignores the tragedy of that struggle with an overwhelming moral problem, slavery. For this was the struggle in which that generation engaged, after its fashion, that is to say after a human fashion. The problem was never posed in absolute purity, and it could not be so posed. The Southerners knew the practical difficulties of abolition; the Northerners had no constitutional right of interference. Union and state rights, and the whole concept of unity or of national diversity, were inextricably mixed up with the problem, and so were material interests on both sides. It is impossible, therefore, to say that in that painful crisis the South was wholly wrong and the North wholly right. This, too, Lincoln knew. In his Second Inaugural he represented the war as just retribution for the evil of slavery, but North and South shared the punishment, because the offense had come by both.

The two main points on which the conventional conceptions of the origins of the war have of recent times been criticized . . . are that of slavery as the central issue, and that of the inevitability of the conflict. As regards the first, I have clearly enough expressed my opinion that neither with the one-sided attention to economic aspects of the Beards nor with Randall's determination to reduce everything to exclusively practical and reasonable terms can the importance of the moral problem be done justice.

As regards the second, I want to guard myself against a possible misunderstanding. I have not been arguing that the war was inevitable, not even—for that is what the discussion is mostly about—in the ten years preceding the outbreak. I have been arguing that Randall's argument in favor of the opposite contention is unconvincing. The question of evitability or inevitability is one on which, it seems to me, the historian can never form any but an ambivalent opinion. He will now stress other possibilities, then again speak in terms of a coherent sequence of causes and effects. But if he is wise, he will in both cases remain conscious that he has not been able to establish a definite equilibrium between the factors, dissimilar and recalcitrant to exact valuation as they are, by which every crisis situation is dominated.

And here I return to a point on which I find it possible to speak more positively. Randall's way of distinguishing between fundamental and artificial causes seems to me inadmissible. With his impressive scholarship and keen intelligence, schooled in historical dialectic, he counts among artificial causes everything that does not agree with the wishes of the majority or with its true interests, defined by himself in accordance with the best rational standards. But in the sequence of cause and effect, of which the human mind will never have complete command, the category of the *imponderabilia,* passion and emotion, conviction, prejudice, misunderstanding, have their organic function. No doubt it is this very fact which makes that command unattainable for us, but we are not therefore entitled to ignore those non-rational factors or to argue them away with the help of wisdom after the event.

------

59.   "THE TRAVAIL OF SLAVERY"

Charles G. Sellers, Jr., in "The Travail of Slavery," in The Southerner As American *(Chapel Hill: 1960), pp. 40–71, believes that the "conflict of values" between slavery and the American liberal tradition produced tensions in Southerners that drove them to aggressive action. This psychological explanation of the Civil War is based on the assumption that slavery was the fundamental issue of the sectional conflict. The following extracts are reprinted with the permission of the University of North Carolina Press.*

The American experience knows no greater tragedy than the Old South's twistings and turnings on the rack of slavery. . . . Like no other Americans before or since, the white men of the ante-bellum South drove toward catastrophe by doing conscious violence to their truest selves. No picture of the Old South as a section confident and united in its dedication to a neo-feudal social order, and no explanation of the Civil War as a conflict between "two civilizations," can encompass the complexity and pathos of the ante-bellum reality. No analysis that misses the inner turmoil of the ante-bellum Southerner can do justice to the central tragedy of the southern experience.

The key to the tragedy of southern history is the paradox of the slaveholding South's devotion to "liberty." Whenever and wherever Southerners sought to invoke their highest social values—in schoolboy declamations, histories, Fourth of July orations, toasts, or newspaper editorials—"liberty" was the incantation that sprang most frequently and most fervently from their lips and pens. . . .

The Revolutionary struggle made this implicit colonial liberalism explicit and tied it to patriotic pride in the new American Union. From this time on, for Southerners as for other Americans, liberty was the end for which the Union existed, while the Union was the instrument by which liberty was to be extended to all mankind. Thus the Fourth of July, the birthday of both liberty and Union, became the occasion for renewing the liberal idealism and the patriotic nationalism which united Americans of all sections at the highest levels of political conviction. . . .

Although a massive reaction against liberalism is supposed to have seized the southern mind in the following decades, the Nullifiers of the thirties and the radical southern sectionalists of the forties and fifties did not ignore or reject the Revolutionary tradition of liberty so much as they transformed it, substituting for the old emphasis on the natural rights of all men a new emphasis on the rights and autonomy of communities. It was ironic that these slaveholding defenders of liberty against the tyranny of northern domination had to place themselves in the tradition of '76 at all, and the irony was heightened by their failure to escape altogether its universalist implications. . . .

What are we to make of these slaveholding champions of liberty? Was the ante-bellum Southerner history's most hypocritical casuist? Or were these passionate apostrophes to the liberty of distant peoples a disguised protest against, or perhaps an escape from, the South's daily betrayal of its liberal self? Southerners were at least subconsciously aware of the "detestable paradox" of "our every-day sentiments of liberty" while holding human beings in slavery, and many Southerners had made it painfully explicit in the early days of the republic. . . .

It is well known that the South's great statesmen of the Revolutionary generation almost unanimously condemned slavery as incompatible with the nation's liberal principles. Though these elder statesmen proved incapable of solving the problem, Thomas Jefferson consoled himself with the thought that it could safely be left to the "young men, grown up and growing up," who "have sucked in the principles of liberty, as it were, with their mother's milk." Such young men did indeed grow up, and they kept most Southerners openly apologetic about slavery for fifty years following the Declaration of Independence. . . .

Though open anti-slavery utterances grew infrequent after the 1830's, the generation which was to dominate southern life in the forties and fifties had already come to maturity with values absorbed from the afterglow of Revolutionary liberalism. . . .

A whole generation cannot transform its most fundamental values by a mere effort of will. Though Southerners tended during the latter part of the ante-bellum period to restrict their publicly voiced libertarian hopes to "oppressed distant lands," the old liberal misgivings about slavery did not die. Instead they burrowed beneath the surface of the southern mind, where they kept gnawing away the shaky foundations on which Southerners sought to rebuild their morale and self-confidence as a slaveholding people. . . .

If the Southerner had been embarrassed by his devotion to liberty and Union alone, he would have had less trouble easing his mind on the subject of slavery. But as a Virginia legislator exclaimed in 1832, "This, sir, is a Christian community." . . . During those early decades of the nineteenth century, when the South was confessing the evils of slavery, it had been swept by a wave of evangelical orthodoxy. Though the wave crested about the time some Southerners, including some clergymen, began speaking of slavery as a positive good, it does not follow that the evangelical reaction against the eighteenth century's religious ideas contributed significantly to the reaction against the eighteenth century's liberalism with regard to slavery.

On the contrary, the evangelical denominations had strong anti-slavery tendencies. Methodists, Quakers, and Baptists nurtured an extensive abolitionist movement in the upper South during the twenties, when the rest of the country was largely indifferent to the slavery question; and the Presbyterians were still denouncing slavery in Kentucky a decade later. It would be closer to the truth to suggest that as Southerners wrestled with their consciences over slavery, they may have gained a first-hand experience with the concepts of sin and evil that made them peculiarly susceptible to Christian orthodoxy. . . .

Even the irreligious found it hard to resist the claims of simple humanity or to deny that slaves, as one Southerner put it, "have hearts and feelings like other men." And those who were proof against the appeals to Revolutionary liberalism, Christianity, and humanity, still faced the arguments of Southerners in each succeeding generation that slavery was disastrous to the whites. Jefferson's famous lament that the slaveholder's child, "nursed, educated, and daily exercised in tyranny . . . must be a prodigy who can retain his manners and morals undepraved," was frequently echoed. . . .

It is essential to understand that the public declarations of Southerners never revealed the full impact of all these anti-slavery influences on the southern mind. Fear of provoking slave insurrections had restrained free discussion of slavery even in the Revolutionary South, and an uneasy society exerted steadily mounting pressure against anti-slavery utterances thereafter. Only when Nat Turner's bloody uprising of 1831 shocked Southerners into open debate over the peculiar institution did the curtain of restraint part sufficiently to reveal the intensity of their misgivings. . . .

[Yet,] . . . when Nat Turner frightened Southerners into facing squarely the tragic ambiguity of their society, they found the price for resolving it too high. The individual planter's economic stake in slavery was a stubborn and perhaps insurmountable obstacle to change; and even Jefferson's nerve had failed at the task of reconstituting the South's social system to assimilate a host of Negro freedmen.

The whole South sensed that a fateful choice had been made.

Slowly and reluctantly Southerners faced the fact that, if slavery were to be retained, things could not go on as before. The slaves were restive, a powerful anti-slavery sentiment was sweeping the western world, and southern minds were not yet nerved for a severe struggle in defense of the peculiar institution to which they were now committed. The South could no longer ease its conscience with hopes for the eventual disappearance of slavery, or tolerate such hopes in any of its people. . . . So southern leaders of the Calhoun school began trying to convince themselves and others that slavery was a "positive good," while southern legislatures abridged freedom of speech and press, made manumission difficult or impossible, and imposed tighter restrictions on both slaves and free Negros. The Great Reaction was under way.

Yet the Great Reaction, for all its formidable façade and terrible consequences, was a fraud. Slavery simply could not be blended with liberalism and Christianity, while liberalism and Christianity were too deeply rooted in the southern mind to be torn up overnight. Forced to smother and distort their most fundamental convictions by the decision to maintain slavery, and goaded by criticism based on these same convictions, Southerners of the generation before the Civil War suffered the most painful loss of social morale and identity that any large group of Americans has ever experienced. . . .

Nowhere . . . was the South's painful inner conflict over slavery more evident than in the elaborate body of theory by which it tried to prove (mainly to itself) the beneficence of its peculiar social system. . . .

Close examination of the superficially impressive pro-slavery philosophy reveals, as Louis Hartz has brilliantly demonstrated, a "mass of agonies and contradictions in the dream world of southern thought." The peculiar institution could be squared theoretically with either the slave's humanity or democratic liberalism for whites, but not with both. Thus the necessity for justifying slavery, coupled with the white South's inability to escape its inherited liberalism or to deny the common humanity it shared with its Negro slaves, inspired "a mixture of pain and wild hyperbole." . . .

It was this inner conflict which produced the South's belligerent dogmatism in the recurrent crises of the fifties. The whole massive pro-slavery polemic had the unreal ring of logic pushed far beyond conviction. . . . If the South's best minds resolutely quashed their doubts, it is small wonder that crisis-tossed editors and politicians took refuge in positive and extreme positions. . . .

How, then, did the fundamentally liberal, Christian, American South ever become an "aggressive slavocracy"? How did it bring itself to flaunt an aristocratic social philosophy? To break up the American Union? To wage war for the purpose of holding four million human beings in a bondage that violated their humanity? The answer is that Southerners did not and could not rationally and deliberately choose slavery and its fruits over the values it warred against. Rather it was the very conflict of values, rendered intolerable by constant criticism premised on values Southerners shared, which drove them to seek a violent resolution.

Social psychologists observe that such value conflicts—especially when they give rise to the kind of institutional instability revealed by the ambiguities of southern slavery—make a society "suggestible," or ready to follow the advocates of irrational and aggressive action. Thus it was fateful that the Old South developed an unusually able minority of fire-eating sectionalists, who labored zealously, from the 1830's on, to unite the South behind radical measures in defense of slavery. Though a majority of Southerners remained profoundly distrustful of these extremists throughout the ante-bellum period, their unceasing agitation steadily aggravated the South's tensions and heightened its underlying suggestibility. By egging the South on to ever more extreme demands, the Calhouns, Rhetts, and Yanceys provoked violent northern reactions, which could then be used to whip the South's passions still higher. At length, in 1860, capitalizing on intrigues for the Democratic presidential nomination, the fire-eaters managed to split the Democratic party, thus insuring the election of a Republican President and paving the way for secession.

Inflammatory agitation and revolutionary tactics succeeded only because Southerners had finally passed the point of rational self-control. The almost pathological violence of their reactions to northern criticism indicated that their misgivings about their moral position on slavery had become literally intolerable under the mounting abolitionist attack. . . .

Superimposed on this fundamental moral anxiety was another potent emotion, fear. John Brown's raid in October, 1859, created the most intense terror of slave insurrection that the South had ever experienced; and in this atmosphere of dread the final crisis of 1860–61 occurred. . . . Southerners believed their land to be overrun by abolitionist emissaries, who were "tampering with our slaves, and furnishing them with arms and poisons to accomplish their hellish designs." Lynch law was proclaimed, and vigilance committees sprang up to deal with anyone suspected of abolitionist sentiments. . . .

From the circumstances of the secession elections—the small turnouts, the revolutionary tactics of the fire-eaters, the disproportionate weighting of the results in favor of plantation areas, the coercive conditions under which the upper South voted, and the hysteria that prevailed everywhere—it can hardly be said that a majority of the South's white people deliberately chose to dissolve the Union in 1861. . . .

Yet it is idle to wonder whether secession represented the deliberate choice of a majority of white Southerners, or to speculate about the outcome of a hypothetical referendum, free from ambiguity, coercion, and hysteria. Decisions like the one that faced the South in 1860–61 are never reached in any such ideal way. And even had the South decided for the Union, its and the nation's problem would have remained unsolved, and a violent resolution would only have been postponed. Slavery was doomed by the march of history and by the nature of Southerners themselves, but so deeply had it involved them in its contradictions that they could neither deal with it rationally nor longer endure the tensions and anxieties it generated. Under these circumstances the Civil War or something very like it was unavoidable. It was also salutary, for only the transaction at Appomattox could have freed the South's people—both Negro and white—to move again toward the realization of their essential natures as Southerners, liberals, Christians, and Americans.

---

60.   SLAVERY AND SECTIONALISM

Kenneth M. Stampp, in America in 1857: A Nation on the Brink *(Oxford University Press, 1990), argues that slavery was at the heart of the sectional conflict. The issue was sometimes confronted directly, sometimes indirectly, but it was a major ingredient in every antebellum political crisis. Extracts from pages 110–13 reprinted with permission of Oxford University Press.*

The [slavery] issue assumed many forms. Northern abolitionists aimed their attacks directly at slavery in the southern states, denouncing it as immoral and its survival as a national disgrace. Most Republicans, who did not consider themselves to be abolitionists, hoped to promote its ultimate extinction indirectly by preventing its expansion, or by resisting enforcement of the Fugitive Slave Act. Others avoided frontal assaults by stressing only the need to check the aggressions of the southern Slave Power. Proslavery Southerners, not without reasons, claimed to see no significant difference between these several forms of attack, regarding each as a dangerous threat, varying only in its degree of subtlety.

Southern editors, politicians, and literary champions, in turn, frequently elected not to speak directly of the need to defend slavery but stressed instead the more abstract and elevated concepts of southern honor or constitutional rights. In most cases the terms were interchangeable, for as they were generally used the concepts of rights and honor were almost invariably linked to slavery. The Richmond *Enquirer* made the linkage explicit when it argued that secession would be justified "only when the honor of the slave states" was "outraged by a Black Republican control of the country. . . . Let Congress enact another boundary line, beyond which slavery shall not go, and we would say repeal it, or the South should go out of the Union." Similarly, Alexander H. Stephens insisted that the territorial issue was important not so much because he expected slavery to expand westward, but because it involved the important principle of "constitutional right and equality. . . . A people who would maintain their rights must look to principles much more than to practical results." But Stephens also linked his principles to slavery. "If the slightest encroachments of power are permitted or submitted to in the Territories," he warned, "they may reach the states ultimately."

Republicans often [echoed] Seward's assertion [in 1858] that an "irrepressible conflict" divided the advocates of free and slave labor, as well as Lincoln's declaration, in his "House Divided" speech, that the Union could not survive half slave and half free but would become "*all* one thing or *all* the other." The Chicago *Tribune* claimed that the sectional conflict was "no accident" but sprang from "the contest between nonslaveholders and . . . the Oligarchs who rule upon *Slave Labor.*" Sectionalism, wrote another Republican editor, had destroyed the old political parties and rendered their platforms obsolete, "and now nothing remains but an issue upon the great principles of humanity and liberty as opposed to wrong and slavery." A substantial segment of the Republican electorate seemed to believe that slavery, or slavery expansion, or the Slave Power, or some combination of these was not only the central issue in national politics but the sole issue. One of Seward's correspondents described a single Republican goal: to "contest every inch of ground, expose every scheme of the slave power, and keep the public mind agitated on the great question of freedom." Looking to 1860, another expected a Republican victory to be the dawn of the day when "that blighting curse of slavery shall be swept from our fair and fertile land."

Proslavery Southerners could, on occasion, speak with equal bluntness about what was at the heart of the sectional conflict. It involved "but one subject," wrote an Alabama editor, and that was slavery. "Other questions may for a time occasion agitation . . . but they can never result in a disruption of the Union." The tariff, federal appropriations for internal improvements, and national banks, said the [New Orleans] editor of *De Bow's Review*, were "but means of ordinary oppression," which the minority South might have to endure. "Slavery restriction and slavery extinction, on the other hand, . . . [would drive] the South back, at a single step, into worse than barbarism." No nation could survive, a Texas Congressman believed, "unless a preponderant majority of its members be one in fundamental opinion."

In a series of editorials the Richmond *Enquirer* developed its own version of the irrepressible conflict. "The slavery question," it claimed, "was the single source of all the intestine trouble" which endangered the Union. For the past fifty years slavery agitation had been "growing greater and fiercer and wilder, widening its circle with each succeeding year." As a result the North and South were "divided into two antagonistic sections," between whom there existed "an intensity of animosity" seldom found "even among separate and distinct nations in times of peace." The *Enquirer* saw a national crisis rapidly approaching and believed that the presidential election of 1860 would, "in all probability determine the result." In that contest "the dangerous doctrine of abolitionism" must be defeated, or the South would "secede at once" and form a southern republic.

Abolitionists, Republicans, and proslavery Southerners, of course, did not speak for the entire body politic. Conservative old Whigs and northern Democrats emphatically rejected the concept of an irrepressible conflict. They denied that the slavery controversy in its various guises had been spontaneously generated by an aroused electorate, thereby forcing reluctant politicians to take up the proslavery or antislavery cause. Rather, they charged, certain opportunistic northern and southern politicians had themselves politicized slavery. Then, for their own partisan purposes, they had exploited the resulting sectional conflict and turned the attention of voters away from more important issues. Northern conservatives accused Republican leaders of recklessly resorting to slavery agitation in order to form a new sectional party through which they hoped to win political power. Their platform needlessly called for the exclusion of slavery from territories that were geographically and climatically unsuited for it. Abolitionist agitation, they claimed, merely intensified the southern defense of slavery, thus postponing the time when natural forces would bring about its demise.

Edward Everett [a conservative Massachusetts Whig] viewed the sectional conflict from this perspective. "In all this wretched struggle," he wrote, "it is mournful to reflect that the real difficulties spring more from the selfish passions of men than the necessities of the case." In the border states, slavery was already declining from "natural causes." If only "intemperate and too often unprincipled agitation of the subject for electioneering purposes at the north could be stopped, Slavery would disappear in 5 years in several of them." Thomas P. Akers, a Democratic Congressman from Missouri, complained of the Republicans' pointless "lectures on the ethics of slavery." . . . Serious national problems demanded the attention of Congress, he said, yet that body ignored them and engaged in a "driveling discussion" of slavery, which all knew could have no other effect than to "deepen the animosity and embitter the strife" between the sections. From the conservative perspective, then, slavery was not the fundamental cause of the sectional conflict. Rather, the politicians and other antislavery agitators were themselves the cause, for they brought it on deliberately, needlessly, and irresponsibly.

Implicit in this conservative explanation was the assumption that there were national problems of greater importance than slavery on which Republicans should have focused, that other available issues would have resonated with voters quite as effectively, that politicians were free to create and politicize whatever issues they pleased, and that they probably would have fared as well with one issue as another. Yet the inability of the remnants of the Whig party, after the decline of nativism, to find and effectively politicize alternative issues, discredited their indictment of antislavery Republicans. Among Democrats no politician tried more desperately than Stephen A. Douglas to keep slavery out of national politics; yet he was obliged repeatedly to grapple with it. . . . Politicians, in fact, can successfully politicize only those issues that have real or at least symbolic significance, and then only when external conditions make them relevant to the concerns of their constituents. Those who joined the slavery debate in one or another of its forms understood not only their constituents but the social climate of the mid-nineteenth-century Western world far better than their critics.

———————

VI. Majority Rule and Minority Rights

THE MANY ISSUES, real or imagined, and the contrasting social and cultural values that divided Northerners and Southerners produced the most serious internal crisis the United States has ever faced. Whether or not it was "inevitable"—an "irrepressible conflict"—the crisis did finally lead to war. This fact might well have some depressing implications for those who believe in democratic processes. If there are some kinds of controversies—for example, controversies that deal with the "fundamental structure of society"—that simply cannot be settled peacefully at the ballot box, then democracy may fail us when we need it most. For it is the capacity of a democracy to deal with fundamental issues directly, decisively, and in time, which provides the real measure of its success.

One way of viewing the Civil War, then, is as "a complete breakdown of the democratic process." Southern secessionists maintained that democracy failed because Northerners did not understand its true nature. They affirmed that rule by an absolute majority free to trample upon the rights of minorities is not democracy but tyranny. Northerners, on the other hand, argued that the South, in effect, demanded that a minority be given the right to dictate to the majority. To them Southern secession represented a refusal to abide by the results of a democratic election and a repudiation of a fundamental principle upon which democracy is based. Many Northerners, therefore, described the Civil War as an attempt to defend popular government—indeed, as a crusade to save democracy for the world.

61.   THE CONCURRENT MAJORITY

John C. Calhoun, reflecting Southern discontent with its minority position in the federal Union, argued that a "concurrent majority" would be a better safeguard against tyranny than a "numerical majority." By this he meant that the majority in each specific interest group should approve federal legislative proposals before they could become law. In effect, this would give the minority South, as an interest group, power to veto obnoxious legislation. Calhoun's conception of how democratic government should function is summarized in the following passages from his A Disquisition on Government, *printed in Cralle (ed.),* The Works of John C. Calhoun, *I, pp. 57–64.*

. . . [The] more perfectly a government combines power and liberty,—that is, the greater its power and the more enlarged and secure the liberty of individuals, the more perfectly it fulfils the ends for which government is ordained. To show, then, that the government of the concurrent majority is better calculated to fulfil them than that of the numerical, it is only necessary to explain why the former is better suited to combine a higher degree of power and a wider scope of liberty than the latter. . . .

The concurrent majority, then, is better suited to enlarge and secure the bounds of liberty, because it is better suited to prevent government from passing beyond its proper limits, and to restrict it to its primary end,—the protection of the community. . . . The tendency of government to pass beyond its proper limits, is what exposes liberty to danger, and renders it insecure; and it is the strong counteraction of governments of the concurrent majority to this tendency which makes them so favorable to liberty. On the contrary, those of the numerical, instead of opposing and counteracting this tendency, add to it increased strength, in consequence of the violent party struggles incident to them. . . . And hence their encroachments on liberty, and the danger to which it is exposed under such governments.

So great, indeed, is the difference between the two in this respect, that liberty is little more than a name under all governments . . . of the numerical majority; and can only have a secure and durable existence under those of the concurrent or constitutional form. The latter, by giving to each portion of the community which may be unequally affected by its action, a negative on the others, prevents all partial or local legislation, and restricts its action to such measures as are designed for the protection and the good of the whole. In doing this, it secures, at the same time, the rights and liberty of the people, regarded individually; as each portion consists of those who, whatever may be the diversity of interest among themselves, have the same interest in reference to the action of the government.

Such being the case, the interest of each individual may be safely confided to the majority, or voice of his portion, against that of all others, and, of course, the government itself. It is only through an organism which vests each with a negative, in some one form or another, that those who have like interests in preventing the government from passing beyond its proper sphere, and encroaching on the rights and liberty of individuals, can co-operate peaceably and effectually in resisting the encroachments of power, and thereby preserve their rights and liberty. Individual resistance is too feeble, and the difficulty of concert and co-operation too great, unaided by such an organism, to oppose, successfully, the organized power of government, with all the means of the community at its disposal; especially in populous countries of great extent; where concert and co-operation are almost impossible. Even when the oppression of the government comes to be too great to be borne, and force is resorted to in order to overthrow it, the result is rarely ever followed by the establishment of liberty. The force sufficient to overthrow an oppressive government is usually sufficient to establish one equally, or more, oppressive in its place. And hence, in no governments, except those that rest on the principle of the concurrent or constitutional majority, can the people guard their liberty against power; and hence, also, when lost, the great difficulty and uncertainty of regaining it by force.

-----

62.   THE TYRANNY OF MAJORITIES

The following editorial from the Richmond Semi-weekly Examiner (January 6, 1860) is typical of many antebellum Southern protests against the theory of majority rule. Quoted in Dumond (ed.), Southern Editorials on Secession, pp. 7–8.

The law which commands obedience to the mandates of the physical force of an unrestrained numerical majority is the operative law, not only with the masses in the free States of the North, but in all communities where no divisions or orders of society are established or recognized, and where the conservative influence of domestic slavery does not supply the deficiency of restraining checks. In the Northern States the popular power has no check but the popular reason and will. A law such as this acting upon a society singularly energetic and adventurous, greedy after wealth and lusting for power, has no limit but the measure of its own power, and that measure is the extent of the physical force of the numerical majority of the people. That force is stimulated to action by one unvarying and universal incentive: the desire for the acquisition and use of power and property. The temper to acquire, the spirit to appropriate, thus unrestrained, operates under a universal law of human nature with a continuous and unremitting energy, against which plighted faith and constitutional checks will ever prove feeble and worthless defenses. There is but one defense of practical value and real efficiency: it is the ability and will of the minority to resist the action of the ruling majority whether seen in the operation of established government, or in the less usual form of unlicensed violence. The majority makes, and construes, and executes the law.— The minority, while living under government, but obeys and submits to the law thus made and construed. No defense provided for it by mere government is in its control or at its service. The majority does not even recognize the existence of the minority where the idea of the supreme authority of the numerical majority prevails, as it does in the Northern States of this Union.

---

63.   THE MONARCHICAL SOUTH

The Philadelphia Press (December 21, 1860) made an accusation that became familiar during the secession crisis—that the secessionists were enemies of democracy and desired to establish a monarchy in the South.

Should the Cotton States go out in a body, we shall then witness the beginning of an experiment to establish, on this continent, a great slaveholding monarchy. With few exceptions, the leaders of the Disunion cabal are men of the most aristocratic pretensions—men who . . . easily adopt the habits and titles of the European nobility. South Carolina, which is at the head of Secession, is almost a monarchy herself. Her representatives in both branches of Congress, for years past, have acted upon the idea that the people of the free States are servile, and Mr. Hammond, the most candid and straightforward of the set, denounced the laboring white masses of the free States as the mudsills of society. . . . That State is, therefore, the fitting pioneer of Southern monarchy, and those who follow in her train in other parts of the South, will, if they speak their honest sentiments, not deny that they heartily sympathize with her in the purpose which she undoubtedly cherishes. What a procession of palatines, and earls, and baronets we shall have after the organization of this new Government!

---

64.   SELF-GOVERNMENT ON TRIAL

The following resolution, adopted at a Union meeting in Chicago on January 5, 1861, expressed a common belief that the future of democracy throughout the world depended upon the success of the "American experiment." Chicago Tribune (January 7, 1861).

That under the Province of God there has been assigned to this nation the high and important mission of working out the great idea of national self-government. That upon the success of that experiment depend the best interests of man. That we owe it to ourselves and to the friends of liberty and humanity throughout the world not to permit the experiment to fail upon the first difficulty which assails it. That this Government having for three-quarters of a century demonstrated to the world its grand capacities for developing the energies and promoting the prosperity and happiness of its people, its utility to meet and conquer its enemies in war and sustain the honor of its flag upon every sea, is now called upon to vindicate before the world its power to preserve our own harmony and integrity, and in case of need its ability to suppress rebellion and sedition at home, to demonstrate that the people in their collective majority are sufficient without the aid of titled monarchs or standing armies to maintain their own government against every treasonable conspiracy for its destruction and every rebellious uprising against its authority.

---

65.   THE MAJORITY MUST RULE

"E Pluribus Unum," in James Russell Lowell, Political Essays *(New York: 1888), pp. 57–58, 63–64.*

It cannot be too distinctly stated or too often repeated that the discontent of South Carolina is not one to be allayed by any concessions which the Free States can make with dignity or even safety. It is something more radical and of longer standing than distrust of the motives or probable policy of the Republican party. It is neither more nor less than a disbelief in the very principles on which our government is founded. So long as they practically retained the government of the country, and could use its power and patronage to their own advantage, the plotters were willing to wait; but the moment they lost that control . . . and saw that their chance of ever regaining it was hopeless, they declared openly the principles on which they have all along been secretly acting . . . . Defeated overwhelmingly before the people, they now question the right of the majority to govern, except on their terms, and threaten violence in the hope of extorting from the fears of the Free States what they failed to obtain from their conscience and settled conviction of duty. Their quarrel is not with the Republican party, but with the theory of Democracy. . . .

We have been so long habituated to a kind of local independence in the management of our affairs, and the central government has fortunately had so little occasion for making itself felt at home and in the domestic concerns of the States, that the idea of its relation to us as a power, except for protection from without, has gradually become vague and alien to our ordinary habits of thought. We have so long heard the principle admitted, and seen it acted on with advantage to the general weal, that the people are sovereign in their own affairs, that we must recover our presence of mind before we see the fallacy of the assumption, that the people, or a bare majority of them, in a single State, can exercise their right of sovereignty as against the will of the nation legitimately expressed. . . . It would seem to be the will of God that from time to time the manhood of nations, like that of individuals, should be tried by great dangers or by great opportunities. . . . The occasion is offered us now of trying whether a conscious nationality and a timely concentration of the popular will for its maintenance be possible in a democracy, or whether it is only despotisms that are capable of the sudden and selfish energy of protecting themselves from destruction.

---

66.   THE CONFEDERATE CHALLENGE TO FREE GOVERNMENT

Chicago Journal (*April 17, 1861*).

The Southern rebellion has started with the contemptuous denial of the right of the majority to rule. Its boasted confederacy is a compact of violence, fraud and treachery levelled against a free government, and the only one that has had the confidence, respect and admiration of mankind. Does any one imagine that a league, long plotted in secret and prosecuted with prolonged treachery, is aiming *only* at independence—*only* at the reconstruction of *free* government? . . .

The unscrupulous character of its leaders, the bold and shameless suppression of all the rights of free men to the minority of their own citizens, and abolition of free speech and free suffrage—all show, in characters of light, that the real and ultimate aim is the total overthrow and annihilation of all republican liberty. . . .

It is no common strife of party, no collision of mere passing opinion, or transitory interest, that awaits the decision of our country. Without a Union that is *free,* without a Constitution that can be enforced, without an authority to command respect and obedience, without acknowledged deference to the voice of the people, in its constitutional majority, which cannot be arrogantly and safely violated or despised, our Republic ceases to be a Government, our freedom will be quickly supplanted by anarchy and despotism, and all the cherished hopes of our country and mankind, for enduring, and national freedom, will be blasted.

---

67.   IN DEFENSE OF THE BALLOT BOX

Philadelphia Public Ledger (*June 7, 1861*).

. . . [We] are fighting for . . . [a] great fundamental principle of republican Government—the right of the majority to rule. When the ballot-box was substituted for revolution, it was thought that all violent changes in established governments, all sudden overthrowing of political structures, would be obviated, for the will of the people could be peacefully known through the ballot, and their legally established rule be patiently submitted to. So long as it answered the purpose of maintaining power in the hands of the would-be-oligarchs, its decrees were acknowledged as binding; but so soon as it threatened to put power really in the hands of the majority, those who labor for their living, then the discovery is made that our institutions rest on a wrong basis, and that political equality is neither desirable for social prosperity, nor practicable for political permanency. We are fighting to expunge this great political error, and to prove to the world, that the free Democratic spirit which established the government, is equal to its protection and its maintenance. If this is not worth fighting for, then our revolt against England was a crime, and our republican Government a fraud.

---

68.   A BATTLE FOR DEMOCRACY THE WORLD OVER

Columbus, Ohio, Gazette (*June 21, 1861*).

It is not only now to be decided whether government shall put down insurrection, or insurgents shall put down government, *but it is a struggle in the decision of which is involved the cause of constitutional liberty the world over.* It is not only in issue whether we have a government or not, here, but we believe it is now being decided whether a free government shall again spring up in any quarter of the globe. If under circumstances as favorable as those under which we have made the experiment, a republican form of government is a failure, what nation will have the audacity to test again an experiment which has so often been tested, and has in every instance so signally failed? . . .

We believe that this struggle rises to a magnitude, equalled by no

former struggle, recorded in history. It is a contest of rightful
authority against rebellion, of order against anarchy, of law against
lawlessness, of constitutional liberty against those trampling under
foot all constitutions. It is to be decided whether we shall have
Courts of Justice or madmen to try American citizens for alleged
crimes; whether Presidents constitutionally elected, or mobs are to
rule. . . .

Give liberty and law to America: then the oppressed in Europe
shall be free. Not before.

69.   "A People's Contest"

*Lincoln summarized the Northern concept of the democratic issue
as a cause of the war in his message to the special session of Congress
which met on July 4, 1861. Richardson* (ed.), Messages and Papers
of the Presidents, *VI, pp. 20–31.*

[This] issue embraces more than the fate of these United States. It
presents to the whole family of men the question whether a
constitutional republic or democracy—a government of the people
by the same people—can or cannot maintain its territorial integrity
against its own domestic foes. It presents the question whether
discontented individuals, too few in number to control administration according to organic laws in any case, can always, upon the
pretenses made in this case, or on any other pretenses, or arbitrarily
without any pretense, break up their government, and thus practically put an end to free government upon the earth. It forces us to
ask: Is there in all republics this inherent and fatal weakness? Must
a government, of necessity, be too strong for the liberties of its own
people, or too weak to maintain its own existence? . . .

This is essentially a people's contest. On the side of the Union it
is a struggle for maintaining in the world that form and substance of
government whose leading object is to elevate the condition of
men—to lift artificial weights from all shoulders; to clear the paths

of laudable pursuit for all; to afford all an unfettered start, and a fair chance in the race of life. . . .

Our popular government has often been called an experiment. Two points in it our people have already settled—the successful establishing and the successful administering of it. One still remains—its successful maintenance against a formidable internal attempt to overthrow it. It is now for them to demonstrate to the world that those who can fairly carry an election can also suppress a rebellion; that ballots are the rightful and peaceful successors of bullets; and that when ballots have fairly and constitutionally decided, there can be no successful appeal back to bullets; that there can be no successful appeal, except to ballots themselves, at succeeding elections. Such will be a great lesson of peace: teaching men that what they cannot take by an election, neither can they take it by war; teaching all the folly of being the beginners of a war.

---

70. THE CIVIL WAR AND THE DEMOCRATIC PROCESS

Avery Craven gives his explanation for the failure of the democratic process in an article entitled "The 1840's and the Democratic Process," Journal of Southern History, XVI (1950), pp. 161–76. Extracts reprinted by permission of the Journal of Southern History.

The most significant thing about the American Civil War is that it represents a complete breakdown of the democratic process. After years of strain, men ceased to discuss their problems, dropped the effort to compromise their differences, refused to abide by the results of a national election, and resorted to the use of force. After four years of bloody civil strife, one side was beaten into submission and the other had its way in national affairs. The emergence of modern America was largely the product of that outcome.

If the breakdown of the democratic process is the significant thing about the coming of the Civil War, then the important question is not *what* the North and South were quarreling about half as much as it is *how* their differences got into such shape that they could not be handled by the process of rational discussion, compromise, or the tolerant acceptance of majority decision. The question is not "What caused the Civil War?" but rather "How did it come about?" The two questions are quite different, yet hopelessly tangled. The effort to distinguish between them, however, is important and needs to be stressed.

If one were to discuss the *causes* of the Civil War, he might begin with geography, move on to historical developments in time and place, trace the growth of economic and social rivalries, outline differences in moral values, and then show the way in which personalities and psychological factors operated. The part which slavery played would loom large. It might even become the symbol of all differences and of all conflicts. State rights, territorial expansion, tariffs, lands, internal improvements, and a host of other things, real and imagined, would enter the picture. There would be economic causes, constitutional causes, social causes, moral causes, political causes involving the breaking of old parties and the rise of sectional ones, and psychological causes which ultimately permitted emotion to take the place of reason. There would be remote or background causes, and immediate causes, and causes resting on other causes, until the most eager pedagogue would be thoroughly satisfied.

The matter of how issues got beyond the abilities of the democratic process is, on the other hand, a bit less complex and extended. It has to do with the way in which concrete issues were reduced to abstract principles and the conflicts between interests simplified to basic levels where men feel more than they reason, and where compromise or yielding is impossible because issues appear in the form of right and wrong and involve the fundamental structure of society. This is not saying, as some have charged, that great moral issues were not involved. They certainly were, and it is a matter of choice with historians as to whether or not they take sides, praise or condemn, become partisans in this departed quarrel, or use past events for present-day purposes.

As an approach to this second more modest problem, a correspondence which took place between Abraham Lincoln and

Alexander H. Stephens between November 30 and December 22, 1860, is highly revealing. On November 14, Stephens had delivered one of the great speeches of his life before the legislature of Georgia. It was a Union speech. He had begged his fellow Southerners not to give up the ship, to wait for some violation of the Constitution before they attempted secession. Equality might yet be possible inside the Union. At least, the will of the whole people should be obtained before any action was taken.

Abraham Lincoln, still unconvinced that there was real danger, wrote Stephens, as an old friend, for a revised copy of his speech. Stephens complied, and he ended his letter with a warning about the great peril which threatened the country and a reminder of the heavy responsibility now resting on the president-elect's shoulders. Lincoln answered with assurance that he would not "*directly*, or *indirectly*, interfere with the slaves" or with the southern people about their slaves, and then closed with this significant statement: "I suppose, however, this does not meet the case. You think slavery is right and ought to be extended, while we think it is *wrong* and ought to be restricted. That I suppose is the rub. It certainly is the only substantial difference between us."

The reduction of "the only substantial difference" between North and South to a simple question of *right and wrong* is the important thing about Lincoln's statement. It revealed the extent to which the sectional controversy had, by 1860, been simplified and reduced to a conflict of principles in the minds of the northern people.

Stephens' answer to Lincoln's letter is equally revealing. He expressed "an earnest desire to preserve and maintain the Union of the States, if it can be done upon the principles and in furtherance of the objects for which it was formed." He insisted, however, that private opinion on the question of "African Slavery" was not a matter over which "the Government under the Constitution" had any control. "But now," he said, "this subject, which is confessedly on all sides outside of the Constitutional action of the Government so far as the States are concerned, is made the 'central idea' in the Platform of principles announced by the triumphant Party." It was this total disregard of the Constitution and the rights guaranteed under it that lay back of southern fears. It was the introduction into party politics of issues which projected action by Congress outside its constitutional powers that had made all the trouble. Stephens used the word "Constitution" seven times in his letter.

The significant thing here is Stephens' reduction of sectional differences to the simple matter of southern rights under the Constitution. He too showed how completely the sectional controversy had been simplified into a conflict of principles. And he with Lincoln, speaking for North and South, emphasized the fact that after years of strife the complex issues between the sections had assumed the form of a conflict between *right* and *rights*.

To the scholar it must be perfectly clear that this drastic simplification of sectional differences did not mean that either Lincoln or Stephens thought that all the bitter economic, social, and political questions could be ignored. It simply meant that *right* and *rights* had become the symbols or carriers of all those interests and values. Yet it is equally clear that as symbols they carried an emotional force and moral power in themselves that was far greater than the sum total of all the material issues involved. They suggested things which cannot be compromised—things for which men willingly fight and die. Their use, in 1860, showed that an irrepressible conflict existed. . . .

The [sectional conflict] had certainly shown the weakness of the democratic process in dealing with issues cast as moral conflicts or having to do with the fundamental structure of society. It seemed to show, as Carl Becker has said, that "government by discussion works best when there is nothing of profound importance to discuss, and when there is plenty of time to discuss it. The party system works best when the rival programs involve the superficial aspects rather than the fundamental structure of the social system, and majority rule works best when the minority can meet defeat at the polls in good temper because they need not regard the decision as either a permanent or a fatal surrender of their vital interests."

That, however, was only half of the difficulty. The [sectional conflict] had also shown that a democratic society cannot stand still. The conservative urge to hold fast to that which has been established may prove as fatal as the fanatic's prod to constant change. Those who profess a belief in democracy must ever remember that alongside the Constitution of the United States stands that other troublesome document, the Declaration of Independence, with its promise of greater freedom and equality. If politicians and parties do not sometimes give it heed, they may learn to their sorrow that the great document was written to justify revolt. That too may be a fatal weakness in the democratic process.

———————

VII. The Conflict of Cultures

THOUGH OFTEN EXAGGERATED, there were some differences between Northern and Southern culture, and both contemporaries and historians have used them to help explain the sectional crisis. From the days of Jefferson, the rural South had romanticized agrarian virtues: the wisdom and integrity of a sturdy landowning yeomanry; the hospitality, good manners, and paternalism of a plantation gentry; in general, the stability and conservatism of a productive, well-ordered society of country folk. The North by no means sneered at such an idyllic portrait of rustic innocence—too many of its people were farmers for that—but even in antebellum years the city exercised a considerable influence upon its culture, an influence reflected in its schools, churches, and literature. The North teemed with bustling, restless men and women who believed passionately in "progress" and equated it with growth and change; the air was filled with the excitement of intellectual ferment and with the schemes of entrepreneurs; and the land was honeycombed with societies aiming at nothing less than the total reform of mankind.

Sectional partisans stressed these cultural differences, invidiously compared their society with the other, and proudly proclaimed the superiority of their own. To Northerners the South was backward, semicivilized, and out of harmony with the ideals of the nineteenth century. To Southerners the North was a hotbed of radical "isms" (feminism, abolitionism, and socialism, among others), of puritan hypocrisy, and of crude parvenus. Each section reduced the other to a cultural stereotype and made it an object of hatred.

71. PURITANS AND CAVALIERS

In its most extreme form the explanation of cultural differences was based upon an alleged difference in population origins. Edward A. Pollard, a Southern partisan, develops this myth in The Lost Cause: A New Southern History of the War of the Confederates *(New York: 1866), pp. 46–52.*

No one can read aright the history of America, unless in the light of a North and a South: two political aliens existing in a Union imperfectly defined as a confederation of States. If insensible or forgetful of this theory, he is at once involved in an otherwise inexplicable mass of facts, and will in vain attempt an analysis of controversies, apparently the most various and confused.

The Sectional Animosity, which forms the most striking and persistent feature in the history of the American States, may be dated certainly as far back as 1787. . . . There was thus early recognized in American history a political North and a political South; the division being coincident with the line that separated the slave-holding from the non-slave-holding States. Indeed, the existence of these two parties and the line on which it was founded was recognized in the very framework of the Constitution. That provision of this instrument which admitted slaves into the rule of representation (in the proportion of three-fifths), is significant of a conflict between North and South; and as a compact between the slave-holding and non-slave-holding interests, it may be taken as a compromise between sections, or even, in a broader and more philosophical view, as a treaty between two nations of opposite civilizations. For we shall see that the distinction of North and South, apparently founded on slavery and traced by lines of climate, really went deeper to the very elements of the civilization of each; and that the Union, instead of being the bond of diverse States, is rather to be described, at a certain period of its history, as the forced alliance and rough companionship of two very different peoples. . . .

The North naturally found or imagined in slavery the leading cause of the distinctive civilization of the South, its higher sentimentalism, and its superior refinements of scholarship and manners. It revenged itself on the cause, diverted its envy in an attack upon slavery, and defamed the institution as the relic of barbarism and the sum of all villainies. But, whatever may have been the defamation of the institution of slavery, no man can write its history without recognizing contributions and naming prominent results beyond the domain of controversy. It bestowed on the world's commerce in a half-century a single product whose annual value was two hundred millions of dollars. It founded a system of industry by which labour and capital were identified in interest, and capital therefore protected labour. It exhibited the picture of a land crowned with abundance, where starvation was unknown, where order was preserved by an unpaid police; and where many fertile regions accessible only to the labour of the African were brought into usefulness, and blessed the world with their productions. . . .

In the ante-revolutionary period, the differences between the populations of the Northern and Southern colonies had already been strongly developed. The early colonists did not bear with them from the mother-country to the shores of the New World any greater degree of congeniality than existed among them at home. They had come not only from different stocks of population, but from the different feuds in religion and politics. There could be no congeniality between the Puritan exiles who established themselves upon the cold and rugged and cheerless soil of New England, and the Cavaliers who sought the brighter climate of the South, and drank in their baronial halls in Virginia confusion to roundheads and regicides.

In the early history of the Northern colonists we find no slight traces of the modern *Yankee;* although it remained for those subsequent influences which educate nations as well as individuals to complete that character, to add new vices to it, and to give it its full development. But the intolerance of the Puritan, the painful thrift of the Northern colonists, their external forms of piety, their jaundiced legislation, their convenient morals, their lack of the sentimentalism which makes up the half of modern civilization, and their unremitting hunt after selfish aggrandizement are traits of character which are yet visible in their descendants. On the other hand, the colonists of Virginia and the Carolinas were from the first distinguished for their polite manners, their fine sentiments, their attachment to a sort of feudal life, their landed gentry, their love of field-sports and dangerous adventure, and the prodigal and improvident aristocracy that dispensed its stores in constant rounds of hospitality and gaiety.

Slavery established in the South a peculiar and noble type of civilization. It was not without attendant vices; but the virtues which followed in its train were numerous and peculiar, and asserted the general good effect of the institution on the ideas and manners of the South. If habits of command sometimes degenerated into cruelty and insolence; yet, in the greater number of instances, they inculcated notions of chivalry, polished the manners and produced many noble and generous virtues. If the relief of a large class of whites from the demands of physical labour gave occasion in some instances for idle and dissolute lives, yet at the same time it afforded opportunity for extraordinary culture, elevated the standards of scholarship in the South, enlarged and emancipated social intercourse, and established schools of individual refinement. The South had an element in its society—a landed gentry—which the North envied, and for which its substitute was a coarse ostentatious aristocracy that smelt of the trade, and that, however it cleansed itself and aped the elegance of the South, and packed its houses with fine furniture, could never entirely subdue a sneaking sense of its inferiority. . . .

The civilization of the North was coarse and materialistic. That of the South was scant of shows, but highly refined and sentimental. The South was a vast agricultural country; waste lands, forest and swamps often gave to the eye a dreary picture; there were no thick and intricate nets of internal improvements to astonish and bewilder the traveller, no country picturesque with towns and villages to please his vision. Northern men ridiculed this apparent scantiness of the South, and took it as an evidence of inferiority. But this was the coarse judgment of the surface of things. The agricultural pursuits of the South fixed its features; and however it might decline in the scale of gross prosperity, its people were trained in the highest civilization, were models of manners for the whole country, rivalled the sentimentalism of the oldest countries of Europe, established the only schools of honour in America, and presented a striking contrast in their well-balanced character to the conceit and giddiness of the Northern people.

Foreigners have made a curious and unpleasant observation of a certain exaggeration of the American mind, an absurd conceit that was never done asserting the unapproachable excellence of its country in all things. . . .

But it is to be remarked that this boastful disposition of mind, this exaggerated conceit was peculiarly *Yankee*. It belonged to the garish civilization of the North. . . . It was Yankee orators who established the Fourth-of-July school of rhetoric, exalted the American eagle, and spoke of the Union as the last, best gift to man. This *afflatus* had but little place among the people of the South. Their civilization was a quiet one; and their characteristic as a people has always been that sober estimate of the value of men and things, which, as in England, appears to be the best evidence of a substantial civilization and a real enlightenment. Sensations, excitements on slight causes, fits of fickle admiration, manias in society and fashion, a regard for magnitude, display and exaggeration, all these indications of a superficial and restless civilization abounded in the North and were peculiar to its people. The sobriety of the South was in striking contrast to these exhibitions, and was interpreted by the vanity of the North as insensibility and ignorance, when it was, in fact, the mark of the superior civilization.

---

72. THE SOUTHERN GENTLEMAN

In an early attempt at a sociological analysis of a class structure, an antebellum Southerner, Daniel R. Hundley, described the Southern gentleman as a distinct type and as the finest product of Southern civilization. Social Relations in Our Southern States (New York: 1860), pp. 7–76.

To begin with his pedigree, . . . we may say, the Southern Gentleman comes of a good stock. Indeed, to state the matter fairly, he comes usually of aristocratic parentage; for family pride prevails to a greater extent in the South than in the North. In Virginia, the ancestors of the Southern Gentleman were chiefly English cavaliers, after whom succeeded the French Huguenots and Scotch Jacobites. . . . In South Carolina, they were Huguenots—at least the better class of them—those dauntless chevaliers, who . . . drained France of her most generous blood to found in the Western Hemisphere a race of heroes and patriots. . . .

Besides being of faultless pedigree, the Southern Gentleman is usually possessed of an equally faultless physical development. His average height is about six feet, yet he is rarely gawky in his movements, or in the least clumsily put together; and his entire *physique* conveys to the mind an impression of firmness united to flexibility. . . . We mention this subject, because the Northern people entertain in regard to it such very erroneous opinions. They have been told so incessantly of the lazy habits of Southerners, that they honestly believe them to be delicate good-for-nothings, like their own brainless fops and nincompoops. . . .

. . . [We] may attribute the good size and graceful carriage of the Southern Gentleman, to his out-of-doors and a-horseback mode of living. . . . By the time he is five years of age he rides well; and in a little while thereafter has a fowling-piece put into his hands, . . . and so accoutred, he sallies forth into the fields and pastures in search of adventure. . . .

. . . [The] natural manner of living in the Slave States helps to cover up a multitude of Southern shortcomings—tobacco-chewing, brandy-drinking, and other excesses of a like character—which would otherwise without doubt render the masses of the Southern people as fickle and unstable, as nervous and spasmodic, as the masses of the North. . . . Such irregularities, however, are not so frequently committed by the gentlemen of the South as by a certain class of underbred snobs, whose money enables them for a time to pretend to the character and standing of gentlemen, but whose natural inborn coarseness and vulgarity invariably lead them to disgrace the honorable title they assume to wear. The real gentlemen of the South are restrained by considerations of family pride, and family prestige, if by none more honorable. . . .

When the Southern Gentleman has fully completed his academic labors—has honorably gone through the University Curriculum—if his means be ample, he seldom studies a profession, but gives his education a finishing polish by making the tour of Europe; or else marries and settles down to superintend his estates, and devotes his talents to the raising of wheat, tobacco, rice, sugar, or cotton; or turns his attention to politics, and runs for the State Legislature. Should, however, the patrimonial estate be small, or the heirs numerous, . . . he then devotes himself to some one of the learned professions, or becomes an editor, or enters either the Army or the Navy. But of all things, he is most enamoured of politics and the Army; and it is owing to this cause, that the South has furnished us with all our great generals, from Washington to Scott, as well as most of our leading statesmen, from Jefferson to Calhoun. . . .

No matter what may be the Southern Gentleman's avocation, his dearest affections usually center in the country. He longs to live as his fathers lived before him, in both the Old World and the New; and he ever turns with unfeigned delight from the bustle of cities, the hollow ceremonies of courts, the turmoil of politics, the glories and dangers of the battle-field, or the wearisome treadmill of professional routine, to the quiet and peaceful scenes of country life. . . . The old hall, the familiar voices of old friends, the trusty and well remembered faces of the old domestics—these all are dearer to the heart of the Southern Gentleman than the short-lived plaudits of admiring throngs, or the hollow and unsatisfactory pleasures of sense. . . .

As it is our desire to present the reader faithful pictures of the home life of the Southern States, we wish we could fitly paint to his mind's eye how the Southern Gentleman appears when reclining under his own vine and fig-tree. Much has been said of his generous hospitality, but this to be fully appreciated should be enjoyed. We doubt if there is any where on the globe its parallel. Certainly in some portions of the South the Southern Gentleman does not live in very grand style . . . but he is always hospitable, gentlemanly, courteous, and more anxious to please than to be pleased. . . .

The natural dignity of manner peculiar to the Southern Gentleman, is doubtless owing to his habitual use of authority from his earliest years; for while coarser natures are ever rendered more savage and brutal by being allowed the control of others, refined natures on the contrary are invariably perfected by the same means, their sense of the responsibility and its incident obligations teaching them first to control themselves before attempting to exact obedience from the inferior natures placed under their charge. This is a fact which it were worth while to ponder thoughtfully, for herein lies the secret of the good breeding of the Gentleman of the South, and the chief reason why they seldom evince that flurry of manner so peculiar to many of our countrymen; and why, also, they manifest on all occasions the utmost self-possession—that much coveted *savoir faire*, which causes a man to appear perfectly at home, whether it be in a hut or a palace. Hence in manners the Southern Gentleman is remarkably easy and natural, never haughty in appearance, or loud of speech—even when angry rarely raising his voice above the ordinary tone of gentlemanly conversation.

---

73. THE ENVIOUS SOUTH

Below are several samples of the hatred that sectional partisans felt toward one another on the eve of the Civil War. The first is from the Chicago Tribune (*February 21, 1861*).

. . . [The] incitements of envy have much to do with the revolution. The North is prosperous and the South is not. The one increases and multiples by a process which freedom and civilization constantly accelerates. The South goes far backward by a process which ignorance and slavery inaugurate. The wealth, the power, the intelligence, the religion and advanced civilization are with the first. The last is stationary and retrograde. It is the infirmity of semi-barbarous men to hate what they cannot imitate; hence the bitterness which marks the utterances and emphasises the actions of the rebels. Dislike of what is above and beyond them is at the bottom of this.

---

74. THE BARBAROUS SOUTH

Milwaukee Sentinel (*April 15, 1861*).

The state of society in the South and their legislation, exhibits a growing tendency to lapse back into barbarism. There are but few schools, and the masses are growing up in ignorance and vice. Men resort to violence and bloodshed, rather than to calm discussion and courts of justice to settle their disputes and difficulties. All classes are impatient of restraint, and indulge in a reckless and lawless disregard and contempt of all institutions of society or religion which obstruct the free exercise of their passions and their prejudices. . . .

The Christian world rose up through just such a state of things to its present mild, moral, peaceable, humane, Christian and enlightened stand-point, and the South has already sunk three centuries back toward the age of barbarism.

---

75. WITH MALICE TOWARD SOUTHERNERS

Franklin Livingston to A. Burnham, March 6, 1861. Zachariah Chandler Papers, Library of Congress.

There is no sett of People on Gods Earth that I despise and hold in such utter contempt as I do those Southern Rebels . . . and I would rather meet them in deadly conflict than any other sett of men in [the] world, in fact I am at peace with the whole world, except them, and with them I confess, I have a deadly hatred. I have no compromise to make, short of a fulfilment of the penaltys of the violated laws.

---

76.   THE BOORISH NORTH

Muscogee, Georgia, Herald, *quoted in New York* Tribune *(September 10, 1856).*

Free society! we sicken at the name. What is it but a conglomeration of greasy mechanics, filthy operatives, small-fisted farmers, and moon-struck theorists? All the northern, and especially the New England states, are devoid of society fitted for well-bred gentlemen. The prevailing class one meets with is that of mechanics struggling to be genteel, and small farmers who do their own drudgery, and yet are hardly fit for association with a southern gentleman's body servant.

---

77.   "WE ARE ENEMIES"

Speech of Senator Alfred Iverson of Georgia, December 4, 1860, Congressional Globe, *36 Congress, 2 Session, p. 12.*

Sir, disguise the fact as you will, there is an enmity between the northern and southern people that is deep and enduring, and you never can eradicate it—never! You sit upon your side, silent and gloomy; we sit upon ours with knit brows and portentous scowls. . . . We are enemies as much as if we were hostile States. I believe that the northern people hate the South worse than ever the English people hated France; and I can tell my brethren over there that there is no love lost upon the part of the South.

---

78. YANKEES VS THE "TROPIC NORDICS"

Hamilton J. Eckenrode offers a novel cultural interpretation of the Civil War which emphasizes the impact of a subtropical environment on white Southerners. Describing his analysis as "an effort to apply anthropological science to American history," Eckenrode suggests that the South produced a new breed of men: the "Tropic Nordics." His interpretation appears in Jefferson Davis: President of the South (New York: 1923), *p.* 12–14, 17–18, 20–24.

The South, strange land of Anglo-Saxon conquerors and negro slaves, had drifted out of the nineteenth century into another epoch all its own. . . .

The world does not understand the ante-bellum South. The South was, in reality, quite as new as it was old: it represented a certain spiritual change in the Anglo-Saxon race. That race is predominantly and characteristically northern: thus, in India and Egypt, the Anglo-Saxon ever remains a stranger. This is because the Englishman has England to look back to. But the Anglo-Saxon in the South had no other country to look back to from his subtropical environment: he was a law unto himself. Consequently, in the South the Anglo-Saxon was feeling the pull of the tropics; he was beginning to be tropical while remaining, in large part, Nordic.

America was mainly settled, in the colonial period, by Nordics. . . . The distinguishing marks of the Nordic race are predominance in war and political capacity, together with the love of adventure. It took adventurous men to cross the sea in the seventeenth century and carve out homes in the forest. For more than a century the Nordic settlers of the various colonies retained most of the racial traits in common. In the Revolutionary period, the South consisted of Maryland, Virginia, North and South Carolina. All of these colonies, with the exception of South Carolina, were really northern, not southern. But when the South expanded into Georgia and Florida and Mississippi and Alabama and Louisiana and Texas, it became really southern subtropical. . . .

The border states were never easy in their minds about slavery.

They protested too much; they treated their slaves . . . well . . . ; they seldom plied the lash; they almost never killed them. It was different in the tropical South. There the Anglo-Saxon was a Nordic towering over inferiors. He worked his chattels; beat them; sometimes though not often, killed them. He did not, like the border Southerner, who was part Northerner, almost believe in his heart that slavery was wrong. No; slavery was right enough to the Nordics in the tropics—in the rice swamps, the cotton fields, the canebrakes. Slavery was so right to them that sometimes they demanded more slaves from Africa, since there were not enough of them to be drafted from the border states.

The Anglo-Saxons in the lower South were becoming tropicized; they were undergoing a transformation which might have had remarkable consequences if the northern Anglo-Saxons had not abruptly halted the process. In other words, the lower Southerners were becoming adapted to tropical life as no Nordics had been for ages. Being tropicals, not temperates, the lower Southerners thought little of the doctrine of the brotherhood of man. In the tropics, the natural relationship is that of master and servant. White men in the tropics do not prate of equality in the presence of elemental inequality. Political cajolery is not the method of managing the masses in the tropics, but naked force. Hypocrisy is not a vice of the south, but of the north. It springs from cold, slow blood, not from ardor and passion. Thus, the Anglo-Saxons in the far South, by 1850, had lost some of their race characteristics while retaining others in stronger form: northern respectability and idealism were gone, along with northern sourness, hardness, ava-rice. What was left was Anglo-Saxon pluck, resourcefulness, initiative. What had been added was a towering race pride and an inclination to ride over racial groups considered inferior. The Southerner was a type as yet new in history: he was the one real creation of America. New Englander, Yankee, was but English super-shopkeeper; Virginian was but English farmer plus imagina-tion and a sense of humor; but South Carolinian and Mississippian represented a distinct phase of human evolution. They were new. . . .

Both Northerner and Southerner had great virtues. New England was the cleanest and sanest community in the world. New Englanders were business men, scholars, athletes, altruists; New England women were cultivated companions. Lower Southerners (when they were not excessively religious) were hot-headed, genial sportsmen who would lend their last dollar to a friend and kill him for an ill-judged word. They were, in fact, partly mad, because they were Nordics baked in the sun, but it was a wonderful madness and better, in some ways, than sanity. Southern women were charming, if uneducated, and many of them were beautiful. With these divergencies, it is not to be wondered at that a rift appeared between the original Nordic race, as it was in the North, and the tropicized Nordics of the South which led to great consequences. This change in the Nordic race—this new development in the hot lands of America, unhampered by European restraints—is the main cause of the Civil War. Constitutional disagreements were only symptoms, economic differences were but a secondary cause. The first cause was tropicalism, and the next cotton; and tropicalism and cotton found expression in states' rights and secession. . . .

The North, with that shrewd Anglo-Saxon trick of putting an adversary in the wrong, called the lower South the Slave Power and its efforts to maintain the supremacy of agriculture the Great Conspiracy. The term "Slave Power" mistakes result for cause. The proper name is the Nordic South. If there had been no negro slaves, the development of the South would have been much what it was. A tropicized Anglo-Saxon population in the Gulf region would have preferred planting to mill-owning, would have attempted to extend farther southward, and would have defied the industrial North. Slavery has been too much glorified. It was but an incident in the conflict, the two determining factors of which were Nordic blood and hot climate. The Civil War was, in essence, a struggle between that part of the Nordic race which was prepared to renounce its tradition of mastery for equality, modernism and material comfort and that part of the race which was resolved, despite modernity, to remain true to its ruling instincts. It was a conflict between a community rapidly becoming un-Nordicized by industry and non-Nordic immigration and a community which had become more thoroughly Nordic than at the settlement by reason of slavery and purely agricultural pursuits. . . .

. . . The North put its faith in modern European theories and practices. It was one with Europe in placing emphasis on material well-being as the great attainable object in life. Humanity had abandoned its religious and political ideals, which distracted it so long, and had come down to an economic basis—an industrial basis. The South was the single exception in the civilized world. It was not materialistic and practical. It was drifting away from equality and the rights of man; from the tepid religion of the times; from Victorian commonplaceness; from the rather dismal civilization of the mid-nineteenth century, with its dull, conventional, ordered life. The South was drifting into the tropics, into a new environment. . . . It was the most remarkable development of the Nordic race in modern history, but it was a development that ran counter to all the tendencies of the North. . . .

. . . As time passed, the modernism of the North and the Nordicism of the South came more and more into conflict, politically and philosophically, foreshadowing the military struggle.

---

79. The Plantation Ideal

James Truslow Adams, in America's Tragedy, *pp. 88–96, describes the characteristics of plantation culture. Reprinted from* America's Tragedy, *by James Truslow Adams, copyright 1934, Charles Scribner's Sons. Used by permission of the publisher.*

The ideal which took root in the South was distinctly that of English country life in which the owners of broad acres should also constitute the dominant class in government. . . . The peaceful Southern planter played no such part as had the feudal lord of the past, but his large plantation, remote from others and on which he exercised a lavish hospitality, was nearer to the English country

estate of the upper middle class than anything else in America. . . .
Families intermarried and built up cliques which ruled socially and
politically. The aristocratic Southerner laid far more stress on
family, land, agreeable manners, and political power than he did on
mere wealth; and the long days on the plantation led him to cherish
social life as an art. His house was no bigger or better than the rich
Northerner's, for the best of the Southern houses . . . were merely
comfortable, moderate-sized country houses, which could easily be
duplicated in New England and elsewhere in the North. Nor was
there more luxury in the South in spite of the romantic tradition.
The silver plate gleamed as lavishly on Northern mahogany as on
Southern.

The difference lay in the hundreds or thousands of acres which
surrounded the Southerners' houses, and made of their owners
something quite different from merely rich men. It lay in the scores
to hundreds of slaves which made of their owners something
likewise quite different from the employer of casual labor in the
North. It lay in the ideal of public life and participation in it as part
of one's social status, and in the presence of a subordinate race, all
of which gave the Southerner the sense of belonging to a genuinely
governing class. . . .

. . . In town, where social life is largely, for men at least, the fag
end of a day during which they have been in contact with all sorts
of other men, it has not the same charm in and for itself that it has
in the country where visits of days or even weeks break the
monotony of otherwise lonely and unchanging life. . . . We need
not insist on the differences further but perhaps it may be accepted
that the able and important man who draws his wealth from the soil
on which he lives, where his family has lived for generations, and
where he expects them to continue to live, whose social position
and political power stem largely from his long association with a
particular estate, is quite different in make-up and outlook from the
man who draws *his* wealth and power from an office in a busy
commercial life where he has no roots. Even when there is no
marked social line drawn between such classes, as there was in
England, they will usually dislike and not understand each other.

The aristocratic Southerner was frequently highly educated, but in this also he differed from the Northerner of equal standing. From the manner of his life, new ideas were less insistent for him. . . . Rather, he steeped himself in history and classical literature, when he was intellectual, and in works on government, as befitted a man of a ruling class. At its best this type of culture produced a Jefferson, a Madison, and a Marshall. In the formative period of the nation, the intellect of the South, as far as the great and pressing problems of the day were concerned, was certainly superior to that of the North. . . .

After about 1830, however, there was a great change. While the North forged rapidly ahead, the South fell behind. This was notable in every direction, although the South was far from being the intellectual desert sometimes pictured. Nevertheless, the new leaders of the South—the Rhetts, Yanceys, Calhouns, Dews, Davises, Stephenses, and others—quite apart from the accident of their leading a cause that was to fail, cannot be compared with the Southern leaders of a generation or two earlier in sheer ability. Nor, if we accept almost any standard, . . . can the writers of the South in pure literature of this period compare with those of the North. . . . In fact the columns of *The Southern Literary Messenger* and other magazines and newspapers were filled with complaints to that effect, lamenting that there were no publishing houses in the section and that even the most ordinary school text books had to be imported from the North and were all written by Northerners. . . .

Even one who loves the South cannot fail to find something pathological in the intellectual life between 1830 and 1860. In the North the fresh winds of new ideas carried many voices on them, of which the often lying screeches of the Abolitionists were but one. In the South there seemed to be no winds, and only the refrain of slavery as against the world. In almost everything the South was aligned against the general movement of the times. In spite of occasional efforts to establish manufactures, the slave economy was essentially agrarian, whereas the world trend was toward industrialism. Southern churches, having to defined what those of the rest of the world mostly condemned, were forced to separate themselves. Authors had to engage largely in painting in the most attractive colors what the rest of the world considered wrong. Statesmen had continually to fight for an institution which was doomed by world judgment. Every political act, every constitutional question, had to be considered in the light of slavery. But this situation was fraught heavily with danger for the healthy spiritual life of both individuals and the people.

Modern psychology has taught us much of the hidden springs of the sub-conscious. It may seem absurd to speak of the proud, haughty, charming South suffering from an inferiority complex; yet it did precisely what a person or people so suffering always does. It not only withdrew itself into something of a dream world of its own, but having its standards and moral values attacked by the rest of the world it set up a defence mechanism by assuming other virtues superior to those of its attackers. . . . Walter Scott provided the escape. As they devoured his novels of feudal life, they came to think of themselves as knights with arms at rest against people who did not understand the laws of chivalry, as an aristocracy forced to defend themselves against plebeians. The theory of every Southerner a lord and every Southern woman a queen of love and beauty was born. . . . But the mechanism of defence did not stop with the setting of the South off in a world of romance. When the pressure became greater, . . . the Southerners evolved the theory that they belonged to a superior race. The extent to which this was carried in the leading journals of the section is only an indication of the degree of mental warping resulting from the necessity, for such it was, of standing out against world opinion with regard to what that opinion had come to consider a morally anachronistic type of civilization.

---

80.   WHERE THE DIFFERENCES LAY

A dispassionate and perceptive analysis of the cultural differences can be found in the following passages from Allan Nevins, Ordeal of the Union, *II, pp. 540–54. Reprinted from* Ordeal of the Union, *by Allan Nevins, copyright 1947, Charles Scribner's Sons. Used by permission of the publisher.*

. . . Asked just where, in detail, the differences of the South lay, we can answer under numerous headings.

The white population of the South was far more largely Anglo-Saxon than that of the North, for despite its numerous Germans, its hundred thousand Irish folk by 1860, its French Huguenots, and others, it was one of the purest British stocks in the world. Its dominant attitudes, as to the color line, were Anglo-Saxon. Its life was not merely rural, but rural after a special pattern; for the section was dotted over with large holdings representing great capital values and employing large bodies of slaves. It was a land of simple dogmatism in religion; of Protestant solidarity, of people who believed every word of the Bible, and of faith frequently refreshed by emotional revivalism. Its churches provided an emphasis on broadly social values contrasting with the intellectualization of morals to be found in the North. . . .

The South drew from its economic position a special set of tenets. . . . With equal inevitability, it drew from its minority position in the political fabric another special set of doctrines. It was a country in which romantic and hedonistic impulses, born of the opulence of nature, had freer rein than in the North. The phrases "the merry South," "the sunny South," connoted a great deal. . . . The remote quality attaching to much Southern life, which made some travellers feel they had dropped into another world, and the sharp contrast of races, added to the atmosphere of romance.

To a far greater degree than the North, the South was a land of class stratification and vestigial feudalism. Various explanations were given for this fact. One was . . . that Southerners were descendants of that portion of the English who were least modernized, and who "still retained a large element of the feudal notion." It is now known that no such distinction existed between Northern and Southern colonists, for honest middle-class folk, not feudal-minded cavaliers, made up the bulk of Virginia as of Massachusetts settlers. Slavery, the large plantation, and the agrarian cast of life, with some traditional inheritances from colonial days, accounted for the class structure. "Slavery helped feudalism," correctly remarked a Southern writer, "and feudalism helped slavery, and the Southern people were largely the outcome of the interaction of these two formative principles." . . .

[Taken] as a section, . . . the South had a life of far more aristocratic tone than the North. Both the central weakness of the South, and the main flaw in American social homogeneity, lay in the want of a great predominant body of intelligent, independent, thoughtful, and educated farmers in the slave States to match the similar body at the North. . . . A really strong Southern yeomanry could have clasped hands with Northern tillers of the soil. But the plantation system was inimical to any such body. . . .

Had Southern and Northern ideals of education been alike they would have done much to erase sectional lines, but they differed sharply. Education for utility was steadily gaining ground in the North; education for character and grace held sway in the South—and the scope of education was far from identical.

The relatively high development of colleges in the South, and the comparatively low provision of common schools, perfectly fitted a semi-aristocratic society sparsely scattered over an area which had all too little of a prosperous yeoman class. The Southern college was in general decently supported, decently staffed, and well attended. . . . The South boasted that it had not only established the first State universities, but had cherished the ideal of a college-trained leadership more fixedly than the North. . . .

Secondary education, too, fared not too ill in the South. In both sections this was the era of the academy, a transitional type of school which was in general privately endowed but sometimes under semi-public control, and which offered a steadily broadening curriculum. The nation by 1850 had just over six thousand academies, of which the very respectable number of 2,640 were in the Southern States. Estimates of the section's enrollment in these schools ran as high as two hundred thousand. . . . Of the nation's public high schools the South had only a handful—about thirty out of 321 listed in 1860. But the academies, practically all of them private institutions, many of them denomination-controlled, . . . were numerous enough to give a host of boys good grammar-school training. . . .

Yet in the elementary field the broad humanitarian ideals of

Jefferson failed. The South was for the most part a land without free public schools—a land where the poor man's son was likely to go untaught, and the workingman or small farmer to be ignorant if not illiterate. Here lay one of the great gulfs separating North from South. . . .

The cultivation of literature in the South was so sorely handicapped by social and economic factors that the effort to create a sectional literature terminated in total failure. The North summed up the reason for this failure in the word slavery. But a more complex explanation is required. The writers recognized that they worked in a highly unfavorable milieu. They needed one or several great cities, with capital and enterprise, where the attrition of intellects would sharpen the general mind; a larger middle class, accustomed to buying books and magazines; and some prosperous, well-circulated periodicals. They needed at least one real publisher; not a printer or bookseller, but a firmly established house like Harper's, Appleton's, or Little, Brown, issuing volumes week after week—ten or twenty a month—and therefore provided with facilities to advertise them, get them into a thousand bookstores, and sell them by mail. They needed the thousand bookshops. And finally, they needed a broader, stronger tradition of literary craftsmanship.

Southern magazines operated under the same disabilities. The *Southern Review*, founded in 1828, published some able contributions by Legaré, Thomas Cooper, Stephen Elliott, and others, but perished within five years. The *Southern Literary Messenger*, begun in 1838, had two editors of ability, Poe and John R. Thompson. In quality it possibly compared with the *Knickerbocker* or *Graham's*, but not with the *Atlantic* or *Putnam's*. And whatever its quality, it made little appeal to Southerners themselves. . . . The *Southern Quarterly Review* was printing three thousand copies in 1854, but it labored under heavy pecuniary embarrassments, and though its editor J. D. B. De Bow wrote that it represented "the last attempt to establish and build up Southern Literature," its influence was slight.

The trait which most heavily stamped Southern literature, whether in books or magazines, was its polemic or defensive quality. Literary expression in the North showed sporadic sectional rancor;

in the South this was a preoccupation which became painful. The section felt that with stormclouds lowering over it, every intellect was needed in the war for the defense of her institutions. Simms, finding his romances neglected, said goodbye to them and took up work instead that fostered Southern regard. From the moment of the Wilmot Proviso, his too-abundant literary productions fell into two channels, one of romantic dreams, the other of doctrinaire nightmares. As much could be said for many another writer. . . .

Altogether, South and North . . . were rapidly becoming separate peoples. The major Protestant denominations had broken in twain; one major party, the Whigs, had first split in half and then disappeared; press, pulpit, and education all showed a deepening cleavage. With every passing year, the fundamental assumptions, tastes, and cultural aims of the two sections became more divergent. As tensions grew, militant elements on both sides resented the presence of "outsiders"; Southerners were exposed to insult at Northern resorts, while Yankees in the South were compelled to explain their business to a more and more suspicious population.

The Southerners loved the Union, for their forefathers had helped to build it, and the gravestones of their patriot soldiers strewed the land. But they wanted a Union in which they could preserve their peculiar institutions, ancient customs, and well-loved ways of life and thought. They knew that all the main forces of modern society were pressing to create a more closely unified nation, and to make institutions homogeneous even if not absolutely uniform. Against this they recoiled; they wanted a hegemony, a loose confederacy, not a unified nation and a standardized civilization. . . .

This schism in culture struck into the very substance of national life. Differences of thought, taste, and ideals gravely accentuated the misunderstandings caused by the basic economic and social differences; the differences between a free labor system and a slave labor system, between a semi-industrialized economy of high productiveness and an agrarian economy of low productiveness. An atmosphere was created in which emotions grew feverish; in which every episode became a crisis, every jar a shock.

1.   THE CULT OF CHIVALRY

According to Rollin G. Osterweis, the unique culture of the antebellum South rested on a tripod: slavery, the plantation system, and a cluster of nineteenth-century ideas known as romanticism. His book, Romanticism and Nationalism in the Old South *(New Haven: Yale University Press, 1949), is an exploration of the third leg of this tripod, romanticism, whose most persistent manifestation he thinks was "the cult of chivalry." While Sir Walter Scott's* Waverly Novels *were popular enough among Northerners, Southerners, according to Osterweis, actually "sought to live them." Southern romanticism, he argues, was a fundamental determinant of Southern culture, and romantic nationalism, which produced the secession movement, was "its most ambitious impulse." Extracts from pages 132–38 reprinted by permission of the publisher.*

The idea of Southern nationalism, which developed chiefly in South Carolina during the decade before the Civil War, was the most ambitious romantic manifestation of the antebellum period. It is not unnatural that this energy-demanding and forward-looking trend should have been cradled in a hard-headed community. These were people anxious to lead—possessing political and intellectual talent, accumulated wealth, influential periodicals, and a past history of fiery, independent thinking. Around 1850 the Cotton Kingdom was looking for leadership; and the Palmetto State stood ready to fill the need. It was soon ahead of the times, waiting for the rest of the South to catch up with its daring plans.

The State of South Carolina, and the city of Charleston, were peculiarly well suited to lead the revolt toward separate Southern nationality. . . . Charleston was the one important center of city life on the Atlantic seaboard below Baltimore. Every February planters from a radius of several hundred miles would gather for a month in their Charleston town houses; during the summer, the threat of malaria in the country would bring many of them back again. While in town, they mingled with informed people from other sections of the South, and from the North as well. Their wide range of experience in plantation management, mercantile activity, and political life gave them powerful advantages for leadership. . . .

The idea of Southern nationalism emerged about 1850 out of an experience mainly native and nonromantic. During the ten years before the war, it took on a distinctive, romantic coloration. It lay rooted in the adventures of the American colonies themselves in 1776; in the Lockian philosophy of Thomas Cooper; in familiarity with the political devices suggested by the onetime American nationalist, John C. Calhoun; in the Tariff and Nullification episode between 1827 and 1833; in the problems produced by the territorial acquisitions of the Mexican War; in the various Southern economic conventions, down to and including the historic Nash-ville meeting of November, 1850. By the latter year, certainly, a group consciousness had developed, an *ethno-centrism*, an impulse for Southern nationalism. The impulse was so similar to the ideas of romantic nationalism, then prevalent in Europe, that it offered a natural affinity for those ideas.

The leadership for the translation of this impulse into action would come first from a group of South Carolinians, headed by Senator Barnwell, A. P. Butler, and the Elder Langdon Cheves. Later, others would take up the torch. . . .

The Carolinian conviction that Southerners comprised a separate cultural unit grew stronger from the concomitant belief that the rest of the country possessed an inferior civilization. So obvious was this attitude by 1860 that the correspondent of the London *Times* could grasp it completely. In a letter dated "Charleston, April 30, 1861," William Howard Russell declared:

Believe a Southern man as he believes himself and you must regard New England and the kindred states as the birthplace of impurity of mind among men and of unchastity of women—the home of Free Love, of Fourierism, of Infidelity, of Abolitionism, of false teachings in political economy and in social life; a land saturated with the drippings of rotten philosophy, with the poisonous infections of a fanatic press; without honor or modesty; whose wisdom is paltry cunning, whose valor and manhood have been swallowed up in a corrupt, howling demagoguery, and in the

marts of dishonest commerce. . . . These [Carolinian] gentlemen
are well-bred, courteous and hospitable. A genuine aristocracy,
they have time to cultivate their minds, to apply themselves to
politics and the guidance of public affairs. They travel and read,
love field sports, racing, shooting, hunting, and fishing, are bold
horsemen, and good shots. But after all, their state is a modern
Sparta—an aristocracy resting on a helotry, and with nothing
else to rest upon. . . .

"Nationalism," according to Hans Kohn, "is first and foremost a
state of mind, an act of consciousness, which since the French
Revolution has become more and more common to mankind." He
goes on to demonstrate that nationalities evolve from the living
forces of history and are therefore always fluctuating. Even if a new
nationality comes into being, it may perfectly well disappear again,
absorbed into a larger or a different nationality. This will happen
when the objective bonds that delimit the group are destroyed, for
nationality is born of the decision to form a nationality. But the
concept, in its developed stage, goes beyond the idea of the group
animated by common consciousness. It comprehends also the
striving by the group to find expression in the organized activity of
a sovereign state. Thus, the nationalism of the nineteenth century
was a fusion of an attitude of mind with a particular political form.

The application of these criteria to the history of the rise and fall
of the Confederacy, and the subsequent reintegration of the South
into the Union, is a documentary implementation of Kohn's
definition.

The movement for Southern independence was a manifestation
of romantic nationalism, as contrasted with the earlier nonromantic
type best exemplified in the creation of the United States of
America. This latter type may be conveniently labeled, "the
nationalism of the American Revolution"; it had been fed by
English national consciousness, evolving since Elizabethan days,
transplanted to the new land—and by the natural-rights philoso-
phies of the seventeenth century. American Revolutionary nationalism was a predominantly political occurrence, with the national
state formed before, or at least at the same time as, the rising tide

of national feeling. The emphasis was on universal standards and values—"inalienable Rights" and "Laws of Nature."

Southern nationalism, on the other hand, stressed the peculiarities of its particular traditions and institutions. In common with the romantic nationalism of central Europe in the nineteenth century, the frontiers of the existing state and the rising nationality did not coincide. The movement expanded in protest against, and in conflict with, the de facto government. The objective was not to alter the existing political organization, as in the case of the thirteen colonies, but to redraw boundaries that would conform to mythical but credited ethnographic needs. That the realities behind the myth were the institution of Negro slavery and the plantation system do not affect the situation. They merely provide the identifying features.

The evolution of the idea of Southern nationalism, by 1860, was thus in the general stream of mid-nineteenth-century romantic thinking. "The Age of Nationalism," Professor Kohn suggests, "stressed national pasts and traditions against the rationalism of the eighteenth century with its emphasis on the common sense of civilization." The tendency in Europe was to weave the myths of the past and the dreams of the future into the picture of an ideal fatherland—an ideal to be striven for with deep emotional fervor.

This tendency was adapted to the Southern scene. From the past Virginia resurrected her George Washington, who had led an earlier crusade for independence; Maryland recalled her heroes in Randall's stirring stanzas; Carolina cherished the cult of Calhoun; Louisiana pointed to her proud Creole heritage.

All this hewed to the line of romantic nationalism in Europe, where "each new nation looked for its justification to its national heritage—often reinterpreted to suit the supposed needs of the situation—and strove for its glorification."

82.   A CONFLICT OF BOURGEOIS AND PREBOURGEOIS CULTURES

Eugene D. Genovese, in The Political Economy of Slavery (*New York: Random House, 1965*), *explains the Civil War as an attempt by a prebourgeois Southern ruling class of planters to maintain its position and protect its distinctive culture from the encroachments of the bourgeois North. Extracts from pages 28–31, 34–36 reprinted with the permission of Pantheon Books, a division of Random House. © 1961 by Eugene D. Genovese.*

The planters commanded Southern politics and set the tone of social life. Theirs was an aristocratic, antibourgeois spirit with values and mores emphasizing family and status, a strong code of honor, and aspirations to luxury, ease, and accomplishment. In the planters' community, paternalism provided the standard of human relationships, and politics and statecraft were the duties and responsibilities of gentlemen. The gentleman lived for politics, not, like the bourgeois politician, off politics.

The planter typically recoiled at the notions that profit should be the goal of life; that the approach to production and exchange should be internally rational and uncomplicated by social values; that thrift and hard work should be the great virtues; and that the test of the wholesomeness of a community should be the vigor with which its citizens expand the economy. The planter was no less acquisitive than the bourgeois, but an acquisitive spirit is compatible with values antithetical to capitalism. The aristocratic spirit of the planters absorbed acquisitiveness and directed it into channels that were socially desirable to a slave society: the accumulation of slaves and land and the achievement of military and political honors. Whereas in the North people followed the lure of business and money for their own sake, in the South specific forms of property carried the badges of honor, prestige, and power. . . .

Slavery established the basis of the planter's position and power. It measured his affluence, marked his status, and supplied leisure for social graces and aristocratic duties. The older bourgeoisie of New

England in its own way struck an aristocratic pose, but its wealth was rooted in commercial and industrial enterprises that were being pushed into the background by the newer heavy industries arising in the West, where upstarts took advantage of the more lucrative ventures like the iron industry. In the South few such opportunities were opening. The parvenu differed from the established planter only in being cruder and perhaps sharper in his business dealings. The road to power lay through the plantation. The older aristocracy kept its leadership or made room for men following the same road. An aristocratic stance was no mere compensation for a decline in power; it was the soul and content of a rising power. . . .

At their best Southern ideals constituted a rejection of the crass, vulgar, inhumane elements of capitalist society. The slaveholders simply could not accept the idea that the cash nexus offered a permissible basis for human relations. Even the vulgar parvenu of the Southwest embraced the plantation myth and refused to make a virtue of necessity by glorifying the competitive side of slavery as civilization's highest achievement. The slaveholders generally, and the planters in particular, did identify their own ideals with the essence of civilization and, given their sense of honor, were prepared to defend them at any cost.

This civilization and its ideals were antinational in a double sense. The plantation offered virtually the only market for the small non-staple-producing farmers and provided the center of necessary services for the small cotton growers. Thus, the paternalism of the planters toward their slaves was reinforced by the semipaternal relationship between the planters and their neighbors. The planters, in truth, grew into the closest thing to feudal lords imaginable in a nineteenth-century bourgeois republic. The planters' protestations of love for the Union were not so much a desire to use the Union to protect slavery as a strong commitment to localism as the highest form of liberty. They genuinely loved the Union so long as it alone among the great states of the world recognized that localism had a wide variety of rights. The Southerners' source of pride was not the Union, nor the nonexistent Southern nation; it was the plantation, which they raised to a political principle. . . .

The South's slave civilization could not forever coexist with an increasingly hostile, powerful, and aggressive Northern capitalism. On the one hand, the special economic conditions arising from the dependence on slave labor bound the South, in a colonial manner, to the world market. The concentration of landholding and slaveholding prevented the rise of a prosperous yeomanry and of urban centers. The inability to build urban centers restricted the market for agricultural produce, weakened the rural producers, and dimmed hopes for agricultural diversification. On the other hand, the same concentration of wealth, the isolated, rural nature of the plantation system, the special psychology engendered by slave ownership, and the political opportunity presented by separation from England, converged to give the South considerable political and social independence. This independence was primarily the contribution of the slaveholding class, and especially of the planters. Slavery, while it bound the South economically, granted it the privilege of developing an aristocratic tradition, a disciplined and cohesive ruling class, and a mythology of its own.

Aristocratic tradition and ideology intensified the South's attachment to economic backwardness. Paternalism and the habit of command made the slaveholders tough stock, determined to defend their Southern heritage. The more economically debilitating their way of life, the more they clung to it. It was this side of things—the political hegemony and aristocratic ideology of the ruling class— rather than economic factors that prevented the South from relinquishing slavery voluntarily.

As the free states stepped up their industrialization and as the westward movement assumed its remarkable momentum, the South's economic and political allies in the North were steadily isolated. Years of abolitionist and free soil agitation bore fruit as the South's opposition to homesteads, tariffs, and internal improvements clashed more and more dangerously with the North's economic needs. To protect their institutions and to try to lessen their economic bondage, the slaveholders slid into violent collision with Northern interests and sentiments. The economic deficiencies of slavery threatened to undermine the planters' wealth and power. Such relief measures as cheap labor and more land for slave states (reopening the slave trade and territorial expansion) conflicted with Northern material needs, aspirations, and morality. The planters faced a steady deterioration of their political and social power. Even if the relative prosperity of the 1850s had continued indefinitely, the slave states would have been at the mercy of the free, which steadily forged ahead in population growth, capital accumulation, and economic development. Any economic slump threatened to bring with it an internal political disaster, for the slaveholders could not rely on their middle and lower classes to remain permanently loyal.

When we understand that the slave South developed neither a strange form of capitalism nor an undefinable agrarianism but a special civilization built on the relationship of master to slave, we expose the root of its conflict with the North. The internal contradictions in the South and the external conflict with the North placed the slaveholders hopelessly on the defensive with little to look forward to except slow strangulation. Their only hope lay in a bold stroke to complete their political independence and to use it to provide an expansionist solution for their economic and social problems. The ideology and psychology of the proud slaveholding class made surrender or resignation to gradual defeat unthinkable, for its fate, in its own eyes at least, was the fate of everything worthwhile in Western civilization.

---

83. "Northern Progress and Southern Decadence"

Eric Foner, in Free Soil, Free Labor, Free Men (*New York: Oxford University Press, 1970*), *stresses the progressive, free-labor, anti-slavery ideology of the Republican party as central to the cultural conflict between North and South. Thus Foner and Genovese together portray two cultures so different in their values and goals as to make sectional conflict well-nigh inevitable. Extracts from pages 38–39, 40–41, 51, 69–72 of Foner's book reprinted with permission of Oxford University Press.*

To the self-confident society of the North, economic development, increasing social mobility, and the spread of democratic institutions were all interrelated parts of nineteenth century "progress." . . . Horace Greeley predicted that the age which had witnessed the invention of railroads, telegraphs, and other marvels could not depart "without having effected or witnessed a vast change for the better, alike in the moral and physical condition of mankind." The important point was that material and moral developments were but two sides of the same coin. "Good roads and bridges," wrote the New York *Tribune*, "are as necessary an ingredient to the spread of intelligence, social intercourse, and improvement in population, as schools and churches." . . . It was but a short step, and one which Republicans took almost unanimously, to the view that for a society as for individuals, economic progress was a measure of moral worth. As Henry Adams later recalled, he was taught in his youth that "bad roads meant bad morals." On this basis, northern society was eminently successful. But when Republicans turned their gaze southward, they encountered a society that seemed to violate all the cherished values of the free labor ideology, and seemed to pose a threat to the very survival of what Republicans called their "free-labor civilization." . . .

The northern image of the South was not, as some historians appear to believe, based merely on the imaginations of abolitionists. Many Republican leaders had first-hand knowledge of economic and social conditions in slave society, and Republican newspapers carried countless reports from travelers to the slave states and the testimony of southern spokesmen themselves. The burden of this evidence was always the same—the southern economy was backward and stagnant, and slavery was to blame. . . .

The whole mentality and flavor of southern life thus seemed antithetical to that of the North. Instead of progress, the South represented decadence, instead of enterprise, laziness. "Thus it appears," wrote the anti-slavery writer and historian Richard Hildreth, "that one plain and obvious effect of the slaveholding system is to deaden in every class of society that *spirit of industry* essential to the increase of public wealth." To those with visions of a steadily growing nation, slavery was an intolerable hindrance to national achievement. Seward . . . saw most clearly the way in which slavery stood in the way of national greatness. Slavery, he declared, was "incompatible with all . . . the elements of the security, welfare, and greatness of nations." . . . The question of restricting and ultimately abolishing slavery, he declared, was the question of "whether impartial public councils shall leave the free and vigorous North and West to work out the welfare of the country, and drag the reluctant South up to participate in the same glorious destinies." . . .

"By 1860," William R. Taylor has written, "most Americans had come to look upon their society and culture as divided between a North and a South, a democratic, commercial civilization and an aristocratic, agrarian one." . . . James S. Pike had written in the New York *Tribune* . . . of the "two opposing civilizations" within the nation, and an Ohio Congressman declared . . . that the sectional struggle was "not between the North and South . . . but between systems, between civilizations." . . .

By 1860, the irrepressible conflict idea was firmly imbedded in the Republican mind. "I regret the facts," Justin Morrill wrote in December, 1860, "but we must accept the truth that there is an 'irrepressible conflict' between our systems of civilization." Not only the labor system of the South and its aristocratic social structure, but its entire way of life seemed alien to the Republicans. . . . Israel Washburn declared that the effects of the peculiar institution could be seen in "the manners, customs, social codes, and moral standards" of the South. Republicans who came into contact with the South commented upon the feeling that they were in an alien land. . . . Aaron Cragin, a New Hampshire Congressman, observed after hearing a southern speech, "this language of feudalism and aristocracy has a strange sound to me." Cragin's use of the word "feudalism" in reference to the South is especially revealing, for to many Republicans the slave states seemed relics from a bygone age. . . .

Whether or not the North and South were in reality so different that the idea of an irrepressible conflict between opposing civilizations has historical validity, is still an open question. . . . There is no doubt, however, that a prominent strain in the ideology of the ante-bellum South . . . stressed aristocratic values and the virtues of an ordered, hierarchical society. . . . As for the Republicans, whatever their differences on specific political issues and strategies, they were united in their devotion to the mores and values of northern society, and in their conviction of the superiority of the North's civilization to that of the South. . . .

The Republicans saw their anti-slavery program as one part of a world-wide movement from absolutism to democracy, aristocracy to equality, backwardness to modernity, and their conviction that the struggle in the United States had international implications did much to strengthen their resolve. They accepted the characteristic American vision of the United States as an example to the world of the social and political benefits of democracy, yet believed that so long as slavery existed, the national purpose of promoting liberty in other lands could not be fulfilled. Lincoln declared in 1854 that slavery "deprives our Republican example of its just influence in the world—enables the enemies of free institutions to taunt us as hypocrites." . . . Yet as they looked at the world around them, Republicans could not but be confident that they were on the side of history. Carl Schurz captured this outlook in 1860 when he said:

> Slaveholders of America, I appeal to you. Are you really in earnest when you speak of perpetuating slavery? Shall it never cease? Never? Stop and consider where you are and in what day you live. . . . This is the world of the nineteenth century. . . . You stand against a hopeful world, alone against a great century, fighting your hopeless fight . . . against the onward march of civilization.

The Republicans were confident that in the sectional struggle, which one newspaper summarized as a contest between "Northern Progress and Southern Decadence," southern civilization must give way before the onslaught of the modern world.

———

84. "The Central Theme of Southern History"

Ulrich B. Phillips, in an article entitled "The Central Theme of Southern History," American Historical Review, XXXIV (1928), pp. 30–43, defines the crucially distinctive element in Southern society far more narrowly. One can easily infer from his article that the Civil War was fundamentally a Southern struggle to maintain the supremacy of the white race and white civilizations. Extracts reprinted by permission of the American Historical Review.

An Ohio River ferryman has a stock remark when approaching the right bank: "We are now approaching the American shore." A thousand times has he said it with a gratifying repercussion from among his passengers; for its implications are a little startling. The northern shore is American without question; the southern is American with a difference. Kentucky had by slender pretense a star in the Confederate flag; for a time she was officially neutral; for all times her citizens have been self-consciously Kentuckians, a distinctive people. They are Southerners in main sentiment, and so are Marylanders and Missourians.

Southernism did not arise from any selectiveness of migration, for the sort of people who went to Virginia, Maryland, or Carolina were not as a group different from those who went to Pennsylvania or the West Indies. It does not lie in religion or language. It was not created by one-crop tillage, nor did agriculture in the large tend to produce a Southern scheme of life and thought. The Mohawk valley was for decades as rural as that of the Roanoke; wheat is as dominant in Dakota as cotton has ever been in Alabama; tobacco is as much a staple along the Ontario shore of Lake Erie as in the Kentucky penny-royal; and the growing of rice and cotton in California has not prevented Los Angeles from being in a sense the capital of Iowa. On the other hand the rise of mill towns in the Carolina piedmont and the growth of manufacturing at Richmond and Birmingham have not made these Northern. . . .

The South has never had a focus. New York has plied as much of its trade as Baltimore or New Orleans; and White Sulphur Springs did not quite eclipse all other mountain and coast resorts for vacation patronage. The lack of a metropolis was lamented in 1857 by an advocate of Southern independence, as an essential for shaping and radiating a coherent philosophy to fit the prevailing conditions of life. But without a consolidating press or pulpit or other definite apparatus the South has maintained a considerable solidarity through thick and thin, through peace and war and peace again. What is its essence? Not state rights—Calhoun himself was for years a nationalist, and some advocates of independence hoped for a complete merging of the several states into a unitary Southern republic; not free trade—sugar and hemp growers have ever been protectionists; not slavery—in the eighteenth century this was of continental legality, and in the twentieth it is legal nowhere; not Democracy—there were many Federalists in Washington's day and many Whigs in Clay's; not party predominance by any name, for Virginia, Georgia, and Mississippi were "doubtful states" from Jackson's time to Buchanan's. It is not the land of cotton alone or of plantations alone; and it has not always been the land of "Dixie," for before its ecstatic adoption in 1861 that spine-tingling tune was a mere "Walk around" of Christie's minstrels. Yet it is a land with a unity despite its diversity, with a people having common joys and common sorrows, and, above all, as to the white folk a people with a common resolve indomitably maintained—that it shall be and remain a white man's country. The consciousness of a function in these premises, whether expressed with the frenzy of a demagogue or maintained with a patrician's quietude, is the cardinal test of a Southerner and the central theme of Southern history.

It arose as soon as the negroes became numerous enough to create a problem of race control in the interest of orderly government and the maintenance of Caucasian civilization. Slavery was instituted not merely to provide control of labor but also as a system of racial adjustment and social order. And when in the course of time slavery was attacked, it was defended not only as a vested interest, but with vigor and vehemence as a guarantee of white supremacy and civilization. Its defenders did not always take pains to say that this was what they chiefly meant, but it may nearly always be read between their lines, and their hearers and readers understood it without overt expression. Otherwise it would be impossible to account for the fervid secessionism of many non-slaveholders and the eager service of thousands in the Confederate army.

-----

85.   A "Crisis of Fear"

Steven A. Channing, in a study of the secession crisis in South Carolina, concludes that fear of the free black was the force that drove that state out of the Union. By linking slavery with "white supremacy," Channing gives support to U. B. Phillips' conception of the distinctive feature of antebellum Southern society. Crisis of Fear: Secession in South Carolina (New York: Simon and Schuster, 1970). Extracts from page 264–65, 282, 286–87, 289, 293 reprinted by permission of Simon and Schuster. Copyright © 1970, by Steven A. Channing.

. . .[The] most powerful force at work in South Carolina contributing to the remarkable unanimity of sentiment in December [1860] was . . . the basic fear of the Negro. The reemergence of a profusion of news stories detailing the activities of suspected abolitionists in the South during the summer campaign has often been noted. . . . There is little doubt that terrible stories of black unrest, and abolitionist infiltration were seized upon by advocates of disunion without regard to their veracity. And the reason was that there was no more potent weapon with which to prove the perfidy of Northerners and the disadvantages and dangers of remaining in the Union; such stories merely played upon the Southern fear of the Negro, they did not create it. The fear-of-insurrection-abolition syndrome was the *core* of the secession persuasion, not its vehicle. The multiplicity of news items reporting incendiary activities of slaves and abolitionists was not the fabrication of a segment of the Southern elite, but a natural result and expression of the anxiety which existed in the mind of the entire white population. . . .

The secession of South Carolina was an affair of passion. The revolution could not have succeeded, and it certainly would not have instilled the astounding degree of unanimity in all classes and all sections that it did, were this not so. The emotional momentum was a function of the intensity of the fear which drove the revolution forward. Divisions, doubts about the wisdom or efficacy of secession were met, or overturned. . . .

Secession was the product of logical reasoning within a framework of irrational perception. The party of Abraham Lincoln was inextricably identified with the spirit represented by John Brown, William Lloyd Garrison, and the furtive incendiary conceived to be lurking even then in the midst of the slaves. The election of Lincoln was at once the expression of the will of the Northern people to destroy slavery, and the key to that destruction. . . . [It] was believed that that election had signalled an acceptance of the antislavery dogmas by a clear majority of Northerners, and their intention to create the means to abolish slavery in America. Lincoln was elected, according to South Carolinians, on the platform of an "irrepressible conflict." . . . Implementing the power of the Presidency, and in time the rest of the Federal machinery, slavery would be legally abolished in time. What would that bring? Baptist minister James Furman thought he knew.

Then every negro in South Carolina and every other Southern State will be his own master; nay, more than that, will be the equal of every one of you. If you are tame enough to submit, Abolition preachers will be at hand to consummate the marriage of your daughters to black husbands.

. . . [The] conclusion is inescapable that the multiplicity of fears revolving around the maintenance of race controls for the Negro was not simply the prime concern of the people of South Carolina in their revolution, but was so very vast and frightening that it literally consumed the mass of lesser "causes" of secession which have inspired historians. . . .

. . . [Somewhere] in the intellectual hiatus of the war the clear and concrete understanding of the cause of it all, an understanding shared by those who joined to tear away from the Union, was lost.

For the people of South Carolina perpetuation of the Union beyond 1860 meant the steady and irresistible destruction of slavery, which was the first and last principle of life in that society, the only conceivable pattern of essential race control. Perpetuation of the Union, according to Senator [James H.] Hammond, meant servile insurrection, and ultimately abolition. "We dissolve the Union to prevent it," he told a Northerner in 1861. . . . Secession was a revolution of passion, and the passion was fear.

---

86.   SECTIONALISM AND AMERICAN POLITICAL CULTURE

Antebellum American culture was inseparable from its political life. Rural and small-town America had few social diversions, and the party rallies, parades, barbecues, and political speeches and debates were major social events and entertainments. Moreover, political campaigns were often waged with the moral fervor of religious revivals. Hence, some historians argue, the cultural roots of sectionalism were in part related to the idiom and beliefs generated over many years in the nation's intense political battles. In short, the rhetoric of sectional partisans was largely the traditional rhetoric of party politics. Joel H. Silbey develops this argument in "The Surge of Republican Power: Partisan Antipathy, American Social Conflict, and the Coming of the Civil War," in Stephen E. Maizlish and John J. Kushma (eds.), Essays on American Antebellum Politics, 1840–1860 (College Station, Texas: Texas A&M University Press, 1982). Extracts from pp. 209–12, 217–18, 227–29 reprinted with permission of the Walter Prescott Webb Memorial Lectures Committee, The University of Texas at Arlington.

To understand the perceptual prism through which secessionists viewed their [Republican] enemies, it is necessary first to comprehend the role, importance, and outlook of the larger community of which many of them were part. What framed political discourse and action, for all of the sectional tensions present, was an older and still powerful stream of political idiom and belief. There was a continuity to a particular kind of political confrontation in America from the 1830s onward that shaped the way events were seen at the moment of crisis. The political memories of southern secessionists contained crucial influences that interacted with their concerns about slavery and the Union to deepen and intensify their fears.

The secessionist prism was partisan. Southern perceptions were intertwined with their long-standing commitments to a particular political party. The most critical of all subcultures in the antebellum period were the political parties. . . . They helped to organize a vibrant, intense politics, one of great feeling, rhetorical exaggeration, and deep commitment. . . . There is strong evidence that they retained their important structuring effect throughout the 1840s and 1850s despite the rise of sectional tensions. . . .

Political parties brought together in disciplined ranks groups of like-minded individuals, their unity rooted in their common enemies, fears, desires, and attitudes. People caught up in partisan politics were schooled in certain unyielding truths. Parties were always at war with their opponents. Their perceptions of each other and their ideological commitments found expression in a divisive and rousing rhetoric. . . . By 1860, both the Democrats and the Republicans had fully developed and articulated clear perspectives about the policies and behavior of their adversaries. These perspectives were highly integrated. . . . Republicans talked about free soil, free labor, and a crusade for white freedom. But it was what the Democrats talked about in return that was central to the secession episode.

It was . . . the southern Democrats who dominated the movement to leave the Union. . . . What drove them were the specifics of Democratic perception and commitment. . . . The Democratic assault throughout the 1850s furnished southerners with a perspective on their immediate political situation. This perspective provided for the faithful an image of Republicans that guided Democrats in their reaction to the rise of the Republican party, the election of Lincoln, and most specifically to the crisis that followed. . . .

[Southerners] viewed the Republicans as meddlesome interventionists willing to crusade persistently against the institution of slavery. But what should not be underestimated was the way northern and southern Democrats in the 1850s rooted such meddlesomeness in ethnocultural conflicts which were, in their view, the centerpieces of Republican advance. . . . Republican rapprochement with nativist movements in the mid-fifties and acceptance, as the Democrats believed, of the program and goals of the latter had made the larger threat clear. The coming of the immigrant, the Democrats suggested, had caused New England Puritans to revert "to the intolerant fanaticism which marked their early colonial history." . . . [Republican] newspapers "boldly" avow "that it is the mission of the Republican party to overthrow Democracy, Catholicism, and Slavery." . . .

But there was a second and much more threatening danger: the willingness of the Republican party to use state power to impose the peculiar standards of Puritanism on everyone else. The use of government for such purpose had been a hallmark of early Puritanism, . . . but it was now brought to a high pitch by the Republicans. . . . The Republicans, Democrats argued, were fostering an aggressive and uncompromising program of coercive cultural legislation [such as prohibition laws] designed to order and direct individual behavior within the Union. . . .

The South was vulnerable to the Republican threat, southern Democrats argued from the mid-fifties on. Republicans were fanatics unable to forgo their commitment to regulate and reform. They might speak conservatively about slavery when it suited them and claim to recognize the South's constitutional rights, but how could they be trusted or believed? . . . The same power used to defeat drunken Irish Catholics could be used to destroy slavery. . . . The Republican conception of a restrictive-coercive government would be as dangerous to slavery as it was proving to be to freewheeling social habits and religious nonconformity. . . .

After the rise of ethnocultural issues, therefore, no southerner could blink his eyes at alleged threats to slavery or ignore the clear evidence that there was no hope at all for any peculiar values, ideas, or institutions if the Republicans won. Years of partisan warfare told all that was at stake. . . . Partisan and sectional ideologies converged and sharpened as they interacted in the fifties. Both ethnocultural and slavery-sectional issues defined the Republicans. Both were part of the same parcel, the plans of a small group of regional fanatics to dominate the Union and their willingness to use state coercion not simply in the name of power but in the name of values rooted in a particular and narrow religious perspective. . . .

Secessionists constantly made the connection between "black" Republicanism and other peculiar "isms" associated with the electoral revolt of the mid-fifties. All of these were united and integrated, and to southerners especially they were devastating. As secessionists read the political world now unfolding, Republican rule would lead to an unacceptably restrictive society with a dominant, snooping, interfering government forcing conformity to a narrow set of behavioral norms. . . . The long adherence to partisan Democratic values and assumptions provided them with a perspective that fortified and intensified the fears constantly stimulated since 1854 over the future of their institutions, values, and chosen behavior. With Lincoln, the interventionist Republican, about to assume office, they acted.

---

87. SOUTHERN HONOR

Bertram Wyatt-Brown, in Yankee Saints and Southern Sinners *(Baton Rouge: Louisiana State University Press, © 1985), does not question the significance of slavery as a cause of the Civil War, but he subsumes it in a broader cultural context, especially in the concept of Southern honor. Extracts from pages 183–89, 197, 198–201 reprinted by permission of Louisiana State University Press.*

Who nowadays would dare to substitute another theory for the long-standing view that slavery was the sole cause for the great catastrophe? . . . At a time when scholars agree about very little, it would be perverse to cast doubt upon so acceptable a proposition. . . .

Nevertheless, it is also true that direct jeopardy to the institution was distant, despite the results of the 1860 [presidential] contest. . . . Moreover, recent studies have cast doubt on the once popular view that disunionism was exclusively the work of the wealthiest Lower South slaveholders defending their gains and livelihood. Instead, the planter class was sharply divided on the right response to Lincoln's installation. . . . The wealthy James Henry Hammond [of South Carolina] . . . believed that the best course would be revival of the old cross-sectional conservative alliance that had held the Union together in the past.

The reluctance of those with the most to lose was only one of several indications that more than just slavery was at work in the secessionist dynamic. Slavery was itself inseparable from other aspects of regional life, most especially from the southerners' sense of themselves as people. That self-perception can be called the principle of honor. . . . [Though] sometimes seen as simply a "romance" to prettify the harsh reality of race control, it was a powerful force in the nineteenth-century South. . . .

In regard to traditional honor, the concept involves process more than merely an idealization of conduct. First, honor is a sense of personal worth and it is invested in the whole person. Yet that whole covers more than the individual—it includes the identification of the individual with his blood relations, his community, his state, and whatever other associations the man of honor feels are important for establishing his claim for recognition. The close bonding of honor with an extended self, as it were, contrasts with the kind of honor that would place country before family, professional duty before other matters of importance. Second, honor as a dynamic connecting self and society requires that the individual make a claim for worthiness before the community, and third, it involves the acceptance of that self-evaluation in the public forum, a ratification that enables the claimant to know his place in society and his moral standing. . . . Unlike the man of conscience, the individual dependent on honor must have respect from others as the prime means for respecting himself. Shifting fortunes, personal rivalries, worrisome doubts that one has been properly assessed make the ethical scheme an elusive, tense, and ultimately insecure method of self-acceptance. Western man has always known that traditional honor, being dependent upon public sanction, is a fickle mistress.

Ambiguities abound. On the one hand, moderation, prudence, coolness under duress, and self-restraint are admired and even idealized.. The southern "Nestors" who urged calm deliberateness before entering on secession hoped to have these qualities approved in the public arena. On the other hand, the man of honor feels that defense of reputation and virility must come before all else. Otherwise he is open to charges of effeminacy and fear. . . .

In political terms, honor was not at all confined to those at the top of the social order. It is the nature of the ethic that it must be recognized by those with less status; otherwise, there would be none to render honor to claimants. In the American South, common folk, though not given to gentlemanly manners, duels, and other signs of superior elan, also believed in honor because they had access to the means for its assertion themselves—the possession of slaves—and because all whites, nonslaveholders as well, held sway over all blacks. Southerners regardless of social position were united in the brotherhood of white-skinned honor. . . .

. . . Politics was an arena in which peers—not necessarily the greatest magnates—were rivals for public acclaim and power. As a forum for self-presentation and public service, politics was a simple system to which elaborate bureaucracies, heavy taxes, statutory refinements, and other complexities were alien. Even the notion of party organization, as opposed to community consensus and unanimity on key principles, was suspect, at least among the firebrands for disunionism. In all societies where honor of this kind functions, the great distinction is drawn between the autonomy, freedom, and self-sufficiency of those in the body politic and the dependency, forced submissiveness, and powerlessness of all who are barred from political and social participation—that is, slaves or serfs. For the southern free white, dependency posed the threat of meaninglessness. Slaveholding ennobled, that is, enhanced one's status and independence because ownership provided the instruments for exercising power, not over the slave alone, but over those without that resource. By the same social perception, thralldom degraded and humbled. . . .

Under these circumstances, the reasons why the southerner felt so threatened by northern criticism should be clear. The dread of public humiliation, especially in the highly charged political setting, was a burden not to be casually dismissed. In general terms, whenever the public response to claims for respect is indifferent, disbelieving, hostile, or derisive, the claimant for honor feels as blasted, as degraded as if struck in the face or unceremoniously thrown to the ground. He is driven to a sense of shame—the very opposite of honor. The response is twofold: first, a denial that he, a persecuted innocent, seeks more than his due; and second, his outraged "honor" requires immediate vindication, by force of arms if need be. This was especially true for the antebellum southerner because he could hardly escape doubts that his section was perceived by the world as inferior, morally and materially. "Reputation is everything," said James Henry Hammond. "Everything with me depends upon the estimation in which I am held," confessed secessionist thinker Beverley Tucker. Personal reputation for character, valor, and integrity did not end there. Individual self-regard encompassed wider spheres. As a result, the southerner took as personal insult the criticisms leveled at slave society as a whole. . . .

Given the character of southern politics and its ethical framework, the road to secession does not seem so puzzling. In responding to northern criticism and self-assertiveness, the South's defenders had to emphasize vindication and vengeance. As a result, the purpose of so much southern rhetoric in the prewar period was to impugn the motives and policies of the abolitionists in and out of Congress. Any number of examples might be cited to show how southern anguish at criticism reflected the psychological processes of injured pride. Abolitionists like Garrison thought that their sermons against slavery would force the slaveholder to listen to his conscience, but the effort was futile. Instead, antislavery polemics evoked feelings, not of guilt, but of anger and indignation. . . .

. . . Southern spokesmen inflated antislavery denunciations to the level of treachery, betrayal, insurrection, and devilish anarchy.

Antislavery attacks stained the reputation by which southern whites judged their place and power in the world. Such, for instance, was the reason why slaveholders insisted on the right to carry their property into the free territories at will. It was not solely a matter of expanding slavery's boundaries, though that was of course important. No less significant, however, was southern whites' resentment against any congressional measure which implied the moral inferiority of their region, labor system, or style of life. Such reflections on southern reputation were thought vile and humiliating. . . . As [Robert] Toombs [of Georgia] remarked in Congress during the sectional crisis of 1850, the right to enter any territory with slaves involved "political equality, [a status] worth a thousand such Unions as we have, even if they each were a thousand times more valuable than this." The issue was no small matter, in his opinion. He elevated the question of slaveholders' territorial prerogatives to the level of a casus belli, at least to his own satisfaction. "Deprive us of this right," he warned the Senate, and it becomes "your government, not mine. Then I am its enemy, and I will then, if I can, bring my children and my constituents to the altar of liberty, and . . . swear them eternal hostility to your foul domination." . . .

In societies where honor thrives, death in defense of community and principle is a path to glory and remembrance, whereas servile submission entails disgrace. . . . Nullifiers . . . as well as secessionists later, often posed the splendors of honor against the degeneracy and cowardly temptation of peaceful capitulation. . . . Dread of shameful subservience became a more pronounced southern theme after Lincoln's election. For instance, Alcibiade De Blanc of Saint Martin Parish introduced to the Louisiana secession convention a resolution that spoke to the southern fear of lost racial honor. The new president's party would force, he said, the southern people to accept an "equality [of blacks] with a superior race . . . to the irreparable ruin of this mighty Republic, the degradation of the American name, and the corruption of the American blood."

Suggested Historiographical Readings

Howard K. Beale. "What Historians Have Said about the Causes of the Civil War," in *Theory and Practice in Historical Studies*, Social Science Research Council Bulletin No. 54 (New York: 1946), pp. 55–102.

Thomas N. Bonner. "Civil War Historians and the 'Needless War' Doctrine," *Journal of the History of Ideas*, XVII (1956), pp. 193–216.

David Donald. "American Historians and the Causes of the Civil War," *South Atlantic Quarterly*, LIX (1960), pp. 251–55.

William Dray. "Some Causal Accounts of the American Civil War," *Daedalus*, IXC (1962), pp. 578–92, and comments by Newton Garner, pp. 592–98.

Don E. Fehrenbacher. "Disunion and Reunion," in John Higham (ed.), *The Reconstruction of American History* (London: 1962), pp. 98–118.

Eric Foner. "The Causes of the American Civil War: Recent Interpretations and New Directions," *Civil War History*, XX (1974), pp. 197–214.

David M. Potter. "The Literature on the Background of the Civil War," in *The South and the Sectional Conflict* (Baton Rouge: 1968), pp. 87–147.

Thomas J. Pressly. *Americans Interpret Their Civil War* (Princeton: 1954).

Charles W. Ramsdall. "The Changing Interpretations of the Civil War," *Journal of Southern History*, III (1937), pp. 3–27.

John S. Rosenberg. "Toward a New Civil War Revisionism," *American Scholar*, XXXVIII (1969), pp. 250–72.

Kenneth M. Stampp. "The Irrepressible Conflict," in *The Imperiled Union* (New York: 1980), pp. 191–245.

Index

ALIEN
VS.
PREDATOR

ALIEN
VS.
PREDATOR

MICHAEL ROBBINS

PENGUIN POETS

PENGUIN BOOKS

Published by the Penguin Group · Penguin Group (USA) Inc., 375 Hudson Street, New York, New York 10014, U.S.A. · Penguin Group (Canada), 90 Eglinton Avenue East, Suite 700, Toronto, Ontario, Canada M4P 2Y3 (a division of Pearson Penguin Canada Inc.) · Penguin Books Ltd, 80 Strand, London WC2R 0RL, England · Penguin Ireland, 25 St Stephen's Green, Dublin 2, Ireland (a division of Penguin Books Ltd) · Penguin Group (Australia), 250 Camberwell Road, Camberwell, Victoria 3124, Australia (a division of Pearson Australia Group Pty Ltd) · Penguin Books India Pvt Ltd, 11 Community Centre, Panchsheel Park, New Delhi - 110 017, India · Penguin Group (NZ), 67 Apollo Drive, Rosedale, Auckland 0632, New Zealand (a division of Pearson New Zealand Ltd) · Penguin Books (South Africa) (Pty) Ltd, 24 Sturdee Avenue, Rosebank, Johannesburg 2196, South Africa

Penguin Books Ltd, Registered Offices:
80 Strand, London WC2R 0RL, England

First published in Penguin Books 2012

10 9 8 7 6 5 4 3

LIBRARY OF CONGRESS CATALOGING-IN-PUBLICATION DATA
Robbins, Michael, 1972–
Alien vs. predator / Michael Robbins.
p. cm.—(Penguin poets)
ISBN 978-0-14-312035-3
I. Title: Alien versus predator.
PS3618.O315244A79 2012
811'.6—dc23   2011040812

Printed in the United States of America
Set in Minion Pro with Trade Gothic Display
Designed by Elke Sigal

For Xa

and for Perdita

CONTENTS

I

II

III

IV

ACKNOWLEDGMENTS

I am very grateful to the editors of the following journals, in which some of these poems, or earlier versions of them, first appeared: *The Awl*, *Boston Review*, *Court Green*, *Fence*, *Five Dials*, *Harper's*, *The Hat*, *LIT*, *The Morning News*, *The New Yorker*, *nonsite*, *La Petite Zine*, *Poetry*.

For the kingdom of grain: Christa Robbins, Frank Robbins, Marcia Borst.

For offending none but the virtuous: Mark Fletcher, Anna Clark, Rose Schapiro, Craig Rawlings, María Rodríguez, William Junker, Paul-Jon Benson, Rachel Furnari, Paul Durica, Mairead Case, Joshua Schwartz, Adam Schreiber, Bobby Baird, Marie McDonough, Anahid Nersessian, David Yium, Kristen Tobey, Tracy Ward, Jennifer Wild, Tricia Lockwood.

For words at the right time: Srikanth Reddy, Oren Izenberg, Ange Mlinko, Jennifer Moxley, Jordan Davis, Dan Chiasson, Zach Baron, Jessica Hopper, Don Share, Nick Demske, Christian Lorentzen, Joshua Scodel.

My personal trainer, Anthony Madrid, read, reread, edited, commented on, color-coded, and generally helped to shape, inspire, and improve every poem in this collection. There is no way in hell I could've written it without him, onlie begetter.

"Pissing in One Hand" is for Anahid Nersessian; "Hold Steady," "Any One I Want," "Desperado" and "Money Bin" are for Tricia Lockwood; "Rosary" is for Rose Schapiro; "Things I May No Longer Bring on Airplanes" is for Anna Clark; "Sway" is for Jennifer Wild.

Thanks to Henry Gould for permission to repurpose a comment he left at the Digital Emunction blog as lines 8–9 of "Downward-Facing Dog."

Thanks to Paul Slovak for taking a chance on this book and to Robert Wrigley for giving him the idea. And thanks to Paul Muldoon for blowing everything open.

RIP Alex Chilton

ALIEN
VS.
PREDATOR

ALIEN VS. PREDATOR

Praise *this* world, Rilke says, the jerk.
We'd stay up all night. Every angel's
berserk. Hell, if you slit monkeys
for a living, you'd pray to me, too.
I'm not so forgiving. I'm rubber, you're glue.

That elk is such a dick. He's a space tree
making a ski and a little foam chiropractor.
I set the controls, I pioneer
the seeding of the ionosphere.
I translate the Bible into velociraptor.

In front of Best Buy, the Tibetans are released,
but where's the whale on stilts that we were promised?
I fight the comets, lick the moon,
pave its lonely streets.
The sandhill cranes make brains look easy.

I go by many names: Buju Banton,
Camel Light, *The New York Times*.
Point being, rickshaws in Scranton.
I have few legs. I sleep on meat.
I'd eat your bra—point being—in a heartbeat.

The elephants ate each other, then they dreamed
of eating elephants till their captors came
to feed them. Then they died. My meth lab
tends to explode. I move to a new one
like a hermit crab. I give the gift of gab.

The truth gets me hard. Song selection
is key. The idiot Swedes do a number on me.
They invent refrigeration and sleep in shifts.
I'm tired of being compared to Britney Spears.
She's so pretty. I'm covered in petroglyphs.

That sorcerer bewitched my penis!
I'm speed and space, an Aztec princess.
The truth makes me hurl, the truth's a mistake.
John Milton jumps out of my birthday cake.

The psyched Mohican oils the beaver.
Fruit Stripe gum soon loses flavor.
Everything's flammable. Everything's flash.
Postmen like doctors and doctors like cash.

I stand and watch lightning
bugs constellate an inch-high sky.
I don't care to learn the secret
of their glow stick–colored snow.
Bechtel and General Mills make bids.
It's enough that Ghostface Killah knows.

Apache, DynCorp, Cobra—
tell me, Ghostface, if you know,
why Baghdad wears a black hood
and the Green Zone's Pizza Hut has power
and the Yankees are six games out.

The rain in Minneapolis is rain-
colored. The poor, purple in the cold,
are lifted up by no white bird.
Ghostface recites the cancer rates
while Prince commands the tide to turn—
our paisley priest, our Swinburne.

Picture?

In these United Arab States, Muslims
are elected wearing roller skates.
Erectile dysfunction in the nation's pets
is just the sort of grievance we petition
to redress. I give my skinny prick
a shake, to ask if there is some mistake.

Hold me closer, tiny reindeer. They saw
Oliver Stone distribute juice boxes.
He counts the headlights on the highway:
one if by reptile, two if by foxes.
Slash is both sad and happy for Axl.
The nation's pets are high on Paxil.

Memory is the bended grass where deer have lain.
It's hard to hold a candle to the cold November rain.

I get up in the evening, dress
the buffalo, slip into its carcass,
a floor too cool for corn. I'm born again
as the Tennessee Valley Authority.
I'm not with you in Rockland, *a fortiori*.

It was the winter of the wayward clone.
The frontier towns were low on phlogiston.
I was a tiny acorn then, but now
I mine the bay and trash the Finns.
My name's in all the magazines.

Little Bo Mercy in heels and hose,
just under the water she usually goes.
She moves grams and ounces, prays for war.
She's not the droid you're looking for.

If I could *mmm* like a mourning dove,
the bonny bears would know.
The final buffalo scrimps and saves.
I come on the uncut hair of graves.

I spit on any fresh green breast.
It's a misdemeanor. You can build the rest
from airplane parts and Listerine.
I get my news from *Meerkat Manor.*
Every Cylon is a mystery.

I get my news from Al Jazeera
and the American Apparel catalog.
Dick Grayson stole my lady friend.
Her muzzle was like yellow fog,
a postconsumer fiber blend.

I wake to Auto-Tune, and take my waking
out into an orchard, where I traipse.
I killed so many bulls the young males went
insane to meet another elephant.
They raped a rhino. They raped some apes.

Mother Mary plows the deep remotely.
She guides the rover to its red thought.
I can't live with or without me.
I etch the speckled cybernaut.
I rape the earth. It's not my fault.

My name is Michael, I'm an alcoholic.
Hi, Michael. Row your boat ashore.
The Christian youth group is sudsing cars.
They get Raptured. They hit the bars.

Cathy Aspirin's a karaoke machine
the size of Racine, Wisconsin.
Cathy, I think I left my uterus in your uterus.
I'd like to know what kind of response you get.

Maybe it's Maybelline. Why can't you be true?
You regifted the VD I wrapped up just for you.
My penis and my brain team up to penis-brain you.
It is now my duty to completely drain you.

Soap me down, children, I'm full of pain pills.
I was born in a barn. Some call it a manger.
The car wash washed in the blood
of the Lamb is full of rainbows.

You homicidal bitch. I killed the boar
'cause boar's the game I came here for.
I clear the jungle with the edge of my hand.
I make love to an ATM. I enrich uranium.
Dude, this aggression will not stand.

I want to watch you bleed. My tongue
doesn't know its right from wrong.
I'm uninsured. I ride the bus,
a loaded gun inside my purse.
My mouth's a roadside bomb.

The boar's inside the mosque and then
the RPG has martyred him.
His favorite song was "Crazy Train."
I pity the Lord, pity the Flash,
I sleep through gynecology class.

They call me Yeti because my carbon
footprint drives the Sherpas round the bend
into the village of the whup-ass can.
When I lie on my back in the ashy rain,
pigs drink from my cavernous groin.

NEW DEVELOPMENTS IN MAOISM

The last living tiger falls
from the research facility. We make pollen.
The plow is covered in fisher runes.
We saw this kind of missile on TV.

The cow powers down on alternate Tuesdays.
The world is empty enough as it is.
When did the first car start being a car?
Best not whack copulating snakes with a staff.

They're working on a self-sufficient tit.
They can rebuild it. All the pageantry a tit!
And the Pathet Lao grow homesick,
and the nose-cone shrouds fall on the homesick.

On the news, a man dressed as Mr. Peanut
showed an eight-year-old boy his penis.
You really should've seen it!
The little boy was also dressed as Mr. Peanut.

Did the astronauts bother to thank us
for torching the looming superstructures
of Bleeding Kansas, our Zippos quick as white-tusked boar?
Please don't get me started on the astronauts.

Good-bye to someone leaving: *annyonghi kaseyo*.
Good-bye to someone staying: *annyonghi kyeseyo*.

This is a poem for the Caterpillar D9.
I, Rachel Corrie, one of the roughs, a kosmos.
This must be nasty little anti-Semitic poem!

All Palestinians are Jews.
I don't follow. I am in the dark.
Hello to someone leaving. We are balloons.

Rachel Corrie bathes in the lee of the *Halve Maen*.
The Wu-Tang Clan has flown a jetliner
into the Nassau Coliseum.
Everyone on earth speaks pretty good Korean.

Next year in Jerusalem
Rachel Corrie stops somewhere waiting for you.

My neighbor's whales keep me up at night.
They may not mean to, but they do.
I turn on Shark Week, plan a killing spree.
I'm all stocked up on Theraflu.

I love the word *chum*. By Kinko's early light,
the Korean children say *swim, swam, swum.*
I'm tangled in the jasmine of your mind.
I'm trying to heat the whole neighborhood.

Whoever has no house now, tough titty.
Whoever is alone will not hook up.
I already told you I think you're pretty.

Your refutation precedes you. I pawn
my iron lung. Whose whales these are
I'll never know. They lawyer up. I'm lying low.

I dare not speak my name, it is so long
and unpronounceable. I enforce the thaw
here among the timbered few. We despise you
and whatever you rode in on—is that a *swan*?
I'm not really like this. I'm over the moon.

Still, we jar marmalade. We plow.
We don't need Neil Young around anyhow.
Your tribe's Doritos are infested with a stegosaur.
That Forever 21 used to be a Virgin Megastore.

Scott Baio in full feathered glory
was everything I'm not. I am everything I am
and then some. I'm coming along nicely.
Don't stick your fork in me till I'm done.

I bit my penis off at three.
Unless—no, wait—that wasn't me.

I stitched my penis, which I hate,
onto the face of my friend Kate.

Why would you want to write such things?
Nothing makes poetry happen.

I look into my heart and creep.
My heart is lovely, dark and deep.

I kiss your trash. My boobs are fake.
I have promises to break.

II

My new asshole's official candy
is cola-flavored, fish-shaped.
I sexually harass it.
It puckers with distaste.

My new asshole could be your friend,
if you had any friends. My new asshole
is making a name for itself.
It is a way of looking at the world.

It tilts at megabucks.
It tithes its chocolate tenth.
It moons over my hammy.
It sings a song of sapience.

Now it wants a puppy.
It wants to open a Red Lobster.
Where did it get that strawberry?
My new asshole has discovered boys.

My new asshole says so much.
My new asshole is being bullied.
It occurs to me I *am* my new asshole.
I am talking about myself again.

Vita brevis, brother. If you die first,
keep your sniveling relations far hence.
You got village girls pregnant with a glance.
Heck, you almost got *me* pregnant once.

I'll never forget your first words to me:
Where's the instructions for this thing?
I said, It's a *pillow*. Your epitaph will read,
IMPROVE YOUR SCORE ON THE A.C.T.!

Don't pull the bell rope if you wake
in your Silver Sapphire casket.
That thing cost a fortune. I hate to dig.
Just go to sleep, recite some Beckett.

Well, the psyche lusts to be wet,
as the kids say. Madrid, it's not cricket!
I'll look after your woman, fear not.
Are you quite sure you're not dead yet?

By the sparklet of certain ciliates, cesium
practices its cricket song.

Am I supposed to be impressed? My smoothie
comes with GPS.

Take a left at that crustacean. You—yes, you,
with the crisis Isis eyes.

By Odin's beard, this is snowier than usual. We can
always burn the first folio.

Go bug a dandelion. You'll have
the elephant of surprise.

You're coated with salmonella. Or am I
confusing you with the kitchen sponge again?
A beautiful phrase, *cellar door*,
but I prefer *You win.* Prefer to sit and spin.

Black people can't swim. Yes we can.
The giant Kool-Aid pitcher doesn't love
a wall. I replace the mirrors with Rorschach blots.
Think some Arnold Horshack thoughts.

I backed over the last passenger pigeon.
The sex was great. The mobled queen
was good. O brave new world
that has such Snapple in it!

I measure my pleasure in AMBER Alerts.
I'm riding to heaven on a camel-sized
needle. Its eye is as big as the Ritz,
but these camels—each hump's wider than the sky.

It's a gorgeous day, not a bat in the sky.
The topography's square with the recon.
Contents may have shifted during rapture.
Let's put the Christ back in Xbox.

This baby is disgusting. Fuck you, baby.
Get a job. You have the worst taste in art.
A real Winston Churchill, this one. Your lot's loss?
So lose. Lose the attitude. Lose the dress.

I was saying something about a baby.
It had eleven dimensions, kind of
a dim bulb. The last of a tiny race.
Just a shadow on a milk carton now.

I saw myself in half then make myself
disappear. Maybe the other way round.
Let's hear it for my lovely assistant.
She's the lower half of my body, sawn.
I open the cabinet and *poof* she's gone.

The moon moves from all to none
of the above. The earth fills in that Scantron oval.
I shoot first, answer questions later,
the fastest titty-twister in Chernobyl.

My theory is, we shine laser pointers
into cockpits of taxiing planes
because we were toilet trained
in tiger pits, in summer rains.

This house I built with my bare hands!
I can see its rusty hasps from Russia.
It's raining collateral and doggerel.
My mind's so clean you could eat off it.

I need your tongue so I can whisper
into these pickled horse thief's ears.
Stack the babies over there.
You'll wake the snake god with your tears.

Every last one of my thirty-eight years
would fit inside Jeffrey Dahmer's freezer.
Thirty-eight clans, thirty-eight Care Bears,
and all I got's this lousy T-shirt.

Sometimes I sag. That's what antlers are for.
You put them in milk, the milk of a stag.
If I had a shoe, I'd bang it on the table.
When I get a shovel, I'll bury you.

You quit smoking! *You* recycle!
These two trochees—Robbins, Michael—
are pronounced with equipoise.
I love this war, girls vs. boys.

I finally passed the Turing test. Everything
I look upon breaks into blossom, I guess.
Life is but the interpretation of a dream.
Gently, gently down the drain.

The morning slathers its whatever
across the thing. It puts the fucking
lotion in the basket. Can't smoke
in the confessional anymore.
If you do, you have to confess it.
So have I heard and do in part believe it.

Old pond, frog jumps in, so what.
Dude speaks Chinese laundry.
My mother like her pussy shave.
Tell her I read in Origen
even Satan might be saved.
Or else it gets the hose again.

Michael J. Fox talks Parkinson's
with the former Miss Arkansas.
The clouds are there for them
to be sick on. Those European
stairwells with the lights on a timer?
You get halfway up and the dark clicks on.

There is four helicopter running after person
and destroy his car. The truth, too, is fourfold:
1) life sucks; 2) for good reason;
3) you can sit under a tree;
4) the movie never ends, it goes on and on

and on and on. To write Nazi poetry
after Auschwitz is barbaric. And so inelegant.
What, you want to live with all those rodents?
Is *this* what you meant? Pay a little rodent rent?
The helicopter destroy four elephant.

Stand back! I am wearing pants! Same nun,
different ATV. God grant me the serenity
to rearrange your face. Grant me a GED.
If the killer whale's a killer, well,
you'd be one too in that whale's place.

Sea World is all that is the case.
Is that a crystal ball in your bosom?
I seem to see my future there.
Didn't your mama tell you it's impolite
to build in the empty house of the stare?

I eat wings. I'm such a pain.
Blue fly, butterfly, airplane, crane,
and everything in between.
I think you'd better hurry.
I think I live in a gooseberry field.

Two hundred miles wide, my mouth!
All these teetering hemlines, college-bound!
I still want—how shall I put this?—cigarettes.
It takes a strong storm to blow over Man-Pig.
Suddenly I begin speaking a language.

It is one I've known from childhood,
the only one, my mother tongue!
Hey, Senor Potato Boob Gun,
you are just so goddamn free.
You're taller than I thought you'd be.

Eleventy thousand degrees outside
with a heat index of kablooey.
The tastiest wings of all are Satan's.
But enough about me
is one of my favorite sayings.

If hell, like Soylent Green, is people,
every little hermit is the one true God.
The Easter Mass begins, *Don't put that
in your mouth, you don't know where it's been.*

I climb. I mean your skull. Its walls.
It's roomy, a man can stretch his legs.
This is the sea, that is a mountain. Now let us say
the prayer for discarded dolls.

A bunch of weird precepts about war—
you call that a religion? I'm fixing
a hole where my mind gets in.

Tonight the locusts ride. The fields are theirs.
Step out into the flensing swarm
if you want to make like a tree and buzz.

You had a woodchuck and an opium ball.
The one ate through the furniture,
the other sat in its cage depressing me.
Now the woodchuck sheds its skin.
I have a cow behind the Dollar Bin.

You shouldn't drink diarrhea
unless you bring enough for everybody.
Turn it into a teaching moment.
Asian American Students for Christ
have the room until two-thirty.

Rumi says no donkey is a virgin,
no, nor any beast that bites the grass.
Maybe it sounds better in Persian.
An unseen force propels the carts
across the Whole Foods parking lot.

The woodchuck hasn't been born yet
I'd rather keep than you as a pet.
You'll sleep on wood shavings, I'll comb your pelt.
That animal loved you, his captor,
whom he hated. I know just how he felt.

THE LEARN'D ASTRONOMER

How long must we hymn the twinkling stars
before we admit they are no more distant
than the glow-in-the-dark stickers adorning
the ceiling of my first girlfriend's boudoir?

Teenage planet swimming into my ken!
Even then, I was so skillful a lover
that when I said "Life is wasted on the living,"
the rivers ran for days with suicides.

Even then, I knew the stars to be empty cans.
There is the great Red Bull, watcher over
fevered gamers. To make me sixteen again—
I'd loose adders on the man who claimed such power.

No, you virgins, blessed in your ignorance,
for whom the night sky holds such romance,
the art of love is less mysterious than you suppose:
a plastic toy in a rubble of caramel corn.

These love poets couldn't write their way
out of a bag of kitty litter. The genitals, the heart,
the burning fantastical heavens themselves—
just junk in a Safeway cart I'm pushing
down to the recycling center.

I feel like a discarded Christmas tree.
Thanks for sharing. I can't hear myself think
about all this racket. As long
as we're discussing "feelings,"
please turn to your information packets.

It took me twelve years to find this socket,
and if you think I'm throwing in the towel
just because my plugs have too many prongs . . .
I don't even *have* a towel. Oh, a *towel*.
No, I have a couple of those.

Tried to use the spoon but
  the spoon shorted out.

Wants its robot raspberries back
  in the box of old receipts.

Bitsy Xanadus from the fever archive
  remix the minesweeper's tiny sex.

The religious left's turntablist
  threw T-shirts into the crowd.

Thus, you no-man-fathom,
  pee-shy, briar-brained, house-proud town mouse.

This episode of *CSI: Miami*
always makes me cry. I throw the Eagles'
Greatest Hits out the window, darkly.
You better take my car keys.

I hope I turn to ashes in the morning sun.
I do whatever a spider woman can.
But I can't stand here listening to
you and your Rastafarian friend.

Them cattle ain't gonna drive themselves.
I hope that in the morning sun
they low apocalyptically. My IQ's
the *E* you get when you divide by zero.

The warm smell of colitas rising
through each woof and wow and warp
takes me to the limit one more time.
It's quiet on the set. That's a wrap.

I up and drown a man who harmed hide
nor hair of kittens or hurts a fly. Might could.
Mite cold. My angel is the centerfold.
I thank too much. I meet you such.
I smoke too little. I speak in blurbs.

You're noncommittal. We just squirm
up on dry land. I want to ask if it's
not too much to ask your husband
for your hand. I append an asterisk.

Twinkle, twinkle. I upend.
I pile up and fender-bend.
I up and drown. Bob up and down.
And I believe—is not that strange?—
I'd re- your very life arrange.

I got a bad desire. I have eyes
in the sack of my dead. Your name is writ
in vitreous humor in the john
at the Ramada, where it's always Ramadan.
The mama-sans get their famine on.

It's dirty because it hasn't bathed.
You clean it like this. You circle
your star-hitched agon. There are more things
in heaven and earth than you're wearing
in my philosophy. You're not the boss of me.

But somehow you give me a raise.
It's my mouth's birthday, and I'm coming
around to its point of view. Its love for you
skeeves out the girls in H&M,
those switchblades made of human skin.

I wash it out with Old English—Anglo-Saxon
if you're nasty. My A game slots into
the bee in your sonnet. Your G-spot
is haunted. I'm the one who wants it
to want me. Let's get this séance started.

I just turned my back for a second and
there you were. I'm not really into breasts.
They remind me of a man wearing a cookie
costume. I've never seen one in the wild.
In the zoo, sure—even the insects have them.

I'm a pussy. Couldn't bench press a wren.
I could care less. I couldn't care less
means the same thing. And now the cat-man
glazes each cat with a tuning fork. Kindness,
I call it, though some call it glazing cats.

You bring the new Bible of Fuck, the Book
of Mormon of Fuck, the Qur'an of—
wait, I am not at war with Islam! I am at war
with Fuck and the Fucking it entails. Fuck
is a Movement I missed out on. I ride

a shrimp boat to Limp City if you take
my meaning. I like mean chicks with private
dicks. The judge sentenced me to use the word
rack in a sentence. Now I'm required
to register as a sex pretender.

Sent to know of the silent wood,
tenants of earthfall, confiscation under
secular pretenses of [line broken off]
The tides which from afar candle,
crash toward [...] eliminate
class distinctions, I can, he said,
only dream of so many at one time,
the leafy shelter of the Skraelings.
It was for your sake the smoke the salt
surrendered spelled nothing at least
nothing this graphite hearth
[six lines missing] birth-days of dead kings.
So you will walk a mile in this polymath's
sand tonight, of which it is said
even the gods [have suffered] to learn the only
way to fall is down a rabbit hole or
[some other kind of hole,] or possibly
there is no burial in that northern ground.
The polestar is visible despite the lamps
of burning city-states, and we can steer
our drowsy boats into that fantastic harbor
[unintelligible] never to thatch huts again
[unknown number of pages used as fuel for cooking fires]
drinks cool spring water from an earthen jar.
And without it, at the solstice's dire genuflect,
we are as one who, composing a hymn,

I glance at a twig, I take the twig to my bed, I tell it of manly love.
I tell my twig of the migratory song of the goose.
I tell it of the new form of companionship I propose in its name.
And now it seems to me I walked with my twig upon the brown
      earth
a thousand years ago, and a thousand thousand, before men were,
or women. It seems to me a twig might sup with the president of
      the United States,
and become president in its turn. And I will drop my twig in the
      gutter,
for I know other twigs in their hour will fall into my uncharted
      path forever.

And I have said I am a brother to twigs, and I say I belong to their
      nation,
and together we embrace the hay . . .

POEM ENDING WITH A LINE FROM *FINAL CRISIS*

I hate—*hate*—the red sweater
and being called a cub reporter.
Stuck forever in a child's skin
while *he* gets Atlas' stamina.

I don't know where I go. A chasm
opens when I say—
well, you know. A wrong needs righting.
Two syllables. Then the lightning.

TUSK

Think of Mick and Stevie fighting
as the great white *Tusk* hove into view,
Lindsey rapt in his indicting
and in the cash and blow they blew.

Stevie Nicks, her nose on fire
like the hills above Malibu,
watches coyotes in fiery coats
trot down to drink from the fiery pool.

Henry pitch his tone so low—
not on stars & sun—
on muskrat, sucker, frog & toad.
Who more low than that?
—Mr. Bones: you like to know.
Triumphant Henry in palaver!

—who tho the ghost of Cotton Mather
his self wade ashore
'd talk of *facts* & objects
to show up phony all his blather, or
refute his taxing that & this.
So in Nature Henry is.

Henry command loaves & fish,
dead upright—archaeologists
never more acute than he
when he fix his mind to furrow.
The doctrine of this hour
Henry mark. A cat most thorough.

Ask the lion who has eaten a bullock
how to crawl stealthily upon the earth.
Ask the bat what hell is like this time of year.
Or let me flap from out the darkness
into your hair. Some beast
has raked its claws across my naked back.
I bought a big bone and bunny food.
And I got to pet the bunny.

Let's go to Laurie in our Eye in the Sky
for a look at traffic. Thanks, Don.
It's an hour in from the Hut of Intelligent Design
to the saddest tapir in the nation.
Nothing left of the Sharper Image but ashes.
All fall down, Laurie? All fall down, Don.

By the sweat of my grave, the dirt of my brow,
by the stage-diving douche bag, the nose-diving Dow,

by the suntanned sphincter and the jelly of roll,
by the mystery meat, by my bargain-priced soul,

by the whip and the fur in the black Cadillac,
by the winter storm warning and the eggs of the ox,

by the suit of hazmat and the muted ass-hat,
by what it's like to be, or to beat on, the bat,

by the milk of the wolfman, by habitat loss,
by the beauty of black, by the red and white cross,

by the fiery furnace, by the frostiest fridge,
by Waco and Jonestown and by Ruby Ridge,

by the donkey with feathers, by dinosaur dung,
by the vaginal fang and the tar in my lung,

by missile defenses and difficult menses,
by tall and by grande, by mochas and ventis,

by the Egyptian dog, by the debonair moose,
by Natasha and Boris and squirrel on caboose,

by the panties that bunch, the knickers that twist,
by the device in my shoe that security missed,

by the saint in the well, by the lion who stank,
by the insignificant people I neglected to thank,

by the man on the street, by American thighs,
by the shit that I took that attracted no flies,

by the orbiting cobra, the comfortable lice,
by getting out of going through everything twice,

by getting out of going through everything twice,
by the saber-dicked tiger, the infinite mice,

by the cow in the moon and the mooncalf of gout,
by the bright boy who wants to know what it's about,

by the millionaire playboy's cape and his cowl,
by that wise old Zen master, the Tootsie Pop owl,

by the erasable duck, by the wascaly wabbit,
by licking the nun and by kicking her habit,

by the brain that I found in the girls' locker room,
by the horrible man-grapes of Fruit of the Loom,

by the bollocks I mind, by the virgin I'm like,
by the smell of teen spirit, the punch that I spike,

by hydro and chronic and eight-legged sparks,
by G-strings and tassels, by bummers and narcs,

by the temples I razed with a swish of my tail,
by the models of Jupiter I built to full scale,

I am a man of few words, each one a thrown switch.
Shall I name the mouth-breathers at whom I pitch

with superstitious loathing these excretions oozing bile?
Then pull up a chair. This could take a while.

IV

I've wasted a lifetime

Not proud of it

—FUCKED UP

> *I used to be carried in the arms of cheerleaders.*
>
> —THE NATIONAL

Somehow I sidle, I kick-start,
I hot-wire my monkey heart.
I take my waking slow.
The president totes a vial of my cremains
and toots a vial of blow.
Nice president! I wish you'd just explode.

This is Uncle Tom to Ground Control.
I'm half awake. I'm a total fake.
The moon's the only natural object
visible from China's Great Wall.
The seasons rearrange themselves.
Winter, winter, Google, fall.

Fuck the moon. It's *pink*.
I was raised on Stax and Stones.
I pledged my troth to Mr. Bones.
The glaciers are melting
at a non-glacial pace. I have no
genes. I learn by going
out alone into America.

Fires, I've lost a few. Bee rustlers
infiltrate my privates. I just
died in my arms tonight,
brown cow. I'll walk into
sky-blue skeet shoots, baby blue.
It was nice of you
to. But you can put me down.

2007

I used to work construction.
I had a hole in my head the size
of an ankh. My gut was a body bag,
full of tanks. Inside every tank, a prize!

No one owns the Loa. I bought a prayer
and a wing, twenty American dollar.
The child's toy poses a choking hazard.
The child, too. Life's a natural disaster.

I capture smoke within my coffin
and offer it to Dr. Strange.
They say that light's the only constant,
but I spend all day watching it change.
I wish people changed half as often.

The white goat is a fertility god.
The black giraffe is a wishbone
in the snow globe of the scorpion. And me?
I'm your host, Jack Kevorkian.

I live by the alien logic we impose on children.
Whoever smelt it dealt it. I'm glazed with K-Y
beside the Goth girls gone haywire.
Talk about cathexis!

You were probably saving them for breakfast.
I stabbed a whale, I freed Tibet. Played
Solo to your Boba Fett.
The rapist they caught's a total sexist.

Very little, perhaps nothing, is known about boats.
It's an ill fish lives in a beehive. The authorities
want you to say it, not spray it. But I'm all,
Whatever floats your goat. Frog got your throat?

And now the Ghanaian poets weep in Guitar Center.
I didn't come on this show to make friends.
Here, hold my drink a sec, I'll teach you
how to know the anteater from the ants.

ROSARY

Love will tear us a new asshole.
Two men are fucking in the gutter
of the picture book on my lap.
That day we read no further.

A man, a plan, Eddie Van Halen.
I can't exactly prove that, you understand.
I think I could turn and live with your vibrator,
it is so placid and self-contained.

I hate interesting children.
I have childish interests. I like you,
for instance. Where two or three women
are gathered together in my name, I like that.

I like to become anorexic
and write a memoir. I like all four
of our assholes. I like that even
our friends are against us.

Last night a DJ almost killed me.
I'm as alive as you can possibly get.
The ash at the end of my cigarette—
who put it there? My wife is asleep.
I hoot like an owl into her hair.

That was a joke, by the way.
Don't get your feelings in a bunch.
The Bible says, *Shawty, you must get loose.*
Augustine cautions against taking this
literally. Its exegesis is abstruse.

Story of my life, my sexual abuse
hotline. One leg at a time, I say.
If you cannot afford a leg, one will
be abandoned on a hot tin roof.
Now you must work a mysterious way.

I never promised you a unicorn.
But still. What is it like to be at bat?
Just having TMI tattooed on my balls.
The heavy lice that hang from them
run in blood down palace walls.

I got a tattoo of God. You can't see it
but it's everywhere. If I seem out of it,
do the math. I was put on earth.
And then you were, making up your feet
as you went along. New thinspo clanks the spank
bank. New emoticon makes a Holocene.

If you want to get in shape you have to jog
your memory of Euclid. Jesus built
a ship in a ship shape and said
there's plenty of loaves in the sea.
Some Idaho you turned out to be.

Some money bin I, a rich duck, swim in!
The coins of you in my feathers like water
off my back. I count each red cent of you.
Now the rain with its funny money din.
The rain beats a tattoo of God any day.

THINGS I MAY NO LONGER BRING ON AIRPLANES:

1. Box cutters
2. Airplanes

All that is sullied melts into flesh.
Hebrew, the original HTML.
How will I open my box on the airplane??

I saw a bat another bat
& two batlike swifts
that might've been bats.

I sing of a fast machine, her eyebrows
hardly eyebrows, little lines. Her smile a carburetor
converting my blood to high-fructose corn syrup.
I sing American thigh-highs, armor-plated.
The lights are on, but everyone's in Europe.

One's self one sings. The business school has softer
toilet paper, so I do my business there.
Even skinny mysteries make deposits.
I'm attracted to my polar opposite,
the white fox in the snow that is not there.

In the snow, that is. *E. coli* makes me plop
and fizz. Keeps my motor clean.
I expel my bloody Ovaltine.
My pancreas is shaped like the inside job
that brought down the World Trade Center.

I think of women as people just like you or me,
even when they eat their young. I know what it's like
to be the only Negro in a thong. And I do thing
my thong. I pee in the think and thigh.
I'll come out to meet you as far as fair My Lai.

The moon is my alibi. My tenders throw hissy fits.
My scalp's at the foot of the precipice.
My lume is spento, there's a creep in my cellar.
You can stand under my umbrella, Ella.

Who put pubic hair on my headphones?
Who put the ram in Ramallah?
I'm just sitting here spinning my spinning wheels—
where are the snow tires of tomorrow?

The llama is burning! My heart is an ovary!
Let's chase dawn's tail across state lines,
sing "Crimson and Clover" over and overy,
till wonders are taken for road signs.

My fish, fast and loose, shoot fish in a kettle.
The boys like the girls who like heavy metal.
On Sabbath, on Slayer, on Maiden and Venom!
On Motörhead, Leppard, and Zeppelin, and Mayhem . . .

Each time I resolve not to do *x*,
I slip to the sound of old T. Rex.
I want more than the world. My heart
unrecompensed disproves Descartes.
The snow that buries all my porn
I consecrate to your shit storm.

In the end your only guerdon
is *Wo Es war, soll Ich werden.*
I'm hung up on Mommy. Exit
wounds us more than the world. Lifted
strains stain the static:
a bra, a briar, my prick,

your panic. Last night I dreamt Marc Bolan
fell from his grave and stole his stolen
corpse away. It's seen much
better days. He stole a horse,
he stole a calf. Before he left,
he gave 'em back.

Until we clear the accounts, leave
it there. Leave each star-fucked nerve
to the beggars' banquet of thin
rats that madden with the rain.
I'll take it from here. I'll rile the Sioux.
All I ever wanted help with was you.

Try this on for size, oy vey!
I got an incandescent logo
and a portable student loan,
you never heard such a din.
Everyone's last name began with *M*.

We simply tipped over
the Housing Ministry's massive tower cranes.
Drive 'em across the border, sell 'em as scrap.
No problem! I bought a
pillowcase at the Chinese Olympics.

Forget these rinky-dink Mickey Mouse
small-and-smaller fist fries.
We're making it out of autoclave parts. Twice
the tensile strength of tungsten.
Put it in a spray can. Use as directed.

Krypto the flying dog, rabid,
tears out the defense secretary's
throat with his heat vision.
See X-Men-eyed Athena stay

the webcast beheading of the camel
spider. See the player haters
with their Paul Robeson dolls.
See the jillion stars of the Bedu camps.

The camel spider is not a spider.
It eats lizards. Its true name
is Lorenzo the Magnificent.

I am the bomb-sniffing dog
whose synthetic-aperture radar
malfunctions at the crucial instant.

Incused on my helmet:
The unexamined life is not worth examining.

Words don't hold you. I'm alive.
Hang me up in silent icicles,
baby, help me build a cross
in the center of crime.
I can walk away at any time.

Oh Jenny, I wish you'd made
this world so I could blame you
for scurvy, feverfew, and fretwork,
and the boys you tell your name to.

Mick Taylor's solos and Prefab Sprout
taught me more than John Donne did about
how to do within and do without.
And since the enamored fish will stay,
I count the hours since you slipped away.

Words don't hold you. I'm thirty-five.
I shine quietly to the riot moon.
"That demon life has got me in its sway"?
A bit rich for early afternoon.

Still, one thing's for sure: there must
be some kind of way out of here, I trust.
It rains in Juárez. It's Eastertime, too.
You're in my light. What is it then between
our buttons? I reach for *Steve McQueen*.

I HEAR YOU HAVE ONE MOUTH

I hear you have one mouth
now. I hear you fly south
past any army closing on
the broken fingers of the dawn.
I can't imagine. I reset.
Space-time takes a cigarette.

Your mouth, the missing one,
enraged the average citizen.
All our cities, busted up
and sold for scrap at cost
—throw in a couple rivers—
are less than what you lost.

Your mouth is now a sepulchre.
The blood stirs as it ought to stir.
Often we're required to return
to a meadow. To watch it burn.
It's only rock and roll. It never forgets.
The gloves are off, as are all bets.

I saw Joe Strummer in the snow,
alive as you or me.
I swear he sailed into the blue inane
above the Pigeon Roost Dairy Bar,

over trucks hauling rabbits and mainframes,
over shuttered firework stands,
over GOD IS PRO-LIFE, ARE YOU?,
over THE LORD JESUS CHRIST IF I BE LIFTED UP,
over half-shot-to-hell county markers.

I was born in the White Castle
right here amid the tiny burgers.
I raised the white flag of winter wire
and winter wet. I stumbled home
in Doppler locomotive wake,
one long cone of light per sleeping rustic.

I never did see Joe Strummer again.

I wandered lonely as Jay-Z
after the Fat Boys called it quits,
before the rapper from Mobb Deep
met up with the Alchemist.

I wandered lonely all along
The Watchtower's office front
in Dumbo, then across the bridge
that tempts the bedlamite to song.

From here you could've seen what planes
can do with luck and delta-v
as that fire-fangled morning
jingle-jangled helter-skelterly.

From *your gravity fails* to *whoops
there goes gravity*, from Céline
to Celan, from "Turn the Beat Around"
to *And the Band Played On*,

from the *Live Free or Die*
of plates from New Hampshire
to Musidora vamping
her way through *Les Vampires*,

from *It Takes a Nation*
of Millions to Hold Us Back
to *Daydream Nation,*
from *Station to Station,*

I take this cadence from the spinning plates
where the DJ plots the needle's fall.
I take it, and I give it back again
to the dollar dollar bill and the yes yes y'all.

Michael Robbins was born in Topeka, Kansas. His poems and criticism have appeared in *The New Yorker*, *Poetry*, *Harper's*, *London Review of Books*, *Village Voice*, *The New York Observer*, and several other journals. He received his PhD in English from the University of Chicago.